KOOBI FORA

RESEARCHES INTO GEOLOGY, PALAEONTOLOGY, AND HUMAN ORIGINS

GENERAL EDITORS

RICHARD E. LEAKEY AND GLYNN LL. ISAAC

Monograph No. 1 of The International Louis Leakey Memorial
Institute for African Prehistory series.

The Koobi Fora Spit from the air

KOOBI FORA
RESEARCH PROJECT

Volume 1

THE FOSSIL HOMINIDS
AND AN INTRODUCTION
TO THEIR CONTEXT
1968–1974

EDITED BY

MEAVE G. LEAKEY

AND

RICHARD E. LEAKEY

CLARENDON PRESS · OXFORD
1978

Oxford University Press, Walton Street, Oxford OX2 6DP

OXFORD LONDON GLASGOW NEW YORK
TORONTO MELBOURNE WELLINGTON CAPE TOWN
IBADAN NAIROBI DAR ES SALAAM LUSAKA ADDIS ABABA
KUALA LUMPUR SINGAPORE JAKARTA HONG KONG TOKYO
DELHI BOMBAY CALCUTTA MADRAS KARACHI

British Library Cataloguing in Publication Data

Koobi Fora Research Project
Koobi Fora research project. Vol 1: The fossil hominids and an introduction to their context, 1968–1974.—(Koobi Fora researches into geology, palaeontology, and human origins).
1. Man, Prehistoric—Kenya—Lake Turkana region I. Leakey, Meave, G. II. Leakey, Richard E. III. Series.
967.6'27   GN865.K/   77-30247

ISBN 0-19-857392-8

Typeset by Eta Services (Typesetters) Ltd.
Beccles, Suffolk, England
Printed in Great Britain by Fletcher & Son Ltd., Norwich, Norfolk

PREFACE

Our earliest ancestors must have ranged over wide areas of Africa, but only in a few places were circumstances favourable for the preservation of their remains. One such was discovered in northern Kenya in 1968. 'East Rudolf', as it was then called, soon became world-famous as more and more proto-human fossils were found, as well as a wealth of evidence of the environmental conditions under which these hominids lived.

Exploration was initiated by Richard Leakey as director of the National Museum of Kenya, and when the importance of the region emerged the Museum sponsored joint Kenyan and international scientific participation in the Koobi Fora Research Project. Although Koobi Fora is the centre of operations, the research extends over a very large area east of Lake Turkana (formerly Lake Rudolf). During the first six years of investigations an extraordinary amount of data was recovered and its publication is clearly a duty for those who work in these favoured places. Kenya takes a justifiable pride in the fact that its national heritage goes back so far into prehistory and that the knowledge obtained is of vital interest to all mankind.

Preliminary reports have appeared in more than a hundred scientific papers, dispersed in many journals and many countries. A series of monographs, of which this is the first, is now being prepared to make the full results of the Koobi Fora Research Project available to scholars all over the world in a readily accessible form. As co-leaders of the scientific work we serve as series editors, but each volume will have an appropriate author or volume editor. The monographs will provide fully illustrated accounts of what has been discovered in the various fields: palaeo-anthropology, palaeontology, stratigraphy, and archaeology. We shall attempt to relate the subjects one to another so that, for example, the salient facts about fossil hominids shall be intelligible to geologists, and that the key factors of stratigraphy, sedimentation, and palaeo-geography shall be apparent to palaeo-anthropologists who may not be expert in the earth sciences.

This first volume in the series appropriately deals with the material which has done most to establish the unique importance of the Koobi Fora region: the fossilized skeletal remains of early hominids, members of the family Hominidae of which *Homo sapiens* is the only surviving species. The volume provides an illustrated catalogue of the 129 specimens recovered up to 1974 and gives basic information on the circumstances of discovery, provenance, and stratigraphic derivation of each specimen. The data have been compiled by the author-editors of the volume, Meave and Richard Leakey. The latter also outlines the history of exploration and research in the Koobi Fora region in Chapter 1. Other authors contribute chapters summarizing the geological and palaeontological contexts of the hominids; and one of the series editors,

Glynn Isaac, provides an outline of the technological capabilities and subsistence patterns of the hominids which made and discarded the stone tools. Future volumes in the series will develop in full the material of these supporting chapters.

In the hominid catalogue (Chapter 5) the representation of anatomical parts in each specimen is stated but no attempt has been made to offer a full account of morphology, nor have taxonomic or phyletic interpretations been discussed except very briefly. Detailed comparative anatomical and systematic studies are currently being undertaken by Drs. M. H. Day, A. C. Walker, and B. A. Wood under the co-ordination of Richard Leakey. Full reports of this work will appear in future volumes of the series.

The region on the north-east shores of Lake Turkana is but one of a series of sedimentary exposures containing a vivid record of early human life. Other important East African localities include Olduvai Gorge, the lower Omo valley, and the Hadar region of the Afar depression in Ethiopia. The results of studies at these and other localities complement one another. In launching this series of monographs our aim is to make the results of the Koobi Fora Research Project known to science, and to help to make the knowledge of human origins more precise. We hope also to share with others our sense of excitement in the participation of a great exploratory journey into remote prehistory.

Nairobi and
Berkeley

RICHARD LEAKEY
GLYNN ISAAC

ACKNOWLEDGEMENTS

There are many people, organizations, and institutions who have collaborated to bring about the Koobi Fora Research Project to whom we would like to express our sincere thanks, although it would be impossible to name them all individually.

We are particularly indebted to the Government of Kenya for permission to work at Koobi Fora and to the National Museum and the Museum Trustees of Kenya for their continued support. We are also grateful for the co-operation of the Kenya National Parks after the area east of Lake Turkana was designated a park in 1972.

We would like to record our appreciation for the continued financial support of the National Geographic Society of Washington from the initial exploratory expedition in 1968 until now. The National Science Foundation, the National Environment Research Council, the William H. Donner Foundation, and the Royal Society have all contributed generously. Without this financial assistance the Koobi Fora Research Project could not have been a reality. Many individuals have also contributed in various ways.

Particular thanks go to the late Dr. L. Carmichael, Dr. M. M. Payne, Dr. M. B. Grosvenor, Mr. C. Winsor, Mr. R. Donner, Mr. G. M. Grosvenor, Professor T. R. Odhiambo, Professor J. M. Mungai, and the late Mr. W. M. Garland, all of whom have provided support, encouragement, and a very genuine interest.

The success of the project is due to a large degree to the skill of the members of the 'hominid team' who by careful searching discovered the majority of the hominid specimens. We thank others who have contributed to the collection (they are acknowledged in the hominid catalogue, Ch. 5), but to the hominid team we are especially grateful. Bwana Kamoya Kimeu directed the search, and other regular members of the team were Dr. John Harris, Bw. K. Kitibi, Bw. Wambua Mangao, Bw. Maundo Muluila, Bw. Mwongela Muoka, Bw. Nzube Mutiwa, Bw. Harrison Mutua, Bw. Bernard Ngeneo, and Dr. Tim White. These people are also responsible for recovering the majority of the specimens in the non-hominid palaeontological collection.

Our thanks go also to Dr. V. J. Maglio, who initiated the detailed palaeontological collecting, and to Dr. J. M. Harris, who took over from him and has continued to supervise and co-ordinate this aspect of the research. A number of people have been involved in the identification and description of the palaeontological material: Dr. M. Beden, Dr. C. C. Black, Professor H. B. S. Cooke, Mme V. Eisenmann, Dr. L. Krishtalka, the late Mrs. S. C. Savage, Dr. J. E. Sutton, Dr. E. Tchernov, Dr. T. D. White, Mr. P. G. Williamson, and Dr. R. Wood have all contributed their expertise and we are grateful to them all. We should also like to thank Dr. R. Bonnefille, who has initiated the palynology study. Taphonomic studies were begun by Miss E. Nesbitt Evans and continued by Dr. A. Hill and Dr. A. K. Behrensmeyer. Miss D. Gifford extended the research to the study of sites abandoned by the local nomadic people. All have freely shared the results of their investigations and are gratefully acknowledged.

The archaeological studies under Professor G. Ll. Isaac have involved a number of people. In particular we thank Mr. J. W. K. Harris, who has made the study of the Karari Industry the topic of his doctoral thesis, and Bw. J. Onyango-Abuje, Mr. J. Barthelme, Miss D. Crader, Miss D. Gifford, Mr. J. Gowlett, Miss I. Herbich, Bw. J. Karoma, Mr. D. Stiles, and Bw. S. Wandibba, who have all supervised the excavation of archaeological sites. Dr. M. D. Leakey described the first tools discovered in 1970.

ACKNOWLEDGEMENTS

The study of the geology of such a large area has been a major and very important under-taking and has involved a large number of people. Particular thanks go to Dr. A. K. Behrens-meyer for her pioneer work and continuing efforts in succeeding years. We are indebted to Dr. I. C. Findlater, whose overall study of the tuffaceous units has led to the formulation of a comprehensive stratigraphic framework essential for the understanding of all other research topics associated with the project. Professor C. Vondra has introduced a number of students to the project: these include Dr. B. E. Bowen, who studied the stratigraphy and petrography of the sediments as a topic for his doctoral thesis and thus made a major contribution to our understanding of the geology; Mr. R. Bainbridge, Mr. D. Burgraff, Mr. H. Frank, and Dr. T. White, all of whom contributed to the study of the microstratigraphy of areas 130 and 131; and Dr. G. Johnson, who, after receiving his doctorate, returned to study the microstratigraphy of areas 103 and 102 and introduced students of his own including Mr. R. Raynolds. We are also grateful to Professor N. J. Skinner and Dr. N. V. Bhatt, who have initiated geophysical studies.

Chemical analysis of the sediments is another important study related to problems of internal correlation. Our thanks go to Mr. T. E. Cerling, who is conducting oxygen isotope studies of the tuffaceous units, and to Dr. P. Abell and his colleagues, who have also undertaken chemical analysis of the sediments.

A number of people have contributed to the dating studies. Our thanks go to Dr. J. A. Miller and Mr. F. J. Fitch, who are responsible for the K–Ar dates, and to their students: Mr. P. Hooker and Mr. A. Hurford have assisted in the laboratory and are now obtaining dates by the fission-track method; and Mr. R. Watkins has attempted to find the source of the sedi-mentary volcanics. Palaeomagnetic studies were initiated by Professor A. Brock and Professor G. Ll. Isaac assisted by Mr. J. D. Hillhouse and Mr. J. Ndombi.

We would particularly like to record our appreciation to Professor M. H. Day, Dr. A. C. Walker, and Dr. B. A. Wood, who described the hominid material. Thanks to their efforts, descriptions of most of the specimens have been published within two years of discovery. This has allowed others to have access to the material very quickly. We acknowledge their generosity in permitting this while their own studies have not yet been completed. They have also spent time in the careful and patient preparation of some of the material. Alan Walker in particular has devoted much time and skill to the preparation of some of the more important specimens, such as KNM-ER 1470, 1805, 1813, and 3230. Mr. Ron Clarke kindly undertook the cleaning and restoration of KNM-ER 407.

Several people have contributed to the expedition in various less obvious ways. We would particularly like to thank Miss S. Abell, Mrs. J. M. Harris, Mrs. A. B. Isaac, Mrs. D. M. Leakey, Mr. J. Matternes, Mrs. J. Rotta, Miss Kelly Stewart, and Dr. H. Wood. We are indebted to Mr. R. I. M. Campbell, who has recorded many of the more exciting discoveries on film.

Many people have been involved in the compilation of this volume. We thank those who have contributed chapters on specific aspects, and also those who have checked the manuscript and provided suggestions and amendments, particularly Drs. M. H. Day, A. C. Walker, and B. A. Wood, who assisted with the hominid catalogue; Mr. T. D. White, who also provided sug-gestions for this chapter and kindly allowed us to publish his measurements in Table 5.2; Dr. I. C. Findlater, who provided Figs. 1.1 and 1.2 and assisted with identifying the environ-ments of deposition for the hominid catalogue; and Dr. J. M. Harris, who has proffered advice on many occasions. Bw. J. Kimunya prepared all the drawings of the hominid specimens, Ms. Judith Ogden drafted the Reference Sections, and Mr. R. Beatty and Mr. J. Day took some of the photographs. Miss L. Gafikin, Miss K. Bell, and Mrs. M. Pomeroy assisted with parts of the hominid catalogue.

Dr. B. A. Wood helped in the early negotiations that led to the establishment of this series. Mrs. Sonia Cole has spent considerable time on the arduous business of preparing the manu-script for publication and her services are gratefully acknowledged.

ACKNOWLEDGEMENTS

Finally we should like to express special thanks to Professor Glynn Isaac and Bwana Kamoya Kimeu. Glynn has acted as co-leader of the expedition since 1971 and has contributed much time and effort to all aspects of the project; its success is very much the result of his enthusiasm and energy. Kamoya has, since the beginning, taken much of the organization on himself; his leadership and dedication have made a very significant contribution.

MEAVE LEAKEY
RICHARD LEAKEY

CONTENTS

LIST OF ILLUSTRATIONS   xiii

LIST OF TABLES   xv

1   INTRODUCTION   1
    Richard E. Leakey

2   STRATIGRAPHY   14
    Ian C. Findlater

3   PALAEONTOLOGY   32
    John M. Harris

4   ARCHAEOLOGY   64
    Glynn Ll. Isaac and John W. K. Harris

5   THE HOMINID CATALOGUE   86
    Richard E. Leakey, Meave G. Leakey, and
    Anna K. Behrensmeyer

    BIBLIOGRAPHY: KOOBI FORA RESEARCH PROJECT CATALOGUE OF   183
        PUBLICATIONS 1970–1976

    INDEX   189

LIST OF ILLUSTRATIONS

TEXT-FIGURES

1.1. The Koobi Fora region showing geographic names   2

1.2. The Koobi Fora region showing locations of the palaeontological collection areas   7

2.1. Generalized stratigraphic column showing stratigraphic nomenclature   15

2.2. Geographic and stratigraphic locations of fossil hominids recovered from the Ileret region   16

2.3. Geographic and stratigraphic locations of fossil hominids recovered from the Koobi Fora region (areas 129, 130, 131, and 105)   17

2.4. Geographic and stratigraphic locations of fossil hominids recovered from the Koobi Fora region (areas 103, 104, 119, and 124)   18

2.5. Generalized stratigraphic sections showing the relative positions of the hominids which can presently be assigned to levels   20

2.6. Environments of deposition related to the generalized stratigraphic sections shown in Fig. 2.5   21

2.7. Palaeogeography   27

2.8. The areal relationships of the five major environments   29

3.1. Known tuffs of the Koobi Fora and Kubi Algi Formations designated by area   33

3.2. Tuffs formerly named and used in provisional correlation   34

3.3. Collection units in major fossiliferous areas   35

4.1. (a) Map showing grid squares used to catalogue the archaeological sites
(b) Detail of sites along the Karari escarpment   68

4.2. Maps showing the distribution of archaeological finds in relationship to localities which have yielded hominid fossils   69

4.3. A representative series of Karari Industry tool forms   74

4.4. A representative series of KBS Industry artefacts   76

5.1–5.70. Hominid specimens   *between* pp. 90–169

5.71. Method of taking mandibular measurements in Table 5.2A   172

5.72. Method of taking mandibular measurements in Table 5.2B   173

Reference Sections 1–49   *between* pp. 91–162

PLATES

PLATES 1–28. Hominid specimens   *between* pp. 93–169

LIST OF TABLES

1.1. The published best apparent ages for the major tuffs in the Koobi Fora Formation ... 11

2.1. Depositional environments in which it is thought that the hominids were buried ... 22

3.1. The distribution of fossil mammal taxa in the Koobi Fora Formation ... 54
3.2. Mollusc concurrent range zones in the Kubi Algi and Koobi Fora Formations ... 56

4.1. The archaeological sites shown in relation to the stratigraphic subdivisions of the Koobi Fora Formation ... 65
4.2. A list of catalogued sites in the Koobi Fora and Guomde Formations ... 66
4.3. The percentage composition of the main excavated assemblages ... 73
4.4. The classification of artefact occurrences ... 78

5.1. Measurements of the cranium ... 171
5.2. Mandibular measurements ... 172–3
5.3. Measurements of upper central incisor ... 174
5.4. Measurements of upper lateral incisor ... 174
5.5. Measurements of upper canine ... 174
5.6. Measurements of upper third premolar ... 174
5.7. Measurements of upper fourth premolar ... 175
5.8. Measurements of upper first molar ... 175
5.9. Measurements of upper second molar ... 175
5.10. Measurements of upper third molar ... 175
5.11. Measurements of lower central incisor ... 176
5.12. Measurements of lower lateral incisor ... 176
5.13. Measurements of lower canine ... 176
5.14. Measurements of lower third premolar ... 176
5.15. Measurements of lower fourth premolar ... 177
5.16. Measurements of lower first molar ... 177
5.17. Measurements of lower second molar ... 178
5.18. Measurements of lower third molar ... 178
5.19. Measurements of upper deciduous central incisor, canine, and molars ... 179
5.20. Measurements of lower deciduous canine and molars ... 179
5.21. Measurements of humerus ... 179
5.22. Measurements of ulna ... 180
5.23. Measurements of radius ... 180
5.24. Measurements of femur ... 181

5.25. Measurements of tibia   180
5.26. Measurements of fibula   180
5.27. Measurements of talus   180
5.28. Measurements of metatarsal   180
5.29. Measurements of phalanges of the foot   182
5.30. Hominid specimens according to parts of the skeleton.   182

I

INTRODUCTION

RICHARD E. LEAKEY

MY interest in the area east of Lake Turkana (formerly known as East Rudolf) began during the course of the 1967 International Omo River Expedition, when I flew in a light aircraft over the extensive exposures of stratified sediments which occur in this region. On one subsequent occasion I was able to use a small helicopter for a ground check. In each locality I visited, I found fragmentary vertebrate fossils which indicated a Plio–Pleistocene age for the deposits. Although the helicopter visit was confined to the border area, the exposures which extended southwards for a distance of about 100 km were potentially all fossiliferous. As a consequence of this limited survey I decided to organize a separate expedition for the following year and to withdraw the Kenya team from the International Omo River Expedition.

Prior to 1967, no detailed investigation of this part of the lake basin had been undertaken. With the exception of Count Samuel Teleki and Ludwig von Höhnel, who visited the lake in 1888 (von Höhnel, 1894), the early European travellers had not visited the region. Teleki and von Höhnel make no mention of fossils in published writing, although the maps of their journey indicate that Teleki spent time in areas where many vertebrate fossils have since been recovered. It is possible that there was considerably more vegetation and grass cover in 1888 and this might explain the absence of palaeontological observation.

During the 1940s, the District Commissioner of Marsabit (an administrative centre some 180 km to the east of Lake Turkana) sent a letter to my father, the late Dr. L. S. B. Leakey, in which he referred to reports of fossil bones at a place called Kubi Fur. It is conceivable that this was a reference to the area we now call Koobi Fora, but owing to the Second World War and lack of opportunity, no follow-up was made at the time and the letter was forgotten. Koobi Fora is the name of the area where the project base camp is now established (see map, Fig. 1.1) and probably refers to a seasonal area for grazing close to fresh water in the river bed near by.

The boundaries of the Plio–Pleistocene sediments currently under study by the Koobi Fora Research Project are: the Kenya–Ethiopian border to the north, the Miocene basalts to the east, and the Miocene basalts to the south in Allia Bay. The lake shore is effectively the western boundary but the sedimentary strata are known to be partly submerged and one important fossil was discovered by an unfortunate bather who stubbed his toe on it while wading in several feet of water. The fossil

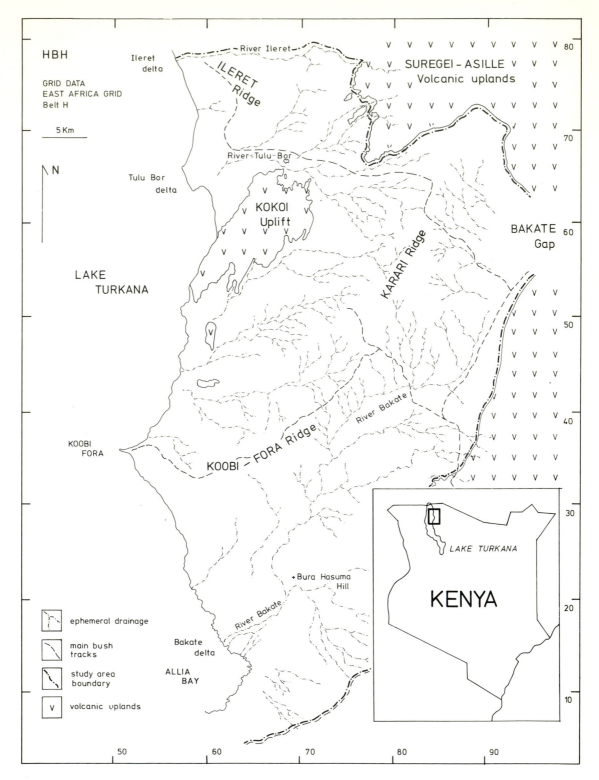

FIG. 1.1. The Koobi Fora region showing geographic names.

localities on the eastern margin of the lake, however, extend beyond these boundaries. Sedimentary exposures are known south of Allia Bay and during investigation of the volcanic margin north-east of the study area, fossiliferous Miocene localities have been discovered (Harris and Watkins, 1974). These Miocene sites have been examined only on a preliminary basis and will be treated as a distinct research project to be undertaken by others. Miocene and Pleistocene fossils are also found on the western margin of the lake and the Pliocene localities of Kanapoi and Lothagam are well known (Patterson, Behrensmeyer, and Sill, 1970; Behrensmeyer, 1976; Smart, 1976).

HISTORY OF THE EXPEDITION

During the initial field season, June–August 1968, the main objective was to traverse the area previously surveyed from the air and so determine the general distribution and potential of the fossil-bearing sediments. During this period water sources were located and we obtained a broad idea of the logistical problems that would be encountered in the course of larger operations.

The party consisted of Mrs. Margaret Leakey, Mr. John Harris, Dr. Paul Abell, Bw. Kamoya Kimeu, Mr. Bernard Wood, and Mr. Bob Campbell with various assistants. A base camp was set up first on the lake shore at Allia Bay and then inland at Nderati. Much of the 1000 km² of sedimentary exposures was visited by using a boat or a vehicle to transport people away from the base camp and then covering long distances on foot. The sediments were found to be remarkably rich in fossils over a large part of the area.

Although some fossil specimens were collected, a deliberate policy was followed whereby most of the finds were left undisturbed for future collection. The reason for this was our awareness that the specimens would be relatively valueless until such time as they could be attributed to a geological framework. The fact that there was no geologist on the first expedition contributed to our caution on the matter of collecting. I felt confident that the few specimens we did collect could subsequently be tied in to the stratigraphy and in most cases this was possible. The vastness of the collecting areas created immense problems of relocation because no accurate maps or large-scale aerial photographs existed. In hindsight, and with our present knowledge of the stratigraphic complexities, it would perhaps have been more prudent to have collected nothing.

The success of this initial expedition, which included the recovery of four hominid fossils, was sufficient to warrant a more extensive project, and a second field season was planned for the following year.

In 1969 Miss A. K. Behrensmeyer joined the expedition as geologist and we made a crude attempt to obtain aerial photographic cover of the area. The base camp was set up at Koobi Fora, which was centrally located and was suitable for a boat anchorage. The presence of flat ground also made it possible to have an airstrip within a few metres of the camp.

The confidence that resulted from returning to a now familiar area and the presence of a geologist with the expedition led to our collecting a number of well-preserved vertebrate fossils. A stone cairn was erected at each collection site and the locality was then referred to a very generalized provisional stratigraphy that Kay Behrensmeyer was developing. Unfortunately we overrated our ability to remember the relationship of each fossil to its cairn in subsequent seasons and it has become abundantly clear that the method was not satisfactory. As in the previous season, a large proportion of the collected specimens could be referred to the site of discovery, but in some instances this has not been possible. It is quite easy to see now that the cairns should have been numbered in some way to give a system of reference for the specimens. The application of plastic-based paint on a stone incorporated in the cairns would have proved adequate and is a system that might be applied elsewhere by others with similar problems.

During 1969 attention was focused mainly on the exposures along the Koobi Fora ridge, although some time was also spent in the Ileret region. Shortly after we began work, a great deal of excitement was generated by the discovery of artefacts *in situ*. Kay Behrensmeyer made the discovery while collecting geological samples from an outcrop of tuff, and a small test excavation subsequently revealed the context of the artefacts within the tuff. As a consequence of this discovery, the site was named the Kay Behrensmeyer Site and the tuff in which the artefacts were recovered is the type locality for the KBS Tuff. Before the end of the field season, several other occurrences of artefacts at outcrops of the KBS Tuff had been noted for future investigation. Dating samples of the tuff were sent to Mr. Frank Fitch and Dr. John Miller of F.M. Consultants Ltd. and a date of 2.6 million years was obtained for these samples (Fitch and Miller, 1970).

Five hominid specimens were recovered during the 1969 field season, including two skulls (KNM-ER 406 and 407) from the Ileret region. These discoveries, the archaeological potential, and the wealth of faunal material established the importance of the area and the need to expand the expedition by including additional scientists. Dr. Glynn Isaac visited Koobi Fora at the end of the 1969 season. After his visit he agreed to join the research endeavour, to take charge of the archaeological research and to assist with the scientific co-ordination.

In 1970 Professor Carl Vondra of Iowa State University joined the expedition, accompanied by two graduate students, Gary Johnson and Bruce Bowen, and took over the mapping and much of the geological investigation. This enabled Kay Behrensmeyer to spend more time on microstatigraphic studies. Dr. Vince Maglio also joined the expedition in 1970 and devoted the field season to the careful collection of vertebrate fossils that were fully documented in relation to stratigraphy. Glynn Isaac, assisted by several graduate students, began excavations at the KBS site and extended the survey for other artefact occurrences. During this survey, the rich localities along the Karari escarpment associated with the Okote Tuff were discovered. Frank Fitch and Jack Miller visited the field and collected additional material for dating studies. The search for hominid fossils was again successful, with the recovery of 16 specimens, including the first postcranial material.

With an enlarged group it became clear that funding would become increasingly difficult in future. It was therefore decided to organize formal co-ordination of research activities and grant applications. The idea of a formal 'Koobi Fora Research Project' with a committee structure to replace the informal 'East Rudolf Expedition' was agreed upon and the first meeting of the committee was held in the field during 1970. The policy of the group was determined by this and subsequent meetings and an attempt was made to initiate thorough co-ordination of all the components of the research endeavour.

At the end of the 1970 field season, Huntings Survey Ltd. was engaged to provide a complete stereo-pair aerial photographic cover at a scale of 1:23,000 for the entire study area. The study of the fossil collections was initiated by several experts who were to concentrate on certain taxa: H. B. S. Cooke, the Suidae; V. Maglio, the Elephantidae; J. M. Harris, the Bovidae; S. C. Savage, the Hippopotamidae; and Meave Leakey the non-hominid Primates and the Carnivora. M. H. Day, A. Walker, and B. A. Wood were invited to describe and study the hominids. Other groups were left pending the recovery of additional material.

The 1971 season resulted in significant progress in various fields. Kay Behrensmeyer undertook an extremely detailed investigation of the geological context of the KBS site and other artefact occurrences in the vicinity. The resulting palaeoenvironmental information has been an important component in the understanding of early hominid activities in this area and has provided the first concept of the palaeogeography during the time of deposition of the KBS Tuff. The increased tempo of exploration resulted in a spectacular yield of fossil hominid remains and it became quite clear that, while the team could revisit an area repeatedly without results, persistence eventually proved rewarding. It seems that the time of day and light conditions are important factors in successfully locating fossils in the field.

The period from 1972 until the end of 1974 saw a continuation of the same research programmes. Microstratigraphic studies of certain areas were undertaken and the broader problems of correlation were investigated. Ian Findlater joined the project in 1972 to investigate the tuffs and to map out marker horizons across the basin. The complexity of the regional geology became very apparent and revisions and refinements of the stratigraphic framework resulted. Vince Maglio left the project at the end of 1971 and John Harris took over the co-ordination of the palaeontological studies. In 1973 M. Beden took over the study of the Elephantidae, and V. Eisenmann the Equidae. The collection and study of the invertebrates was also initiated in 1973 when Peter Williamson joined the group. The rarity of microfaunal remains was considered to be partly the result of prospecting techniques, and Craig Black with a team of assistants joined the project in 1974 to concentrate on the problem.

The problems of absolute dating became the subject of widespread debate and an attempt was initiated to locate the source area for the various tuffs. Ron Watkins incorporated this objective as part of his study of the volcanics to the north-east of the study area, but so far his efforts to locate sources have been in vain. Palaeomagnetic studies were initiated by Andrew Brock working in conjunction with a graduate student, Joab Ndombi, and Glynn Isaac. In the later stages of this study Jack

Hillhouse joined the effort under the supervision of Alan Cox at Stanford University. While a considerable amount of data has been accumulated, various problems of interpretation remain.

At the end of 1974 it was realized that the volume of data accumulated during the previous seven field seasons was such that it was unreasonable to continue to collect more information without first assessing the data in the laboratory and writing up the results. A geological and archaeological moratorium was, therefore, called in 1975 and this is considered to mark the end of Phase I of the research project. Fossils collected during the 1975 field season amounted to one-third of the total sample retrieved from the Koobi Fora and Kubi Algi Formations. The study of this material by John Harris and Tim White (who was a member of the palaeontology team in the 1974–5 seasons) led to a revision of former provisional lithostratigraphic correlations and resulted in the informal collection unit scheme employed in the body of the text (see p. 36). Phase II will include more detailed studies of specific aspects and problems realized during Phase I. Thus the information contained in this volume concerns only data collected between 1968 and 1975.

GEOGRAPHICAL NAMES

As a matter of policy, local names have been used for the geographical features in the study area. Until recently the lake was known internationally as Lake Rudolf, having been so named in 1888 by Count Teleki after the Crown Prince of Austria at the time. In 1975 the Government of Kenya decreed that the lake would be officially called Lake Turkana. The Turkana people occupy the southern and western regions of the lake basin and many are now active as fishermen.

The eastern side of Lake Turkana is today sparsely inhabited by the Rendille people who range over the area between Loiyengalani and Allia Bay. When the research project was initiated in 1968, a number of Gabra families made use of the grazing areas near Allia Bay and northwards to Koobi Fora during the dry months. Similarly, a scattered community of Dassenetch, known locally as the 'Shangilla', occupied the area from Koobi Fora northwards and beyond the Kenya–Ethiopia border.

The creation of a National Park in 1972 by legislation of the Government of Kenya effectively removed human habitation from the area north of Allia Bay and south of Ileret. The Dassenetch villages are now in the area around Ileret and northwards, where the inhabitants herd sheep, goats, and cattle as their principal means of livelihood.

The geographical names for geological nomenclature have incorporated both Gabra and Dassenetch words. A list of the principal terms used is as follows:

Allia Bay, an embayment on the eastern shore of the lake.

Bura Hasuma, a large seasonal river with several permanent waterholes south of Koobi Fora. The head waters or source area of this river is known as Ol Bakate.

Galana Boi, the lake, also known as Lake Turkana.

6

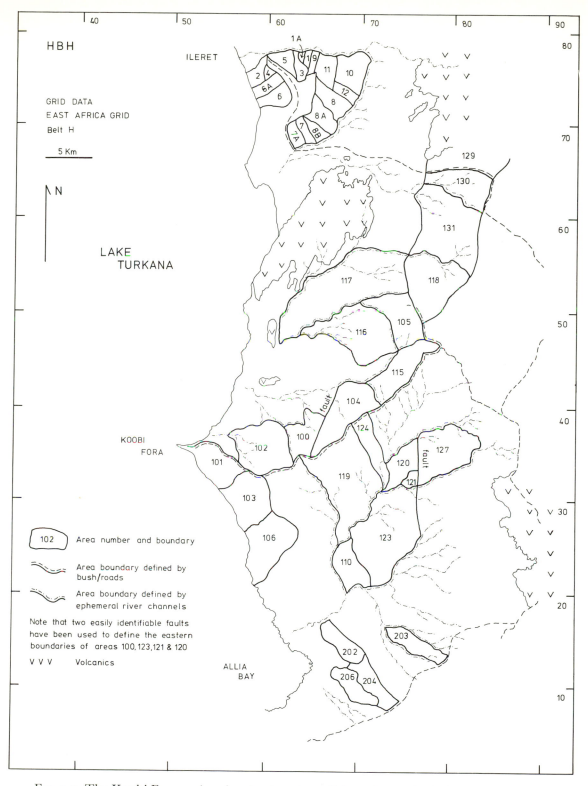

FIG. 1.2. The Koobi Fora region showing locations of the palaeontological collection areas.

Ileret, the name of the police post near the Ethiopian border. Ileret is a contraction of Il Erriet, a large seasonal river which has several permanent waterholes of local importance.

Karari, an escarpment running north–south and generally defining the eastern margin of the extensive exposure of sediments to the east of Koobi Fora.

Kokoi, the name used to describe the volcanic hill north of Koobi Fora and more specifically a permanent waterhole at the southern end of these volcanics.

Koobi Fora, the distinctive sandy peninsula that extends into the lake. Also known as Kwiro Renya by the Dassenetch.

Kubi Algi, a permanent waterhole to the east of Allia Bay on the margin of the volcanics and sedimentary exposures.

Okote, the area east of the Karari escarpment.

Sibilot, a distinctive volcanic hill east of Allia Bay.

Suregei, the volcanic hills to the north-east of the study area.

Tulu Bor, a large ephemeral river course draining the volcanic plateau to the north-east of the study area.

LOCALITY REFERENCE

The large geographical extent of the fossil-bearing sediments required a system of locality references. Owing to the discontinuous nature of the exposures, the three major regions of Ileret, Koobi Fora, and Allia Bay have been divided into a number of areas. Each area has been numbered and is bounded either by natural vegetation cover or by easily recognizable topographic features (sand rivers, etc.). The areas are detailed in the map in Fig. 1.2. Numbers 1–99 are allocated to areas in the Ileret region, 100–199 to areas in the Koobi Fora region, and 200–299 to areas in the Allia Bay region.

PALAEONTOLOGICAL COLLECTING PROCEDURES

The vertebrate fossil collection consists of specimens that were in most instances surface finds. The rate of erosion varies between localities but in general seems to be gradual; as a consequence, the collection probably represents a concentration or lag resulting from many years of exposure by wind and rain. Most collected specimens are in reasonably good condition, but when necessary they are treated before removal with frequent application of very dilute Bedakryl, an alcohol-based hardener. One of the critical factors that accounts for the completeness of specimens has been the care given to the field collection procedure. As is noted by Findlater (Chapter 2), the character of sediment deposition is such that the stratigraphic provenance of most surface finds can be ascertained to within one or two metres.

The non-hominid vertebrate collection has been obtained over successive seasons, with a significant proportion of specimens being collected since 1971 when aerial photographs permitted exact locations to be recorded. These specimens are individually marked on the photographs by a pin-prick locating the spot of collection. In the intensively collected areas, additional copies of the same photo have been used successively. As the work in the area continues these records will be transferred to a master set of photographs, which will be maintained as a permanent museum record. In this way it will be possible to refer the palaeontological material to the geological interpretation of any locality, regardless of periodic revisions and refinements occasioned by future field work.

For the hominid fossils, the collection procedure has been more elaborate and the site of discovery has been marked by a concrete post bearing the National Museum of Kenya accession number for the specimen. Many of the hominid fossils were discovered in a fragmented condition which required very careful field recovery and restoration. In certain instances fragments were widely scattered on slopes and extensive screening was undertaken to recover the many pieces. A commentary on the provenance of the specimens is given in Chapter 5. Wherever a specimen was recovered *in situ* this has been stated; unless so stated the specimens are surface recoveries.

Kay Behrensmeyer and Ian Findlater have examined the majority of locations of hominid recovery and have compiled geological notes and sections. Some of these sections are presented in Chapter 5.

In the case of KNM-ER 164, 730, 732, 803, 1481, and 1805, small excavations were carried out in the hopes of recovering additional material. All of these proved futile, although more extensive excavation at the same sites and others could yet provide results. One of the problems to be considered is the most expedient use of skilled manpower: while excavating a locality for ten weeks critical specimens already exposed by natural erosion might disintegrate, or be damaged by the trampling hooves of animals. It is my belief that it was appropriate to concentrate on seeking out material naturally exposed during the first phase of the project and subsequently to undertake excavations when the surface material had, to a large extent, been recovered safely. There are several examples, such as KNM-ER 406, 407, 1805, and 1813, where recovery was only just in time and a further year of weathering would have resulted in considerable damage to the specimens.

ARCHAEOLOGY

As already noted, the area to the east of Lake Turkana offers considerable potential for archaeological investigations at various time levels. The general scarcity of stone artefacts, with the few low-density occurrences of artefacts below the KBS Tuff, may be a reflection on hominid activity at that time, but it could also reflect the absence of suitable raw material locally. The potential for further discoveries in the region is excellent, and subsequent field work will incorporate extensive surveys in the earlier sediments, especially around the eastern margin of the old lake.

The sites along the Karari escarpment are of a critical age, for few localities of this time period (1–1.5 million years B.P.) are represented elsewhere in eastern Africa. The wealth of material and the large number of sites in differing palaeogeographical settings will offer many years of useful study. It is conceivable that evidence will be forthcoming which might tie the development of large complex tools to the emergence of the *Homo erectus* phase of hominid evolution. This will be one focus for continuing research.

The Holocene deposits, mainly Galana Boi beds, offer considerable evidence for the late Stone Age and early pastoralist activities. Numerous sites exist where pottery, bone harpoons, and stone tools are plentiful. John Barthelme working under Glynn Isaac has initiated research on this phase of the archaeological record and further studies will be undertaken in future.

TAPHONOMY

The existence of large numbers of herbivores and some predators along the eastern shore of the lake provides a useful opportunity for taphonomic studies. Additionally, the presence of 'hunter-gatherers' living today along the shore illustrates one pattern of human existence in an ecological zone that is well represented in the fossil context.

The relative proportion of bone refuse that survives after predator kills or natural death is of great importance to the ultimate reconstruction of animal populations in the palaeontological environment. The survival of bone waste away from the lake shore can be documented in a variety of situations ranging from flood plain and high-water flood zones to deltaic situations and high-energy channels. While much is destroyed, a proportion of bone is being incorporated in the present-day sedimentation process. Considerably more research on these processes can be carried out following the work initiated by Andrew Hill and Kay Behrensmeyer.

The study of bone refuse and artefacts at short-term camps occupied by known numbers of Dassenetch tribesmen has been undertaken by Diane Gifford. The observation of daily activities and a pattern of re-using preferred camp sites has provided important data of the greatest interest to the interpretation of the archaeological sites. The exclusion of these people from the study area by the National Park has reduced the opportunity for ongoing research, but a small number of Dassenetch still persist in the traditional pattern of life at the north-east end of the lake.

Kay Behrensmeyer has attempted to elucidate possible relationships between fossil vertebrate assemblages and particular environments of sediment deposition. Initially this was approached by means of surface samples from a large series of squares and these results have been summarized by Behrensmeyer (1975). Additional investigations will incorporate excavation of localities where surface data have provided an overall pattern.

A detailed account of the taphonomic studies and the use of this data in the interpretation of fossil situations will appear in a subsequent volume in this series.

DATING AND CORRELATION

It is now well known that controversy has arisen from the published reports of radiometric dating of the tuffaceous units within the Koobi Fora Formation. A considerable effort has been made to obtain absolute ages for these horizons and an extensive body of data has accumulated; much of this is yet to be published but will appear as part of a subsequent volume in this series. Particular problems are associated with the KBS Tuff, which was dated by Fitch and Miller at 2.61 ± 0.26 million years (Fitch and Miller, 1970), and more recently at 2.42 ± 0.01 Myr (Fitch, Hooker, and Miller, 1976); and at 1.60 ± 0.05 and 1.82 ± 0.04 Myr by Curtis et al. (1975).

The research group has always been aware of the problems, and our publication of data has been on a provisional basis with a note of caution. The ongoing research has led to review and revision and there has been a remarkable degree of frank discussion and openness throughout. While I would certainly like to have our provisional reports confirmed, there is nothing sacred about any published interpretation, and as new data become available they will be presented. There are certainly some important issues raised by the alternative chronology presented by Curtis et al. (1975) and it is our intention that these be examined and tested.

I am impressed by the magnitude of the present dilemma where two different potassium–argon laboratories produce dates that are so much at variance. There is clearly a need for further radiogenic studies and a refinement of the techniques when applied to relatively young rocks. It is possible that an alternative dating technique will have to be employed to resolve the problem, and attention is being given, where possible, to the application of fission-track investigations and palaeomagnetic studies.

The potential of fission track work has only recently been recognized and this work was not started in connection with the Koobi Fora Formation until 1974. Preliminary results indicate that it may be possible to develop a chronology independent of the potassium–argon dates.

Instability in the magnetic properties of some of the sediments at Koobi Fora lead to ambiguity in the palaeomagnetic results, so that these studies seem unlikely to provide conclusive answers to dating or correlation questions.

Table 1.1 gives published best apparent K–Ar dates and fission-track dates for the major tuffs in the Koobi Fora Formation.

TABLE 1.1. *The published best apparent ages (Myr) for the major tuffs in the Koobi Fora Formation*

Tuff	K–Ar irradiation technique (Fitch and Miller, 1976)	(Fitch, Hooker, and Miller, 1976)	Conventional K–Ar (Curtis et al. 1975)	Fission track (Hurford et al. 1976)
Chari	1·22 ± 0·01	—	—	—
Lower/Middle	1·48 ± 0·17	—	—	—
Karari	1·32 ± 0·10	—	—	—
Okote	1·56 ± 0·02	—	—	—
Koobi Fora	1·57 ± 0·00	—	—	—
KBS	2·61 ± 0·26	2·42 ± 0·01	1·82 ± 0·04 and 1·60 ± 0·05	2·44 ± 0·08
Tulu Bor	3·18 ± 0·09	—	—	—
Suregei	—	—	—	—

PUBLICATIONS

A number of reports on various aspects of the research undertaken by the project have already been published. These are given in the bibliographical references (p. 180). Summary chapters are included in this volume as a background to the catalogue of hominid remains, serving to introduce in a general manner the geology, palaeontology, and archaeology of the region. In addition I have made some specific comments on certain aspects of the research programme in this chapter.

The planned series of monographs, of which this is the first, will include a full treatment of the palaeontology, geology, archaeology, and the fossil hominids.

The policy on the publication of the hominids has been the early announcement of discoveries in preliminary notes published in *Nature*, followed by more detailed descriptions in the *American Journal of Physical Anthropology*. The collection of fossil hominids has provided an unprecedented volume of data but initially very little attention was given to the interpretation of the material with regard to taxonomy, functional studies, and comparisons with other material. The reason for this was the very rapid annual growth of the collections which led to a group policy to refrain from interpretive studies until the anatomical descriptions had been published. Drs. Michael Day, Alan Walker, and Bernard Wood have devoted much time to the anatomical descriptions and they now have the task of preparing two separate volumes within this series which will give full consideration to anatomy, function, and taxonomic affinities of the hominid collection. Meanwhile some brief comments on taxonomy are given on p. 88. Casts of the hominid material referred to in this volume are available for purchase from the National Museum of Kenya.

CONCLUSION

It is unlikely that another locality of the size and richness of Koobi Fora will be found in Kenya. Although there are regions in Africa where vast tracts of unknown desert remain to be investigated, the 'discovery' of Koobi Fora must constitute an important landmark in the history and development of Quaternary research. The vastness of the site presented new problems in terms of logistics but, more important, the investigation required the collaboration of many scientists from different nations, different institutions, and different viewpoints. This interaction and collaboration has resulted in fresh concepts, and the profession has moved away from the historical situation of individualism.

Interpretations are always subject to further evaluation, but seldom before have so many facets of palaeontological project been the subject of such close review and discussion in the investigative stage. The extent of the geological area required the involvement of many geologists; the large collection of fossil vertebrates required the participation of many experts and the introduction of new people to take on specific problems. The numerous hominid fossils presented the opportunity of avoiding premature discussion on taxonomic issues, and the commitment of three anatomists was necessary to maintain an up-to-date schedule of publication on the basic descriptions. Had there been fewer specimens, the need for the three experts would not have arisen and a consequence might have been the traditional treatment of the material: brief descriptions and lengthy discussions on a single specimen's complex affinities. It is appropriate to record here my appreciation of the good-natured co-operation that I have enjoyed from Drs. Day, Walker, and Wood on this approach.

REFERENCES

BEHRENSMEYER, A. K. 1976. Lothagam Hill, Kanapoi and Ekora: a general summary of stratigraphy and faunas. In *Earliest man and environments in the Lake Rudolf Basin* (ed Y. Coppens *et al.*), pp. 163–70. University of Chicago Press.

CURTIS, G. H., DRAKE, R., CERLING, T. E., and HAMPEL, J. H. 1975. Age of KBS Tuff in Koobi Fora Formation, East Rudolf, Kenya. *Nature, Lond.* **258**, 395–8.

FITCH, F. J. and MILLER, J. A. 1970. Radio-isotopic age determinations of Lake Rudolf artefact site. *Nature, Lond.* **226**, 226–8.

——, 1976. Conventional potassium–argon and argon-40/argon-39 dating of the volcanic rocks from East Rudolf. In *Earliest man and environments in the Lake Rudolf Basin: Stratigraphy, paleoecology and evolution* (eds. Y. Coppens, F. C. Howell, G. Ll. Isaac, and R. E. F. Leakey), pp. 123–47. University of Chicago Press.

——, HOOKER, P. J., and MILLER, J. A. 1976. ^{40}Ar/^{39}Ar dating of the KBS Tuff in the Koobi Fora Formation, East Rudolf, Kenya. *Nature, Lond.* **263**, 740–4.

HARRIS, J. M. and WATKINS, R. T. 1974. A new early Miocene fossil mammal locality near Lake Rudolf, Kenya. *Nature, Lond.* **252**, 576–7.

HÖHNEL, L. VON. 1894. *Discovery of Lakes Rudolf and Stefanie: A narrative of Count Samuel Teleki's exploring and hunting expedition in eastern Equatorial Africa in 1887–1888.* Longmans and Green, London.

HURFORD, A. J., GLEADOW, A. J. W., and NAESER, C. W. 1976. Fission-track dating of pumice from the KBS Tuff, East Rudolf, Kenya. *Nature, Lond.* **263**, 738–40.

PATTERSON, B., BEHRENSMEYER, A. K., and SILL, W. D. 1970. Geology and fauna of a new Pliocene locality in northwestern Kenya. *Nature, Lond.* **226**, 918–21.

SMART, C. 1976. The Lothagam 1 fauna: its phylogenetic, ecological and biogeographic significance. In *Earliest man and environments in the Lake Rudolf Basin* (ed. Y. Coppens *et al.*), pp. 361–9. University of Chicago Press.

2

STRATIGRAPHY

IAN C. FINDLATER

INTRODUCTION

THIS chapter serves to introduce aspects of the geological studies in the Koobi Fora region (study area) used in identifying the areal and sequential positions of the fossil hominid localities (Figs. 2.2, 2.3, 2.4, 2.5).

The first section summarizes the formal and informal stratigraphic nomenclature used within the study area. The subsequent sections deal with the sedimentary environments of deposition, the history of sedimentation, and the fundamental controls of sedimentation. Taken together these sections outline the geological context of the sites at which hominid fossil remains were recovered.

Some specimens were found *in situ* and in one instance in an archaeological excavation; in these cases the stratigraphic and geological context can be determined exactly. However, the majority of fossils have been recovered as surface specimens exposed by the processes of erosion. It is clear from examination of the localities that the great majority of such specimens have been recently derived from beds that crop out in the vicinity. Inevitably, the degree of precision that is possible in assigning such specimens to a particular stratigraphic interval and to an environment of deposition varies considerably from case to case.

The final section discusses the use and limitations of the stratigraphic catalogue (Figs. 2.5 and 2.6) and the maps (Figs. 2.2, 2.3, 2.4) which show the distribution of the fossil localities. The sections and the maps together enable the relative position of individual fossil localities to be identified both in an areal and temporal sense. It should be clearly understood that the stratigraphic and lithologic studies that form the basis for defining the geological context are capable of defining only the *relative* sequential position of a fossil locality. To imply absolute time differences requires chronometric data from geophysical sources.

Inevitably in such a brief survey of the geology it is necessary to present many interpretations without the supporting evidence. These data will be considered fully in the geological monograph.

FORMAL AND INFORMAL STRATIGRAPHIC NOMENCLATURE

The stratigraphic correlation of sediments in the study area was investigated by Bowen (1974) as part of a doctoral thesis on the stratigraphic and petrographic

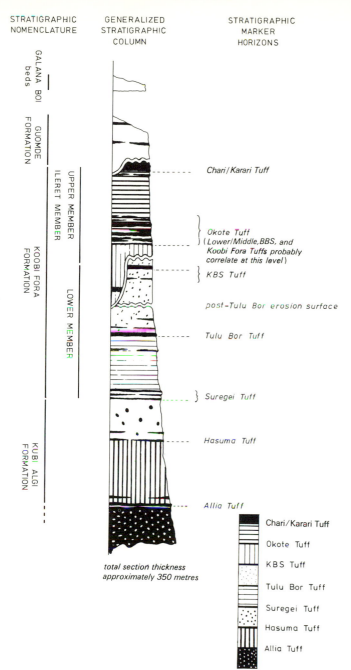

STRATIGRAPHIC NOMENCLATURE	GENERALIZED STRATIGRAPHIC COLUMN	STRATIGRAPHIC MARKER HORIZONS

FIG. 2.1. Generalized stratigraphic column showing stratigraphic nomenclature (after Bowen and Vondra, 1973).

aspects of the sediment body. From these studies it proved possible to erect a *formal* stratigraphic nomenclature (Bowen and Vondra, 1973) and this is shown in Fig. 2.1. The basis of the correlation was the identification of three laterally extensive tuff/tuffaceous horizons, the Suregei, KBS, and Chari Tuffs. Bowen and Vondra further introduced and formalized the name Tulu Bor Tuff for a widespread tuff/

15

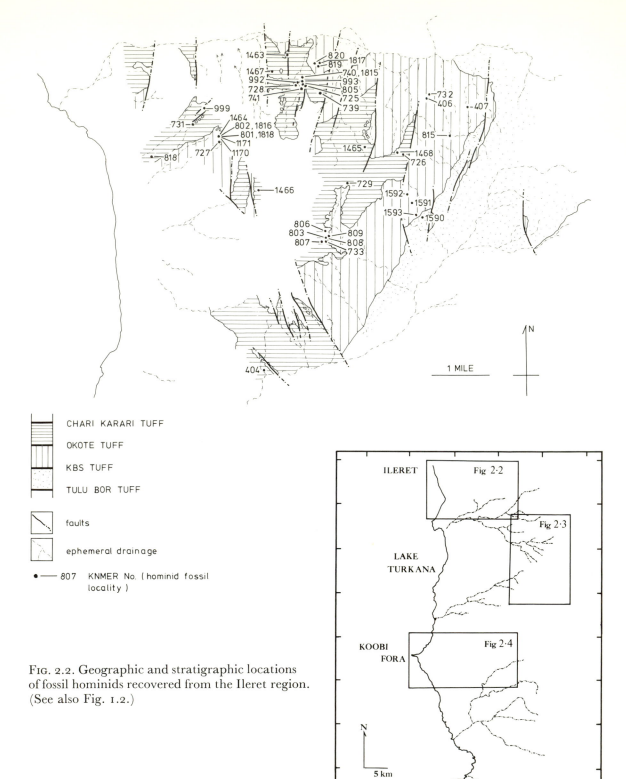

FIG. 2.2. Geographic and stratigraphic locations of fossil hominids recovered from the Ileret region. (See also Fig. 1.2.)

16

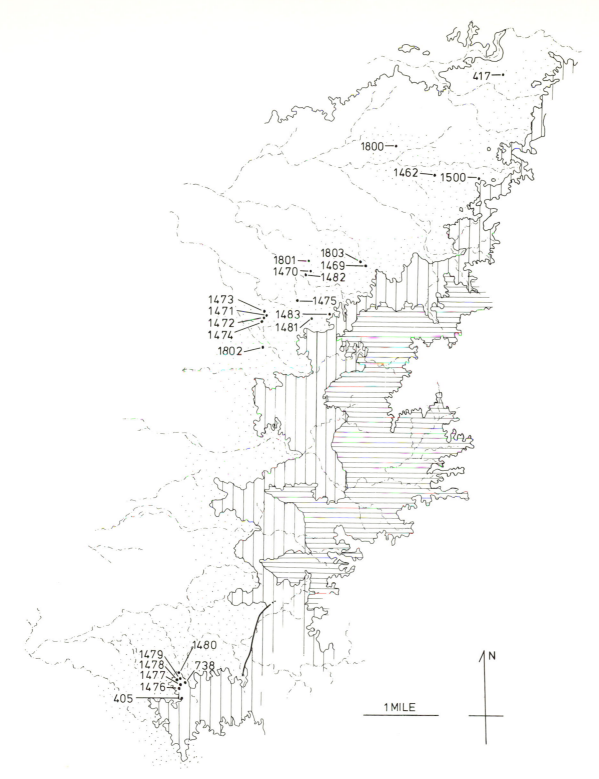

FIG. 2.3. Geographic and stratigraphic locations of fossil hominids recovered from areas 129, 130, 131, and 105. (See also Fig. 1.2 and inset map Fig. 2.2.)

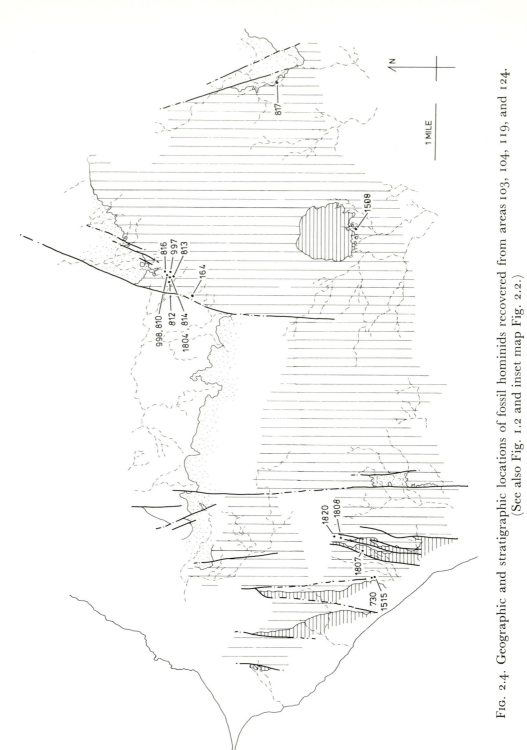

FIG. 2.4. Geographic and stratigraphic locations of fossil hominids recovered from areas 103, 104, 119, and 124. (See also Fig. 1.2 and inset map Fig. 2.2.)

tuffaceous horizon occurring between the Suregei and the KBS Tuff. The present author has formally named a further three tuffs, the Okote, Hasuma, and Allia Tuffs (Findlater, 1978).

The tuffs were chosen as the major correlation horizons because of their obvious field character both in colour and petrography. For the most part the tuffs were deposited from an aqueous medium and are therefore present only where declining energy conditions allowed deposition. This original depositional distribution was further modified by penecontemporaneous erosion so that the tuff or tuffaceous sediment is usually restricted in outcrop. The chief exception to this is along the Karari ridge, an area that was immediately downstream of the proto-Bakate Gap (Fig. 1.1). The palaeoriver flowing through the gap transported tuff into the study area and deposited much of it on the river floodplains which are today exposed along the flanks of the Karari ridge. The tuffs are seen as a nearly continuous blanket.

The tuffs used as the correlation marker horizons are not the only tuffs present in the succession (Fig. 2.1), and the possibility of incorrect correlation is always present. This is most likely to occur in the area around Koobi Fora and in the Allia Bay region where tuff outcrops are usually sparse and of restricted lateral extent. The Koobi Fora Tuff which occurs in areas 102 and 103 is retained in Figs. 2.5 and 2.6 although this has been provisionally correlated with the Okote Tuff, which crops out along the Karari ridge. The correlation of Bowen and Vondra (1973) between Ileret and the Karari ridge at the Tulu Bor, KBS, and Okote Tuff stratigraphic levels is considered satisfactory. The correlation of the Chari and Karari Tuff stratigraphic level is also considered satisfactory. The correlations are, however, best viewed as working hypotheses until further work has been completed and the author should point out that he is not always in agreement with the methods of stratigraphic subdivision used in this volume.

SEDIMENTARY ENVIRONMENTS OF DEPOSITION

Discussion of the geological context and the use of the stratigraphic catalogue (Figs. 2.5 and 2.6) is facilitated by reference to five major sedimentary environments that have been identified in the study area. These will be discussed fully in the geological monograph. They are briefly outlined as follows:

Alluvial Valley Plain	(AVP)
Alluvial Coastal Plain	(ACP)
Alluvial Delta Plain	(ADP)
Lacustrine High Energy	(LHE)
Lacustrine Low Energy	(LLE)

The environments adjoin each other (Fig. 2.8) and represent a broad classification of the potential depositional sites in the Plio–Pleistocene sediments of the study area.

The alluvial valley plain encompasses the established fluviatile channels and their floodplains. The environment is far enough upstream from the lake to be unaffected

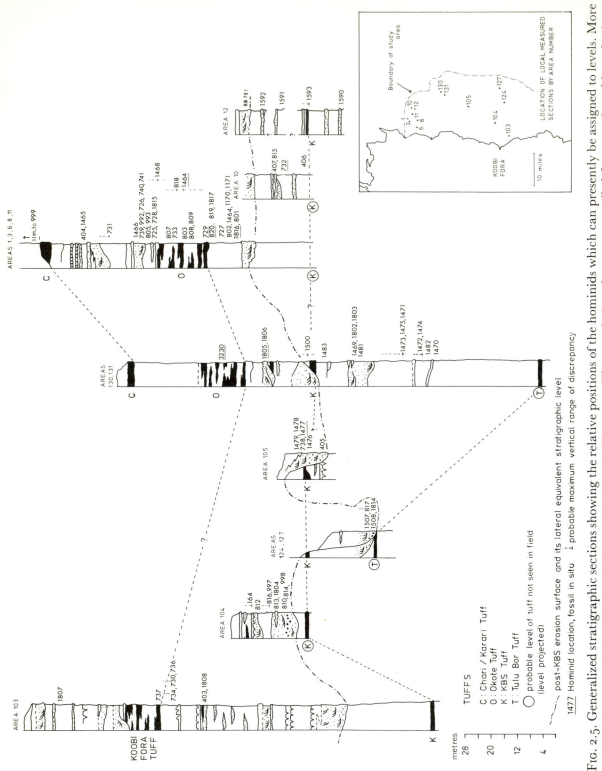

FIG. 2.5. Generalized stratigraphic sections showing the relative positions of the hominids which can presently be assigned to levels. More detailed placement is given in the Reference Sections in Chapter 5. The correlation chart was compiled from stratigraphic and micro-stratigraphic studies by I. C. Findlater, A. K. Behrensmeyer, and B. Bowen. The stratigraphic positions of hominids not included on the chart have yet to be determined with certainty.

Correlations between sections are based on the identification of marker units such as tuffs and similarity of stratigraphic sequences. Vertical dashed lines above or below hominid site markers indicate uncertainty ranges for placement of the hominid in the generalized sections.

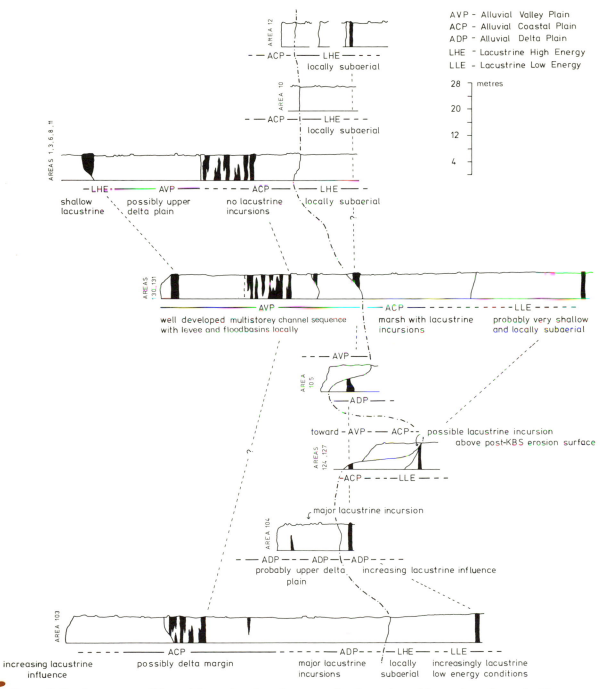

AVP – Alluvial Valley Plain
ACP – Alluvial Coastal Plain
ADP – Alluvial Delta Plain
LHE – Lacustrine High Energy
LLE – Lacustrine Low Energy

28 ⌐ metres

20

12

4

FIG. 2.6. Environments of deposition related to the generalized stratigraphic sections shown in Fig. 2.5.

TABLE 2.1. *Depositional environments in which it is thought that the hominids were buried*

The broad-scale environmental interpretations of Findlater (this chapter) are here presented together with finer-resolution interpretations of Behrensmeyer (Chapter 5).

Area	KNM-ER No.	After Findlater	After Behrensmeyer	Section No.
			Environments of deposition	
1	725	AVP	floodplain associated with $CaCO_3$ nodule horizon	10
	728	AVP	floodplain associated with $CaCO_3$ nodule horizon	10
	739	AVP	channel	18
	740	AVP	floodplain associated with $CaCO_3$ nodule horizon	19
	741	AVP	fluvial, probably edge of channel	20
	805	AVP	floodplain	10
	819	ACP	floodplain	—
	820	ACP	floodplain	25
	992	AVP	channel	26
	993	AVP	floodplain	10
	1463	ACP	floodplain	—
	1817	ACP	floodplain	—
1A	2595	—	—	—
3	1467	—	—	—
	1819	—	—	—
6	1466	AVP	channel	27
	2592	—	—	—
	2593	—	—	—
6A	727	ACP	distributary channel	11
	731	AVP	—	—
	801	ACP	distributary channel	11
	802	ACP	distributary channel	11
	818	ACP	—	—
	999	ACP	lake margin beach sand	—
	1170	ACP	distributary channel	11
	1171	ACP	distributary channel	11
	1464	ACP	edge of distributary channel	11
	1816	ACP	distributary channel	11
	1818	—	—	—
	1823	ACP	distributary channel	—
	1824	ACP	distributary channel	—
	1825	ACP	distributary channel	—
	3737	ACP	distributary channel	—
7A	404	ACP	interdistributary	2
8	729	ACP	floodplain channel edge	12
	733	ACP	small channel or levee on floodplain	15, 22
	803	ACP	levee or floodplain	21
	806	ACP	—	—
	808	ACP	—	21
	809	ACP	—	—
8A	807	ACP	floodplain or levee	15, 22
10	406	LHE	small distributary	8
	407	LHE	transgressive shoreline	9
	732	LHE	distributary channel or overbank	14
	815	LHE	delta margin, probably distributary or offshore	—
11	726	AVP	channel	—
	1465	ACP	delta margin, probably shoreline	—
	1468	AVP	channel	—
12	1590	LHE	delta margin	41
	1591	LHE	delta margin distributary	—
	1592	LHE	distributary channel or deltaic plain	42
	1593	LHE	delta margin	—
15	2596	—	—	—
	2597	—	—	—
	2598	—	—	—
	2599	—	—	—

Table 2.1—continued

Area	KNM-ER No.	Environments of deposition		Section No.
		After Findlater	After Behrensmeyer	
103	403	ADP	large distributary channel	23
	730	ACP	delta margin	13
	734	ACP	delta margin	—
	736	ACP	probably small distributary channel	16
	737	ACP	transgressive shoreline	17
	1515	—	—	—
	1807	ACP	large channel	47
	1808	ADP	delta margin probably distributary channel or transgressive sand	26
	1820	ADP	—	—
104	164	ADP	probably delta margin distributary	—
	810	ADP	channel	23
	811	—	—	—
	812	ADP	channel	24
	813	ADP	near the top of a channel	24
	814	ADP	channel	23
	816	ADP	upper part of channel	23
	997	ADP	probably channel	23
	998	ADP	probably channel	23
	1804	ADP	channel	45
105	405	AVP	channel	3
	738	AVP	channel	5
	1476	AVP	channel	4
	1477	AVP	channel	6
	1478	AVP	top of channel or floodplain	7
	1479	AVP	upper part of channel or floodplain	6
	1480	AVP	channel	6
	2607	AVP	channel	6
117	2602	—	—	—
	2603	—	—	—
	2604	—	—	—
	2605	—	—	—
	2606	—	—	—
118	1648	—	—	—
119	1509	—	—	—
121	1506	—	distributary channel	39
	1809	—	delta margin, probably distributary channel	—
123	1501	—	probably delta margin	36
	1502	—	delta margin	37
	1503	—	delta margin	38
	1504	—	delta margin	38
	1505	—	delta margin	38
	1810	—	delta margin, probably transgressive sand	—
	1811	—	delta margin, probably distributary channel	48
	1812	—	delta margin	37
	1813	—	delta margin, offshore or interdistributary	49
	1821	—	—	—
	1822	—	—	—
124	817	AVP	—	—
127	1507	AVP	channel	40
	1508	AVP	channel	40
	1814	AVP	floodplain	—
129	417	—	—	—
130	1462	—	—	—
	1500	ACP	channel	35
	1800	ACP/LHE	channel	43
	1805	AVP	channel	46
	1806	AVP	channel	46
	2600	—	—	—

Table 2.1—continued

| | KNM-ER | Environments of deposition | | Section |
Area	No.	After Findlater	After Behrensmeyer	No.
	2601	—	—	—
	3230	AVP	floodplain	—
131	1469	ADP	distributary channel	28
	1470	ACP/LHE	delta margin, upper part of distributary channel	29
	1471	ACP/LHE	delta margin	30
	1472	ACP/LHE	delta margin	31
	1473	ACP/LHE	delta margin	30
	1474	ACP/LHE	probably delta margin	31
	1475	ACP/LHE	delta margin	—
	1481	ADP	delta margin, distributary or interdistributary	32
131	1482	ACP/LHE	delta margin	33
	1483	ADP	channel or levee	34
	1801	ACP/LHE	—	—
	1802	ACP/LHE	delta margin	44
	1803	ADP	delta margin, probably shallow offshore	28

Where no entry occurs opposite a KNM-ER number, the fossil has not been placed in palaeoenvironmental context.

by lacustrine influence excepting for the grading of the long profiles of the channels to changing base level. The alluvial delta and alluvial coastal plains are transitional between the alluvial valley and the lacustrine environments. The deltaic plains occupy regions of maximum subsidence; sedimentation is often rapid, and relative to the alluvial coastal plain greater thicknesses of sediment are deposited in unit time. The alluvial coastal plain is tectonically relatively more stable than the delta situation and significantly less sediment is deposited in unit time. All three of the alluvial environments have intergrading boundaries. Their landward boundaries are defined by the contact with the actively eroding hinterland and therefore they include colluvia. Lakeward the delta and coast plains have a sharp boundary defined by the contact between subaerial and subaqueous conditions.

The lacustrine environment is divided into high- and low-energy depositional situations. The high-energy condition is found where the competency of the lacustrine currents flowing above the depositional surface prohibits the deposition of silt and sediment of finer grade. Effectively this means that the lacustrine high-energy environment receives only sand and coarser-grade sediment and is therefore geographically restricted to delta distributary mouths, upper delta slope, and shores affected by waves of high energy. The lacustrine low-energy environment is found where silt and finer sediments are deposited and the sand grades excluded because of insufficient current energies.

This fivefold environmental classification allows the major sedimentary environments and the palaeogeographic framework of the study area to be described. Thus it is possible to attribute each fossil to the depositional environment in which it was buried or from which (in the case of surface finds) recent erosion is presumed to have exhumed it (Table 2.1).

24

REVIEW OF THE FUNDAMENTAL CONTROLS OF SEDIMENTATION WITHIN
THE STUDY AREA

The history of sedimentation in the study area is that of westward prograding
alluvial deltaic and alluvial coastal plains which were themselves later overlain by
alluvial valley plains. This westward extension of subaerial conditions in late Pliocene
and Pleistocene times is in detail a complex history of transgressive and regressive lake
stages.

The factors affecting sedimentation are:

(a) *subsidence* reflecting both local and regional tectonic deformation;
(b) *sediment supply*, which is a function of catchment area relief (tectonic deformation), climate, and vegetation cover;
(c) *base level* static or dynamic lake level, which again reflects both climate and the
changing relief.

Long-term transgressive or regressive stages reflect imbalance between sediment
supply and subsidence relative to an approximately static base level. When sediment
supply exceeds subsidence the land is built out into the lake, appearing in the stratigraphic record as a long-term regression. When subsidence exceeds sediment supply
a long-term transgression occurs. The maintenance of static base level is considered
to have resulted from periods when there was sufficient rainfall to maintain a lake
level high enough to give outflow from the lake basin.

These long-term conditions were interrupted by shorter-term regressions with
penecontemporaneous incision of the earlier sediments and then subsequent inunda-
tion of the newly incised surfaces. During these periods the lake basin was probably
internally drained (evaporation exceeding inflow and rainfall) and the relative fall in
base level induced erosion. An increase in inflow would reverse this process and the
lake would rise until it again overflowed. Once the externally drained condition was
re-established the interrupted long-term regressive or transgressive lake stage would
continue. Such oscillating changes in base level are a feature of the lake basins in the
Eastern Rift. In the Western Rift, by contrast, stable lake levels are the rule today
and have been so through much of the late Cenozoic (Butzer *et al.* 1972).

Lake basins within the Eastern Rift are subject to tectonic movements interfering
with the outflow altitude and this induces fluctuations in lake level independent of
climate. At present little is known of the detailed tectonic development of the Lake
Turkana basin and this limits discussion. Thus an oversimplified picture may have
been given in this section.

SUMMARY OF THE HISTORY OF SEDIMENTATION

During Kubi Algi Formation times (Fig. 2.1) sediment was derived from the region
to the south of the study area and is almost totally of volcanic origin. Prograding
deltaic lobes advanced from the south in the Allia Bay region causing a regression of
the proto-lake that reached a maximum development around Hasuma Tuff times.
Unfortunately these stratigraphic levels are not exposed in the Koobi Fora and Ileret

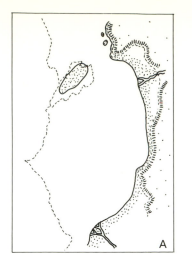

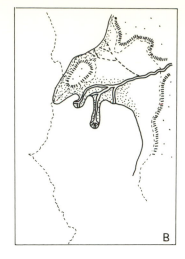

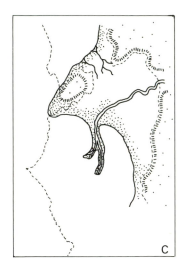

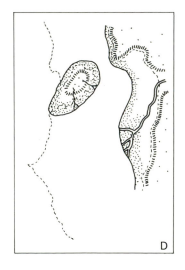

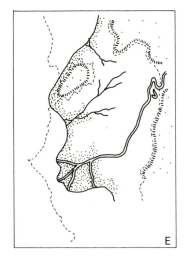

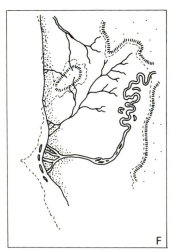

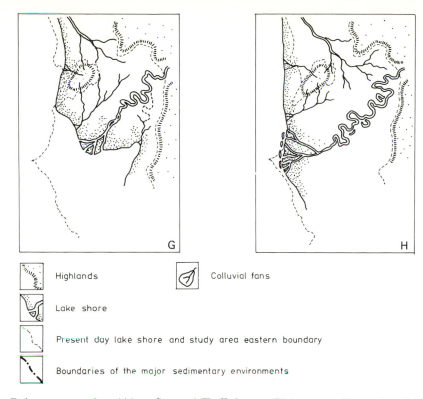

Highlands

Colluvial fans

Lake shore

Present day lake shore and study area eastern boundary

Boundaries of the major sedimentary environments

FIG. 2.7. Palaeogeography, (A) at Suregei Tuff times; (B) between Suregei and Tulu Bor Tuff times; (C) at Tulu Bor Tuff times; (D) at the maximum post-Tulu Bor transgression; (E) at KBS Tuff times; (F) at the maximum extent of the post-KBS erosion surface; (G) at the maximum transgression following the post-KBS erosion surface; (H) at Okote Tuff times.

regions except for a small inlier in area 102; consequently nothing is known about the palaeogeography in these regions.

By Suregei Tuff times (Fig. 2.7(A)) a major transgression of the proto-lake had inundated the entire study area, the shore being located along the present-day boundary between the sediments and the volcanics to the east and isolating the Kokoi volcanic uplift as an island.

During Koobi Fora Formation times, sediment derived from a catchment east of the study area, presumably along the rift axis, began to be transported into the study area via the proto-Bakate Gap. These sediments are dominated by material from the metamorphic rocks of the regional basement complex. Westward prograding deltaic conditions reached a maximum at or just after Tulu Bor times (Fig. 2.7(C)). By this time subaerial conditions existed between the Kokoi and the volcanic uplands to the east. After Tulu Bor Tuff times the proto-lake steadily transgressed the newly formed land surface and at its maximum (Fig. 2.7(D)) probably again isolated the Kokoi uplift. Between Kokoi and the Karari–Koobi Fora ridge, sediment infilling appears to have almost kept pace with the deepening depression formed by subsidence, so that through much of this time conditions of sedimentation were probably those of a swamp, with straggling low-gradient distributaries and frequent channel switching. A probably short but significant period of internal drainage interrupted the long-term transgression, and an incised land surface was formed—the post-Tulu Bor erosion surface. The time required for the incision of the land surface is unknown but it may be significant that the lacustrine sediments that overlie the erosion surface show no observable change in their molluscan fauna from the sediments underlying the surface. The long-term transgression reached its maximum after the erosion surface was incised.

Regression of the lake again commenced as sediment input exceeded the rate of subsidence. The shoreline withdrew to occupy a fluctuating position not far from the present lake margin, and this phase continued throughout the remainder of Koobi Fora Formation times. A major interruption to this long-term regression occurred after the deposition of the KBS Tuff. A major land surface was incised, the post-KBS erosion surface (Fig. 2.7(F)). In area 103, where deltaic conditions are found, a marked and sudden change in the molluscan faunas is observable (Williamson, 1978). Up to one-third of the identified lineages are terminated, and of those lineages that continue through the erosion surface there is a significant diminution in size of some taxa. While this marked change in the molluscan fauna may indicate a substantial period of time lost, it may equally be related to a short-term change in lake-water chemistry. As with the post-Tulu Bor erosion surface it is not possible using stratigraphic analysis alone to infer the period of time occupied by the formation of these land surfaces.

Above the post-KBS erosion surface an initial transgression inundated parts of the erosion topography (Fig. 2.7(G)). Regression again followed with the continuing long-term westward prograding of alluvial conditions. The post-erosion-surface transgression did not reach far inland though traces are present in areas 104 and 127 (Fig. 2.7(G)). Elsewhere all upper member deposits represent subaerial conditions. Delta and coastal plain were the predominant sedimentary environments in the Ileret region and areas 123 and 104. In area 103 alluvial delta plain dominates the depositional environment with major high-energy lacustrine incursions. Inland along the Karari ridge (areas 130, 131, 108, 105) above the erosion surface alluvial valley plains extended, with time, further and further westward toward Koobi Fora and north-westward into the Ileret region.

The Chari Tuff defines the upper boundary of the Koobi Fora Formation and by the time of its deposition in the Ileret region the lake was again expanding. These stratigraphic levels are not present in the Koobi Fora region.

A further episode of erosion locally truncated the Chari Tuff, then renewed sedimentation gave rise to the Guomde Formation. This is predominantly comprised of shallow lacustrine sediments, but includes alluvial deposits. Though their age is not known, it is clear that they predate the grid faulting that dislocates the entire sedimentary sequence. The faulting coincides with, and is probably responsible for, the cessation of major sedimentation in the study area.

Erosion appears to have dominated the post-faulting landscape through to the present day. The only known sediments in the study area younger than the faulting

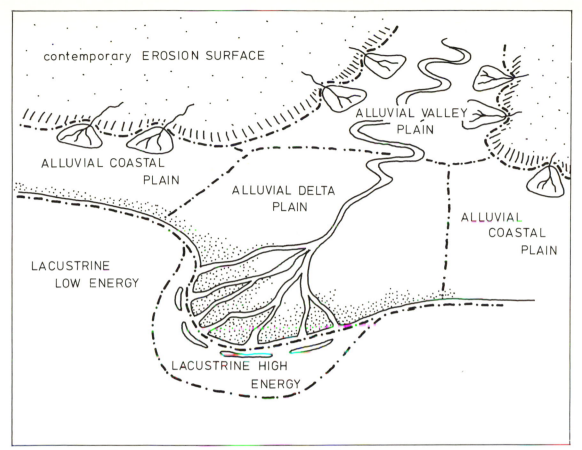

FIG. 2.8. The areal relationships of the five major environments.

are the Galana Boi beds which locally blanket the high-relief erosion topography. These beds, rich in molluscan fauna, probably represent a period when the lake rose to its overflow level and flooded large areas inland from the present shore line. This transgression belongs to the early Holocene and has been well dated to a period between about 10,000 B.P. and 4000 B.P. C[14] samples from sediments of this age are reported elsewhere in the Lake Turkana Basin (Butzer *et al.* 1972). The absence of lacustrine sediments from the time interval between the Guomde Formation and the Galana Boi beds could be due to: (1) prolonged internal drainage of the basin; (2) a different tectonically determined relation between the fault block of the study area and that controlling the altitude of the outlet; or (3) successive thin veneers of lake beds may have been deposited and then stripped off, just as erosion is now rapidly disposing of the Galana Boi beds.

USE OF THE STRATIGRAPHIC CATALOGUE

Figs. 2.5 and 2.6 illustrate generalized stratigraphic sections in the major fossil collecting areas. Fig. 2.5 was compiled by A. K. Behrensmeyer with additional material by the author. Each generalized stratigraphic section has been assembled from one or more local measured stratigraphic sections. It should be noted that for some sections, notably in areas 124 and 127, and also Ileret areas 1, 3, 6, 8, and 11, there may be considerable distances between local sections. In these situations every effort was made to ensure reasonable correlation.

The post-KBS erosion surface is well defined in the Karari ridge, exposures being identified by a distinct change in lithology above and below the surface. Westward, toward the lake shore, however, the lithologic contrast diminishes as the environments of deposition both above and below the surface become increasingly deltaic. The surface is not obvious in the areas 102 and 103 and its inferred level is a projection. The depth of incision of the surface decreases lakewards, and the potential loss of time between sediments above and below the surface will therefore increase landwards. A spectacular example of this is in area 127 where the post-KBS erosion surface is incised to the level of the Tulu Bor Tuff. The time loss across the erosion surface in this case is very substantial. This illustrates that it is wrong when using Figs. 2.5 and 2.6 to assume that equal time loss is represented wherever the erosion surface is identified. In the Ileret region the erosion surface level is probably represented by major regressive beach sands but the correlation is not well understood. In Figs. 2.5 and 2.6, where correlation is only provisional, broken lines have been drawn with question marks.

The stratigraphic position of those hominid fossil localities (the majority) that occur off the generalized sections have been determined by projecting the stratigraphic level of their occurrence laterally to intersect the nearest local measured section. The level of reliability of such projections varies, for it is sometimes difficult to identify the time-equivalent level between fossil and section. However, the lateral projection was established with reasonable confidence because many of the fossil localities are in alluvial delta and coastal plain sediments. In these environments minor transgressive and regressive sand lag sheets are often good marker horizons. Soil horizons, aeolian lag sheet sands, bioclastic sands, calcrete, and concretionary horizons have also been used locally as marker horizons.

In the alluvial valley plain environment, multistorey channel complexes and their equivalent floodbasin deposits often make the identification of time-equivalent surfaces difficult. To a certain extent this problem can be overcome by passing the traverse of the line of the local measured section(s) through as many of the fossil localities as possible (as occurs in area 104), or as close as possible to the localities, to minimize the errors associated with projection. However, it remains true that in the alluvial valley deposits the precision of sequential location is in general much lower than in the lake margin environment.

When precise attribution is in any doubt, this is noted on the generalized stratigraphic sections by a vertical broken line indicating the probable maximum vertical range of uncertainty (Fig. 2.5). More detailed stratigraphic placement is given in Chapter 5.

The sedimentary environments of deposition (Fig. 2.6) are shown at two scales of resolution. The more generalized scheme of environmental categories is detailed on p. 19. It defines the dominant environments represented in the beds containing the fossils. The second, finer scale of resolution (after Behrensmeyer, see reference sections in Chapter 5 and Table 2.1) identifies within these dominant environmental categories interpretations of particular sub-environments that will enable the reader to place associated fossils in a more restricted palaeogeographical context.

ACKNOWLEDGEMENTS

The author wishes to acknowledge his debt to those geologists who have been associated with the geological studies in the Koobi Fora region. First, Dr. B. E. Bowen, who laid the foundation of stratigraphic and environmental interpretation in this study area. Dr. A. K. Behrensmeyer's early geological investigations and later palaeoenvironmental interpretations form a substantial part of the geological context of the hominids (Chapter 5). Helpful discussions in the field were held with Dr. G. Johnson, Robert Raynolds, Thure Cerling, Hal Frank, and Russel Bainbridge. Drs. F. J. Fitch and C. F. Vondra supervised much of the work that led to this synthesis of the study area geology.

REFERENCES

BOWEN, B. E. 1974. The geology of the Upper Cenozoic sediments in the East Rudolf embayment of the Lake Rudolf basin, Kenya. Ph.D. thesis (unpublished). Iowa State University.

—— and VONDRA, C. F. 1973. Stratigraphical relationships of the Plio-Pleistocene deposits, East Rudolf, Kenya. *Nature, Lond.* **242**, 391–3.

BUTZER, K. W., ISAAC, G. LL., RICHARDSON, J. L., and WASHBOURN-KAMAU, C. 1972. Radiocarbon dating of East African lake levels. *Science,* **175**, 1069–76.

FINDLATER, I. C. 1978. Isochronous surfaces within the Plio/Pleistocene sediments east of Lake Turkana, Kenya. In *Geological background to fossil man* (ed. W. W. Bishop). Geol. Soc. Lond. Special Publ. No. 6. Scottish Academic Press, Edinburgh.

WILLIAMSON, P. G. 1978. Evidence for the major features and development of rift palaeolakes in the Neogene of East Africa from certain aspects of lacustrine mollusc assemblages. In *Geological background to fossil man* (ed. W. W. Bishop). Geol. Soc. Lond. Special Publ. No. 6. Scottish Academic Press, Edinburgh.

3

PALAEONTOLOGY

JOHN M. HARRIS

INTRODUCTION

THE sedimentary rocks exposed to the east of the northern half of Lake Turkana range in age from Miocene to Recent. Although investigations are in progress on, or are planned for, the earlier and later fossiliferous levels, only the Pliocene and Pleistocene fossiliferous sequences have so far been sampled in any great detail. The resultant collection of more than four thousand specimens provides an illustration of faunal change in the region over a period exceeding two million years.

The sediments from which the fossils were obtained reflect phases in the development of the Lake Turkana basin. Parts of the sedimentary succession that represent major expansions of the lake were not conducive to preservation of terrestrial faunas and such lacustrine episodes are virtually barren of mammalian fossil material. In consequence Pliocene mammal-rich fossiliferous horizons are infrequent. Fluviatile and terrestrial sediments predominate in the early and middle Pleistocene succession and have yielded a more continuous faunal record.

The Pliocene and Pleistocene sequences include a number of tuffaceous units, many of which have been employed as stratigraphic marker horizons. The tuffs employed as markers were originally labelled by a restricted set of names, each derived from a type outcrop. Use of these names has, however, been extended to areas that are geographically remote from the type localities. Many of the mapped tuffs and their projected horizons do define valid stratigraphic intervals over wide areas, and the majority of provisional regional correlations proposed by Bowen and Vondra (1973) and Findlater (this volume) can be substantiated by evidence from the fossil vertebrate faunas. Difficulties encountered in unequivocally matching tuff sequences in the basin are in large part due to the limited lateral extent of the tuff exposures and their lack of unique identifiable field criteria. The work of stratigraphic revision is being undertaken under the direction of I. C. Findlater, and laboratory investigation of the component particles of the tuffaceous horizons is being pursued by T. E. Cerling. Both investigations should in due course lead to a refinement of formal rock-stratigraphic and time-stratigraphic nomenclature for the region. In the meantime there is a need for a system of labels for the local marker beds that are currently in use.

It is felt that as far as possible the labelling system must avoid prejudging the

ILERET

Areas: 1A	01	02	03	04 06 6A	05	07 7A	08 8A	8B	09	10	11	12	14	15
L/M	CH	CH	CH	CH	CH	CH	L/M		L/M		CH	II	II	IV
	L/M	L/M	L/M	L/M		L/M	I				L/M	I	I	III
														II
													SU	SU

KOOBI FORA

Karari Ridge				KBS–Kokoi Area				Koobi Fora Ridge								Bura Hasuma		
118	129	130	131	105	115	116	117	100	101	102	103	104	106	119	127	110	121	123
KAR	V	KAR	KAR	III	I	KBS	VI	II	KF	KF	KF	III	KF	KF	III	III	I	
OK	IV	OK	OK	KBS		III	V	I	I	VII	IV	II	II		II	II		
II	III	II	III	I		II	IV			VI	III	I	I		I	I		
I	TB	I	II			I	III			V	II							
	I		I				II			IV	I							
							I			III								
										II								
										I								

KUBI ALGI

202	203	204	206	250
IV	V	IV	I	I
III	IV	III		
II	III	AL		
HA	II	I		
	I			

Named tuff abbreviations: KAR; Karari; CH; Chari; L/M; Lower/Middle; KF; Koobi Fora; OK; Okote; KBS; KBS; TB; Tulu Bor; SU; Suregei; HA; Hasuma; Al; Allia

FIG. 3.1. List of known tuffs of the Koobi Fora and Kubi Algi Formations, designated by area. Roman numerals are assigned in vertical sequence within each area and *do not* imply correlation between areas. Named tuffs (or letter abbreviations) indicate correlations which are direct and secure between the type area and adjoining areas. The base of each tuff enclosed within a box has been employed as a palaeontological marker horizon. (Fig. 3.3.)

Column groupings — **ILERET** (Areas): 1A–15; **KOOBI FORA**: Karari Ridge (118, 129, 130, 131), KBS–Kokoi Area (105, 115, 116, 117, 100), Koobi Fora Ridge (101, 102, 103, 104, 106, 119, 127), Bura Hasuma (110, 121, 123); **KUBI ALGI**: 202, 203, 204, 206, 250.

	1A	01	02	03	04/06/6A	05	07/7A	08/8A	8B	09	10	11	12	14	15	118	129	130	131	105	115	116	117	100	101	102	103	104	106	119	127	110	121	123	202	203	204	206	250
Karari		CH	CH	CH	CH	CH	CH	CH				CH				KAR		KAR	**KAR**																				
Okote	L/M	L/M	L/M	L/M	L/M		L/M	**L/M**		L/M		L/M					**OK** / V	OK	OK						**KF**	KF	KF	KF	KF	KF	KF / III								
KBS													II	II	IV		IV	II	I	**KBS**	I	KBS (VI)	I			(VI)	(II)	(II)	II										
Tulu Bor																	**TB**					(II)	III	(II)		(IV)													
Suregei														SU	**SU**								I				(II)								(IV)				
Hasuma																																				**HA**	II	IV	
Allia																																					**AL**	I	I

FIG. 3.2. Tuffs formerly named (**bold type**) and used by Bowen and Vondra (1973), Vondra and Bowen (1976), and Findlater (this volume and in press) in their provisional regional rock-stratigraphic correlation, which is now being re-examined in terms of lateral relationships of the tuffs and other marker horizons. The names, hitherto used over a wide area, are retained only in areas where relationship with the type locality is direct and secure. This figure should *not* be used as a guide to correlations between named and numbered tuffs until further geological work has been completed.

ILERET

Collection units	1A	01	02	03	04 06 6A	05	07 7A	08 08A 8A	8B	09	10	11	12	14	15
6		CH	CH	CH	CH	CH	CH					CH			
5	L/M	L/M	L/M	L/M	L/M	X	L/M	L/M L/M	L/M	L/M		L/M			
4	X	X		X	X		X	X	X	X	X	X	II	III	IV
3											X		X	X	X
2														SU	SU
1															

KOOBI FORA

Collection units	Karari Ridge 118	129	130	131	KBS-Kokoi Area 105	115	116	117	Koobi Fora Ridge 100	101	102	103	104	106	119	127	Bura Hasuma 110	121	123
6	KAR		KAR	KAR															
5	OK	V	OK	OK						KF	KF	KF		KF	KF	III			
4	II	IV	I	I	KBS	I	KBS		II	X	X	X	X	X	X	X	X	X	X
3	X	TB	X	X	X	X	I		X		X								
2							X	I			?								
1								X			?	?							

KUBI ALGI

Collection units	202	203	204	206	250
C	HA	II	IV		
B	X	X	AL	I	I
A		X		X	X

FIG. 3.3. Collection units in the major fossiliferous areas east of Lake Turkana. The *base* of each collection unit is, where possible, related to a numbered or named tuff. The occurrence of collection units whose lower boundaries cannot presently be defined litho-stratigraphically is denoted by X.

correlations that are being tested. An index has therefore been prepared in which each known tuff occurrence in each area is assigned a serial number from the lowest to the highest. For example, the second tuffaceous unit up from the base of the section in Area 129 is designated 129/T II, and so on (Fig. 3.1). Previously published names for tuffs (e.g. KBS, Tulu Bor, etc.) will be retained only in the type area and in adjoining areas where correlation amounts to certainty. The named tuff beds are also assigned numbers in their type areas although, in general, they will be referred to by name rather than number. Formerly accepted lateral correlations of named tuffs are shown in Fig. 3.2. Many more tuff beds are known than those which have been used as markers and all have been assigned numbers. The proposed system is a working device that should facilitate studies of biostratigraphy independent of prior correlation hypotheses.

Subsequent advances in the comprehension of both local faunas and stratigraphy indicate that continued use of the biostratigraphic zonation proposed by Maglio (1972) would lead to confusion unless the zones were redefined to incorporate necessary nomenclatorial changes, updated interpretations of associated faunal assemblages, and redefinition of zonal boundaries. In effect such required changes necessitate total redefinition of Maglio's concurrent range zones and this will be possible only when further proposed microstratigraphic surveys have been completed and when all elements of the fauna have been studied in greater detail. Meanwhile it is desirable that the known fossiliferous sequences should be divided and grouped in such a manner that faunal changes within and outside the basin can be discussed.

The vertebrate fossil faunas recovered from the Pliocene and Pleistocene strata have been collected with reference to their exact geographic location (marked on aerial photographs) and to their position in the sequence *vis-à-vis* local tuff outcrops. Information provided from study of the fossil Suidae confirms some of the provisional regional tuff correlations and suggests that others are erroneous. However, in-sufficient samples have been obtained to test all the provisional tuff correlations. At this stage in the investigation a combination of faunal and lithostratigraphic evidence is therefore necessary to construct temporal criteria essential to further study of represented faunal elements. Accordingly, nine informal collection units have been established to facilitate the collection of faunal samples from different segments of the local succession. The main biological basis for the collection units is observed gradualistic evolutionary change exhibited by suid species (Harris and White, in press; White and Harris, 1977). This is comparable to that observed in other fossil suid populations from Pliocene and Pleistocene localities of sub-Saharan Africa. The upper and lower collection unit boundaries are expressed in terms of marker horizons present in those local areas that have yielded fossil suids, the boundary in each case being defined as the base of such marker horizons. The collection unit boundaries are indicated in Fig. 3.3.

Three collection units (A–C) are restricted to the southern (Allia Bay) part of the region. Collection units 1–5 are recognized in the greater part of the basin (Bura

Hasuma northwards). Suid, bovid, and primate evidence suggests that there is an as yet unresolved amount of temporal overlap between the northern and southern collection units.

Collection units A–C comprise that part of the sequence forming the type section of the Kubi Algi Formation and the *Notochoerus capensis* zone of Maglio (1972). The new collection unit scheme is to be preferred to the former terminology for two reasons. First, the lower boundary of the Koobi Fora Formation is defined by the Suregei Tuff, but the latter may not be unequivocally equated with any tuff or other marker horizon occurring south of Bura Hasuma. Second, nomenclatorial changes have resulted in *Notochoerus capensis* (*sensu* Maglio) now being interpreted as *N. euilus* (*sensu* Harris and White). At least two different fossil mammalian assemblages are now known to occur in the southern succession, one of which is characterized by *Notochoerus capensis* (*sensu* Maglio) and the other by *Notochoerus capensis* (*sensu* Harris and White).

Similar reasons require at least temporary abandonment or interim redefinition of former nomenclature applied to the northern succession. Collection units 1–5 include those parts of the succession formerly including exposed portions of the Kubi Algi Formation around the Kokoi horst and at Ileret plus the former Koobi Fora Formation. Collection unit 1 equates essentially with the northern exposures of the Kubi Algi Formation. Collection unit 2 is known only from areas 117 and 129 and is apparently either condensed or missing from above the level of the Tulu Bor Tuff in the latter area. Collection unit 3 equates essentially with the upper fossiliferous portion of the former lower member of the Koobi Fora Formation and with Maglio's *Mesochoerus limnetes* zone. Collection unit 4 equates with the lower part of the former upper member of the Koobi Fora Formation and in part with both the Ileret Member of the latter formation and with Maglio's *Metridiochoerus andrewsi* zone. Collection unit 5 is equivalent to the upper portion of both the former upper member and Ileret Member of the Koobi Fora Formation, with Maglio's *Loxodonta africana* zone and with part of his *M. andrewsi* zone. The former terms 'upper' and 'lower member' of the Koobi Fora Formation are recognized as useful informal subdivisions of the Koobi Fora sequence but cannot be employed without further qualification because their defined junction—the KBS Tuff—is now recognized only in two areas (105 and 116). In this chapter informal use of 'lower member' and 'upper member' corresponds with collection units 2–3 and 4–5 respectively, their junction being that of zones 3–4 as seen in Fig. 3.3.

Collection unit 6 corresponds to the former Guomde Formation, whose lower boundary is equivalent to the top of the Chari Tuff. Collection unit 6 is currently restricted geographically to the Ileret region.

The recognition that tuffaceous marker horizons can be confidently used only locally has in effect greatly restricted the validity of formal and informal terms formerly applied to the Pliocene and Pleistocene sequences east of Lake Turkana. The collection unit scheme as outlined above is put forward as an interim device to facilitate discussion of the collected faunas pending the resolution of lithostratigraphic correlative problems and formal proposition of comprehensively defined biostratigraphic concurrent range zones.

The majority of specimens collected from the Koobi Fora Formation have been retrieved through surface prospecting and few excavations have been undertaken other than those at hominid, microfaunal, or archaeological sites. Circumstantial evidence makes it clear that the great majority of specimens do derive from layers that crop out at the localities where they were collected and we have adopted such attribution as a working hypothesis for the entire collection. Specimens of fossil *Phacochoerus* and fossil *Equus* remains that occur as 'float' in areas that are capped by the high lake level Galana Boi beds do, however, provide notable exceptions to such an hypothesis and are not considered as part of the Koobi Fora or Kubi Algi Formation faunas.

Since 1971 the exact location of each fossil collected has been noted on aerial photographs. Since geological mapping is done in the first instance as a series of overlays on aerial photographs, the relationship of the collected fossils to current geological interpretation can always be ascertained despite any necessary revised interpretations of the stratigraphy in any one area.

In addition to general surface collecting a systematic sampling programme to investigate the palaeotaphonomy of the fossiliferous horizons has been undertaken (Behrensmeyer, 1975). This has yielded valuable information on the mode of accumulation of the fossil material. It has also provided an independent means of discerning the relative abundance of the various fossil taxa. It has, furthermore, shown that certain of the fossil species are restricted to particular depositional facies and this has important connotations for interpretation of the preferred habitats of such species. The same techniques have been applied to localities at which hominid fossils have been found, and preliminary results are suggestive of possible differences in the ecologic preferences of the several recognized hominid species (Behrensmeyer, 1976, in press, *a*, *b*). Further work and an enlarged sample will be necessary to verify such preliminary indications and excavations will be needed to assess the degree to which surface samples, exposed by erosion, fairly reflect the composition of assemblages *in situ*.

A total of well over 4000 mammalian fossil specimens has now been collected from the Koobi Fora Formation. Enough fully provenanced specimens have been retrieved to permit detailed investigation of most mammalian groups represented in the faunas. Such investigations are currently being pursued. The well preserved and complete nature of much of the material from the Koobi Fora Formation has already proved of vital importance in the correct identification of more fragmentary material from other East African Plio–Pleistocene localities. It is evident that the faunas from east of Lake Turkana will play a vital role in the comprehension of evolutionary, biogeographic, and environmental changes during the late Pliocene and early Pleistocene. This in turn will help place into context our knowledge of early man and his activities.

Seventy-five extinct mammalian species (exclusive of micro-mammals) and twelve extant species are known from the Koobi Fora Formation. The bovids are the most prominent group in terms of both number of species and total number of specimens, but primates, carnivores, and suids are also numerous and diverse. Many of the mammalian families were represented by a greater number of geologically synchronous species in the Koobi Fora Formation than they are today. In the modern fauna of the region only the carnivores retain a similar species diversity. Human activities and an increase in the aridity of the region have, even in historic times, appreciably reduced the variety of extant wild fauna. It is also interesting that of the domestic animals introduced into the region in historic times, the donkey, camel, and cow were also represented by closely allied forms during the early Pleistocene.

Discrete ecological zonation can today be recognized within the confines of the sedimentary basin and this affects the regional distribution of ungulate species. *Equus burchelli* and *Damaliscus korrigum* are apparently confined to the grassy lake margins; *Giraffa camelopardalis* (and *Diceros bicornis?*) to the sparse riverine forest fringing the larger sand rivers; *Oryx beisa*, *Gazella granti*, *Tragelaphus strepsiceros* and *T. imberbis*, *Litocranius walleri*, *Rhynchotragus guentheri*, *Phacochoerus aethiopicus*, and *Equus grevyi* inhabit the semi-desert bushland away from the lake. Contrasting zones must almost certainly have been in existence during the Plio–Pleistocene although it is probable that somewhat more humid climatic conditions prevailed. The geological and faunal evidence is consistent with a pattern of well-vegetated lake margins, perennial and ephemeral rivers fringed by gallery forest, and with wooded or bush grassland predominating away from the lake. Periodic minor climatic fluctuations affected the lake level and perhaps modified the vegetation pattern also.

The apparent species diversity of the fauna from the Koobi Fora Formation is noteworthy and is difficult to explain. Seasonal climatic changes may have controlled the composition of the biota so that any resultant fossil accumulation may, at any one locality, represent an admixture of taxa with different habitat preferences. Transport of carcass elements post mortem and the inevitably coarse temporal definition of any local fauna may also contribute to the apparent diversity of fossil faunas. The variety of fossil carnivore species is not unexpected and reflects the diversity of prey animals on which they depend. The large total number of suid species assumes less dramatic proportions once it is appreciated that no more than three species are common at any one horizon, and that each presumably had different dietary requirements and habitat preferences. Palaeotaphonomic work (Behrensmeyer, 1975) has already indicated that some fossil taxa are restricted to particular depositional environments although the latter are not necessarily the original habitats. The presence of anomalously large numbers (by modern standards) of pig, primate, hippo, giraffe, and bovid species tends to suggest that each of the fossil taxa had a more rigorously defined niche specificity than is exhibited by most constituents of extant African faunas. The reduction in total number of herbivores after the Pleistocene may be due to decrease in the number of available niches (through human agency or climatic change) or to the assumption of less specialized dietary requirements by the successful surviving forms.

A brief synopsis of the fauna and flora from the Koobi Fora Formation follows. The larger mammalian fossils have so far received more attention and are thus emphasized accordingly. Each mammalian species is, where possible, dealt with separately. The provenances cited are those known as at the end of the 1975 field season. The references quoted represent published results of current and previous investigations. More detailed accounts of the fauna will be given in a subsequent volume in this series.

MAMMALIA

INSECTIVORA

Material: mandibles, isolated teeth.
Collection unit: 3.
Remarks: Microfaunal prospecting was not initiated until the 1974 field season but representatives of three insectivore families—Chrysochloridae, Erinaceidae, and Soricidae—have subsequently been recovered from collection unit 3. As yet only a small proportion of the field area has been surveyed for micromammals.

PRIMATES

CERCOPITHECIDAE

Cercopithecinae

Theropithecus oswaldi
Material: crania, dentitions, postcranial elements.
Collection units: 3–5.
Remarks: This is the most common cercopithecoid taxon and though absent from collection unit 2 occurs throughout the remainder of the Koobi Fora Formation. *T. oswaldi* appears to replace *T. brumpti* in Omo Shungura Member F (G. Eck, pers. comm.).
Evolutionary changes: Increase in size and in complexity and hypsodonty of the cheek teeth through the succession. Posterior cheek teeth increase in size relative to the anterior teeth.
Reference: M. G. Leakey, 1976a.

Theropithecus brumpti
Material: cranium, mandibles.
Collection unit: 2; Kubi Algi Formation.
Remarks: This species is not contemporary with *T. oswaldi* east of Lake Turkana but more advanced representatives are found with *T. oswaldi* in Omo Shungura Members F and G. *T. brumpti* is the predominant species at Omo (Eck, in press).
Evolutionary changes: Specimens from the Kubi Algi Formation and collection unit 2 have smaller, less hypsodont, and less complex teeth and the mandibles have smaller masseteric fossae than those from Omo Shungura Members C–G (G. Eck, pers. comm.). Only one female cranium is known (from collection unit 2) but its zygoma is slighter than in specimens from the Omo.
Reference: M. G. Leakey, 1976a.

Papio sp.
Material: crania, mandibles.
Collection units: 3–4.
Remarks: This species is a relatively short-nosed baboon and an almost complete skull from the collection unit 4 shows clear affinities with extant *Papio*. A relatively complete muzzle of *Papio* from Omo is much longer than the Koobi Fora specimens.
Evolutionary changes: A short-nosed monkey (cf. *Papio*) from the Kubi Algi Formation may well be ancestral to the specimens from the Koobi Fora Formation.

Papionini indet.
Material: mandibular specimens.
Collection unit: 3; Kubi Algi Formation.
Remarks: Three specimens from collection unit 3 and one from collection unit C are so fragmentary that they cannot be assigned to a single taxon with confidence. They evidently represent a small baboon-like monkey. Similar specimens are known from most levels in the Omo Shungura sequence.
Reference: M. G. Leakey, 1976a.

Cercopithecinae indet.
Material: two mandibular specimens.
Collection unit: 2.
Remarks: These mandibles are similar in size to those of *T. oswaldi* but show an unusual combination of characters which at present prevents precise taxonomic allocation. The teeth appear to be papionine but have some theropithecine features. This taxon is not present in the Omo Shungura Formation.

Cercocebus sp.
Material: crania, isolated teeth.
Collection units: 4–5.

Remarks: With the exception of four South African specimens (B. Eisenhart, pers. comm.), these are the only known fossil *Cercocebus* remains. The specimens show a mixture of characters seen in several extant mangabeys but their relationship to extant species is unclear. The occurrence of *Cercocebus* in the Koobi Fora Formation is restricted to very few localities and this may suggest a specific habitat preference. Mangabeys are today always restricted to forested regions. A small Papionini species which may have affinities with *Cercocebus* has been recorded from the Omo Usno Formation and from Shungura Members B and C (Eck, 1976).
References: Leakey and Leakey, 1976; M. G. Leakey, 1976a.

Cercopithecus sp.
Material: isolated molar, femur.
Collection unit: 4.
Remarks: The femur shows affinities with *C. aethiops* but the incomplete nature of the material precludes positive identification. A smaller, talapoin-sized *Cercopithecus* is known from the Kubi Algi Formation. *Cercopithecus* of similar size to the collection unit 4 specimens has been recorded from the Omo Usno Formation and from Shungura Members B, G and J (Eck, 1976; Eck and Howell, 1972).
Reference: M. G. Leakey, 1976a.

Colobinae
Colobus sp.
Material: cranial fragments and isolated teeth.
Collection units: 4–5.
Remarks: The five known specimens are too fragmentary to identify with certainty but show closest affinities to the extant red colobus. *Colobus* are nearly always associated with forests and it is interesting that these specimens were mostly recovered from the same areas as the *Cercocebus* specimens.
Reference: M. G. Leakey, 1976a.

Cercopithecoides sp. nov.
Material: crania, mandibles, postcranial elements.
Collection units: 3–4.
Remarks: This large colobine is most common in collection unit 3. It is characterized by a shallow mandible with a low, slightly angled ascending ramus. The supraorbital tori are thick and the braincase is rounded but without a marked postorbital constriction. The zygoma is relatively narrow. The teeth are relatively wide. A significantly smaller *Cercopithecoides*, slightly larger than

the South African species, is known from the Kubi Algi Formation and may be ancestral to the Koobi Fora Formation species. *Cercopithecoides* is not recorded from the Omo.
References: Leakey and Leakey 1973; M. G. Leakey, 1976a.

Colobinae gen. et sp. nov.
Material: crania, mandibles, postcranial elements.
Collection units: 2–3.
Remarks: This large colobine is characterized by a deep mandible with a tall ascending ramus that was elongate anteroposteriorly. It has a marked postorbital constriction on the cranium, a relatively small braincase, thin supraorbital tori, and a wide zygoma. The teeth are relatively narrow and the premolars large. It is common throughout the Shungura sequence (Eck, 1976).
References: Leakey and Leakey, 1973; M. G. Leakey, 1976a.

Colobinae gen. indet.
Material: mandibles.
Collection unit: 3; Kubi Algi Formation.
Remarks: The specimens represent small- to medium-sized colobines but are too fragmentary to permit positive identification.

RODENTIA
Material: mandibles, isolated teeth.
Collection units: 3–4.
Remarks: Several species of thryonomid and murid rodents are represented but the material has yet to be fully studied.

LAGOMORPHA
Material: cranium and associated skeletal elements.
Collection unit: 3.
Remarks: The only lagomorph specimen yet known from the Koobi Fora Formation comprises a poorly preserved articulated skull and mandible with associated postcranial elements. The specimen was discovered at the end of the 1975 field season and has not yet been studied in detail.

CARNIVORA
CANIDAE
Canis cf. **mesomelas**
Material: cranium, mandibles.
Collection units: 3–4.
Remarks: Although these specimens show close resemblances to the extant *C. mesomelas*, the minor nature of cranial differences between

extant jackal species preclude precise identification of the fossil specimens.
Reference: M. G. Leakey, 1976*b*.

cf. **Lycaon** sp.
Material: Associated cranial and postcranial remains, edentulous mandible.
Collection units: 3–4.
Remarks: Known specimens represent a canid slightly smaller than the extant *L. pictus*. The postcranial elements show closer similarities to those of wild dogs than to those of jackals.
Reference: M. G. Leakey, 1976*b*.

MUSTELIDAE
Lutra sp. nov.
Material: crania, mandibles, postcranial elements.
Collection units: 2–4.
Remarks: The material provides information about the skull and skeleton of this species that is not available from other localities. The new species is significantly larger than *L. lutra* and twice the size of *L. maculicollis*. The teeth clearly belong to *Lutra* rather than *Aonyx*. The skull is more elongate with a wider muzzle and less exaggerated postorbital constriction than in *L. lutra*. A cranial vault and upper first molar from Olduvai incorrectly referred to *Aonyx* by Petter (1973) are clearly conspecific with *Lutra* sp. nov. A lower first molar is known also from Omo (Howell and Petter, 1976).
Reference: M. G. Leakey, 1976*b*.

Enhydriodon sp. nov.
Material: hemimandible (M_1) and isolated M_2.
Collection units: 2–3.
Remarks: This very large species of otter is known also from Omo (Howell and Petter, 1976) and Hadar (D. C. Johanson, pers. comm.).

Mellivorinae gen. et sp. indet.
Material: mandible (M_1).
Collection unit: 3.
Remarks: The specimen resembles *Mellivora capensis* in size and morphology but the fossil molar is narrower. Two specimens of Mellivorinae are known from Shungura Member E but are much larger than the collection unit 3 specimen (Howell and Petter, 1976).

VIVERRIDAE
Genetta cf. **genetta**
Material: palate, maxillary fragment.
Collection units: 3–4.
Remarks: The specimens are indistinguishable from the extant *Genetta genetta* but are similar also to other extant species.
Reference: M. G. Leakey, 1976*b*.

Pseudocivetta ingens
Material: cranial vault, isolated teeth.
Collection units: 3–4.
Remarks: Petter (1973) showed that the posterior dentition of Olduvai specimens was large and specialized. The Koobi Fora material indicates that the anterior dentition was also large and specialized. A cranial vault which has relatively large sagittal and nuchal crests, a large extension to the jugular process and an exceptionally large pterygoid, all features that are consistent with a specialized masticatory apparatus, is also assigned to *P. ingens*. This species is represented from Omo by a P^4 and partial humerus (Howell and Petter, 1976).
Reference: M. G. Leakey, 1976*b*.

HYAENIDAE
Hyaena hyaena
Material: crania, mandibles, postcranial elements.
Collection units: 3–5.
Remarks: Two spectacularly complete crania from collection unit 3 show affinities with the small *Hyaena hyaena makapani* from South Africa in size and in several primitive morphological features. The specimens from collection units 4–5 are also small with relatively gracile limbs, but are insufficiently complete for detailed comparison with the earlier material. This species is relatively rare at Koobi Fora although common in the Omo Shungura sequence where it is seen to increase in size through the succession (Howell and Petter, 1976).
Reference: M. G. Leakey, 1976*b*.

Crocuta crocuta
Material: cranial, dental, postcranial.
Collection units: 3–5.
Remarks: This species is most common in collection unit 4.
Reference: M. G. Leakey, 1976*b*.

Hyaenidae gen. et sp. indet.
Material: mandibles.
Collection units: 2–3.
Remarks: These specimens clearly differ from *C. crocuta* and *H. hyaena* but are too fragmentary for more precise identification.

FELIDAE
Felinae
Panthera cf. **leo**
Material: postcranial elements.
Collection unit: 4.

Remarks: This is a tentative identification but the specimens are clearly not those of *Homotherium*, the only other large felid present in this collection unit.
Reference: M. G. Leakey, 1976*b*.

Panthera pardus
Material: hemimandible (RI$_3$–M$_1$).
Collection unit: 3.
Remarks: There may be several postcranial specimens also referable to this species, which is more common in the Omo Shungura sequence.

Panthera cf. crassidens
Material: maxilla fragment, postcranial elements.
Collection units: 2–4.
Remarks: This species was originally recorded from fragmentary South African material and the assignation is therefore tentative.
Reference: M. G. Leakey, 1976*b*.

Felis sp.
Material: hemimandible (M$_1$).
Collection unit: 3.
Remarks: The specimen is of similar size to the extant caracal but is too incomplete for positive identification. Similar material is known from the Omo (Howell and Petter, 1976).

Machairodontinae
Homotherium sp.
Material: crania, postcranial elements.
Collection units: 2–5.
Remarks: More specimens are known from Koobi Fora than any other locality and some of the postcranial material is very well represented. This is the most common felid from Koobi Fora although possibly its large size provides a favourable bias for preservation and collecting.

Megantereon eurynodon
Material: cranium, cranial fragments.
Collection unit: 4.
Remarks: The cranium is less distorted than the one known South African specimen but less complete than some European specimens of *M. megantereon*. This species is less common at Koobi Fora than at Omo and is known only from a single collection unit.
Reference: M. G. Leakey, 1976*b*.

Dinofelis barlowi
Material: crania, mandibles, postcranial elements.
Collection unit: 3.
Remarks: The cranium is rather better preserved than one from Omo although good specimens are also known from South Africa.

Reference: M. G. Leakey, 1976*b*.

Dinofelis piveteaui
Material: mandibles, postcranial elements.
Collection units: 4–5.
Remarks: This species is the second most common felid at Koobi Fora. *Dinofelis* is often included in the Felinae but has many features in common with the Machairodontinae, seeming to be a sabretooth without a 'sabre tooth'. There may have been parallel evolution but the genus is here attributed to the machairodontines.
Evolutionary changes: Distinct changes in cranial features related to enlargement of the incisors and lengthening of the carnassials are seen from *D. barlowi* to *D. piveteaui*. The canines become shorter and stockier. The skull increases in width with enlarged sagittal and nuchal crests and the muzzle becomes shorter. Given sufficiently complete specimens, such changes can be used for correlative purposes.
Reference: M. G. Leakey, 1976*b*.

PROBOSCIDEA
DEINOTHERIIDAE
Deinotherium bozasi
Material: cranium, immature mandibles, isolated teeth.
Collection units: 2–4; Kubi Algi Formation.
Remarks: This species apparently evolved in East Africa from the Miocene *Prodeinotherium hobleyi*. It is known from many East African Pliocene and Pleistocene sites and was the last surviving representative of the family. It became extinct after Omo Shungura Member K, Lower Bed II at Olduvai, and collection unit 4. The Koobi Fora cranium was the first known of this species but a more complete specimen is now known from Hadar.
Reference: J. M. Harris, 1976*a*.

ELEPHANTIDAE
Elephas recki
Material: crania, mandibles, isolated teeth.
Collection units: 2–5; Kubi Algi Formation.
Remarks: *Elephas recki* is the predominant elephantid from the Koobi Fora Formation where it is well represented by cranial and dental material. Maglio (1969) and Beden (1976) have defined evolutionary stages for this species. The majority of specimens from collection units 2–3 and the Kubi Algi Formation can be referred to *E. recki* stage II$_A$, those from units 4–5 to stage II$_B$. A few specimens from unit 5 may belong to stage III. Specimens from the Koobi Fora Formation

previously attributed to *Elephas ekorensis* (Maglio, 1972, 1973) are now interpreted as part of the *E. recki* lineage (M. Beden, pers. comm.).

Evolutionary changes: A number of progressive changes in molar morphology are evident in the sequence and include increase in hypsodonty, plate number and enamel folding and decrease in enamel thickness.

Reference: Maglio, 1973.

Loxondonta adaurora

Material: palate, mandible, isolated teeth.

Collection unit: 2; Kubi Algi Formation.

Remarks: This species predominates in the Kubi Algi Formation, but in the Koobi Fora Formation it is restricted to collection unit 2.

Reference: Maglio, 1973.

Loxodonta sp. indet.

Material: isolated teeth.

Collection unit: 4.

Remarks: A species of *Loxodonta* that is somewhat more advanced than *L. adaurora* is known from collection unit 4. The material is, however, too fragmentary or too worn for more precise identification (M. Beden, pers. comm.).

TUBULIDENTATA

ORYCTEROPODIDAE

Orycteropus afer crassidens

Material: crania, mandibles, associated postcranial elements.

Collection units: 3–5.

Remarks: Aardvarks are uncommon in the Koobi Fora Formation. Some of the less complete specimens from collection units 4–5 were described by Pickford (1975), who assigned them to the extinct subspecies *O. afer crassidens* on the basis of their small body size but large teeth. The fossil subspecies is also known from Pleistocene sites at Rusinga and Kanjera. Further unusually complete specimens have recently been excavated from collection units 3–4 but have yet to be studied in detail.

Reference: Pickford, 1975.

PERISSODACTYLA

EQUIDAE

Hipparion sp.

Material: cheek teeth, astragalus.

Collection unit 2; Kubi Algi Formation.

Remarks: This large *Hipparion* species has a caballine lower cheek tooth pattern. Ectostylids are present but not very well developed. This taxon is more advanced than specimens of *H.*

primigenium from Oued el Hammam and Ngorora, and similarly advanced specimens occur at Lothagam, Kanapoi and in the Chemeron Formation (V. Eisenmann, pers. comm.).

Hipparion cf. ethiopicum

Material: immature cranium, mandible, dentitions, postcranial elements.

Collection units: 3–5.

Remarks: This species has reduced third incisors, well-developed ectostylids and is smaller than *Hipparion* sp. It is very close to the species of *Hipparion* that is present in the Omo Shungura Formation from Member E upwards (V. Eisenmann, pers. comm.).

Reference: Eisenmann, 1976.

Equus cf. numidicus

Material: partial crania, mandibles, dentitions, postcranial elements.

Collection units: 3–4.

Remarks: This species is smaller and with more slender limb bones than the other *Equus* species common to the same levels. *E. numidicus* was originally described from Aïn Boucherit and similar specimens are present in the Omo Shungura Formation (Members G and H) and at Olduvai. This species was previously referred to *E. oldowayensis* (Eisenmann, in press) but as the type specimen of the latter is lost it seems better to avoid that name until a revision of the species has been undertaken (V. Eisenmann, pers. comm.).

Reference: Eisenmann, 1976.

Equus sp. A

Material: cranium, upper cheek teeth.

Collection units: 3–4.

Remarks: The cranium is larger than that of any extant wild species and than the Villafranchian *E. stenonis* of Europe. This taxon is possibly also represented in Omo Shungura Member G (V. Eisenmann, pers. comm.).

Reference: Eisenmann, 1976.

Equus sp. indet.

Material: postcranial elements.

Collection units: 4–5.

Remarks: One metacarpal and several first phalanges are close in size and slenderness to recent asinine and hemionine species. Three phalanges fall within the range of variation exhibited by *E. tabeti* from Aïn Hanech.

Reference: Eisenmann, 1976.

RHINOCEROTIDAE

Ceratotherium simum germanoafricanum

Material: crania, mandibles, dentitions, postcranial elements.

Collection units: 2–5.

Remarks: The specimens are assigned to the fossil subspecies on the basis of the transverse orientation of the metaloph in the upper teeth and the more upright inclination of the occiput. An immature skull from collection unit 3 bears some resemblances to *Ceratotherium praecox* but no undoubted specimens of the latter species have yet been retrieved from collection units 2–3.

Evolutionary changes: *C. simum germanoafricanum* changed gradually and almost imperceptibly into the extant white rhinoceros by the late Pleistocene. A slight increase in hypsodonty is evident within the Koobi Fora Formation.

References: J. M. Harris, 1976*b*, *e*.

Diceros bicornis

Material: cranium, mandibles, dentitions, postcranial elements.

Collection units: 3–5.

Remarks: The Koobi Fora material differs only slightly from extant specimens of this species. The cranium was the first complete fossil skull known of this species but another less well preserved specimen is now known from Omo Shungura Member E (Hooijer, 1973).

Evolutionary changes: A slight increase in hypsodonty is evident within the succession.

References: J. M. Harris, 1976*b*, *e*.

ARTIODACTYLA

SUIDAE

Nyanzochoerus cf. kanamensis

Material: mandibles, dentitions, postcranial elements.

Collection unit 2; Kubi Algi Formation.

Remarks: The teeth of this taxon from Koobi Fora differ from other East African representatives by virtue of their greater width and cingular development. The differences are, however, insufficient to warrant the erection of a new species.

Reference: Harris and White, in press.

Mesochoerus limnetes

Material: cranial, mandibles, dentitions.

Collection units: 3–5; C.

Remarks: Perhaps the best collection of *Mesochoerus* specimens in terms of relatively complete crania and mandibles comes from Koobi Fora. The majority of the crania are male and few undoubted female skulls are known. Material assigned to this taxon includes specimens that have elsewhere been assigned to *M. olduvaiensis* and some that approach *M. paiceai* in terms of

length, hypsodonty and enamel thickness of the molars. Available evidence suggests that the Koobi Fora individuals belong to a single evolving lineage and that subdivision into different species would be both arbitrary and difficult to substantiate. Earlier and more primitive examples of *Mesochoerus* are known from the Kubi Algi Formation, the lower Shungura Formation, and from Laetolil and Kaiso.

Evolutionary changes: Gradual increase in length, height, and number of pillars on the third molar is seen throughout the succession. The cranium shape changes from one reminiscent of *N. kanamensis* to one similar to that of the extant *Hylochoerus*. Individual variation (including sexual dimorphism) of the cheek teeth is very great at any one level and a large sample is required before using evolutionary tendencies for correlative purposes.

Reference: Harris and White, in press.

Potamochoerus sp.

Material: isolated teeth.

Collection unit 2; Kubi Algi Formation.

Remarks: This species, apparently a late Pliocene immigrant to Africa, is known from more complete material at Hadar and Laetolil. The teeth are rather smaller in size than those from the latter sites but are similar to isolated teeth from the Chemeron and Aterir Formations in the Lake Baringo region.

Reference: Harris and White, in press.

Notochoerus euilus

Material: crania, mandibles, dentitions, postcranial elements.

Collection unit 2; Kubi Algi Formation.

Remarks: Two skulls, one with an articulated skeleton, were retrieved from collection unit 2, although the majority of specimens comprise isolated teeth. The teeth are somewhat smaller than those of this species from Hadar but are similar to those from Shungura B.

Evolutionary changes: This is a conservative species although a slight increase in hypsodonty is evident in the succession.

Reference: Harris and White, in press.

Notochoerus scotti

Material: partial cranium, mandible, dentitions and isolated teeth.

Collection unit: 3.

Remarks: This species appears to have been an offshoot from *Notochoerus capensis* but at Koobi Fora is confined to a single unit. Its absence from the subjacent unit may have been ecologically controlled. The teeth are more hypsodont and with a greater pillar number in the third molar in *N. euilus* but the pillar number is seen to be variable. The teeth are neither as hypsodont nor as elongate as specimens from the later part of the Omo Shungura sequence (H. B. S. Cooke, pers. comm.).

Evolutionary changes: Specimens from collection unit 3 are highly variable in morphology but no trends are evident in this unit.

Reference: Harris and White, in press.

Metridiochoerus andrewsi
Material: crania, mandibles, dentitions.
Collection units: 3–4.
Remarks: As in *Mesochoerus limnetes*, specimens of *M. andrewsi* appear to have belonged to a single evolving lineage. The initial stage occurs in Shungura Member B and at Makanpansgat in South Africa. Three informal stages are evident in East Africa. Stage 1 occurs only in the lower half of the Omo Shungura Formation. Early examples of stage 2 are equivalent to *M. jacksoni* from other localities and are known only from the lower portion of collection unit 3. Later examples of stage 2 were formerly assigned to *M. andrewsi*. Stage 3 is equivalent to specimens elsewhere assigned to *Metridiochoerus* or *Tapinochoerus meadowsi*. It is confined to the upper portion of collection unit 4 and represents the culmination of this lineage.
Evolutionary changes: The sexually dimorphic crania bear some close resemblances to those of *Phacochoerus* and are relatively conservative in morphology but increase in size through the sequence. The third molars increase in length, hypsodonty, and pillar number gradually through the succession.
Reference: Harris and White, in press.

Metridiochoerus modestus
Material: isolated teeth.
Collection unit: 4.
Remarks: Although only known from isolated teeth this species forms a distinct entity in collection unit 4 where, by virtue of its small size, it may be easily differentiated from *M. andrewsi*. It is apparently an offshoot from *M. andrewsi* stage 1 and may represent the lineage that culminated in the extant *Phacochoerus*.
Reference: Harris and White, in press.

Metridiochoerus hopwoodi
Material: dentitions and isolated teeth.
Collection units: 4–5.
Remarks: A species of *Metridiochoerus* distinguished

by the symmetry and relative isolation of the paired pillars of the third molar. Early representatives of the species are rather similar in size to late stage 1 or early stage 2 of *M. andrewsi* (from which it was apparently derived) but later stages can be readily separated from *M. andrewsi* stage 3 or *M. compactus*. The last recognized occurrence of this taxon is at Olorgesailie.
Evolutionary changes: Gradual increase in tooth size and symmetry throughout its known range.
Reference: Harris and White, in press.

Metridiochoerus compactus
Material: incomplete cranium, mandibles, isolated teeth.
Collection units: upper 4, 5.
Remarks: The third molars of this species are similar to, and could logically have been derived from, those of *M. andrewsi*. The canine morphology and orientation is, however, sufficiently different from that of *Metridiochoerus andrewsi* to warrant a separate species. Teeth of this species tend to be variable in size but those from collection unit 5 are, in general, smaller and less hypsodont than those from Upper Bed II at Olduvai.
Reference: Harris and White, in press.

HIPPOPOTAMIDAE
Hexaprotodon karumensis
Material: crania, mandibles, dentitions, postcranial elements.
Collection units: 2–4; Kubi Algi Formation?
Remarks: This species is common in collection units 3–4 but is absent from unit 5. Specimens attributable to this species are known also from collection unit 2 and perhaps from the Kubi Algi Formation. *H. karumensis* is apparently derived from *Hexaprotodon harvardi* of Kanapoi as is *Hex. protamphibius* from the early part of the Omo Shungura Formation. The Koobi Fora species never quite achieves the large size, or the elevated orbits, of *Hippopotamus gorgops*. The medial incisor becomes progressively enlarged and laterally aligned; in advanced forms the lateral incisor of the mandible is lost entirely and the canine becomes smaller. The limbs of this species are more gracile and elongate than those of *Hip. gorgops* and the teeth are brachyodont. *Hex. karumensis* is interpreted as a riverine hippo and is largely confined to the region east of Lake Turkana although an isolated specimen is known also from late in the Omo Shungura Formation (S. C. Coryndon, pers. comm.).
Evolutionary changes: The species exhibits a pro-

gressive increase in size coupled with lengthening of limbs. Reduction of the lateral incisor culminates in a large diprotodont form.

Reference: Coryndon, 1976.

Hippopotamus gorgops

Material: crania, mandibles, dentitions, post-cranial elements.

Collection units: 2–5; Kubi Algi Formation?

Remarks: This large tetraprotodont species predominates in collection units 4–5 but is less common in units 2–3. Isolated teeth and post-cranial elements suggest that a primitive form of the taxon may have occurred in the Kubi Algi Formation. *Hip. gorgops* may be readily distinguished from *Hip. aethiopicus* by its large size and from *Hex. karumensis* by its canine and incisor morphology, its hypsodont cheek teeth, and its more massive but shorter limbs. *Hip. gorgops* is also known from the upper part of the Omo Shungura Formation and from Olduvai and has been interpreted as a lacustrine rather than riverine species (Coryndon, 1976).

Evolutionary changes: *Hip. gorgops* is seen to increase in size through time. The orbit becomes progressively more elevated on the cranium and the anterior orbital part of the face becomes elongate. The medial incisor enlarges at the expense of the (retained) lateral incisor.

Reference: Coryndon, 1976.

Hippopotamus aethiopicus

Material: crania, mandibles, dentitions, post-cranial elements.

Collection units: 2–5.

Remarks: This small tetraprotodont hippo species is not uncommon in collection units 4–5 but is only a rare element in units 2–3. This species is known also from the later portion of the Omo Shungura Formation and perhaps from Bed I at Olduvai (Coryndon and Coppens, 1975).

Evolutionary changes: Specimens from the Koobi Fora and Shungura Formations exhibit a progressive reduction in the length of the premolar row (by comparison with the length of the molar row) together with a general decrease in overall size.

References: Coryndon and Coppens, 1975; Coryndon, 1976.

Hippopotamidae gen. et sp. indet.

Material: mandible.

Collection unit: 2.

Remarks: A mandible of a small hexaprotodont hippo was recovered in 1975. Larger hexaprotodont mandibles are known from the Kubi Algi Formation but the relationship (if any) of the collection unit 2 specimen to other hippo taxa from east of Lake Turkana has yet to be determined.

CAMELIDAE

Camelus sp.

Material: mandible, premaxilla, isolated teeth, postcranial elements.

Collection units: 2 and 4.

Remarks: The mandible is the most complete specimen so far known from East Africa. The species is of intermediate size between the extant *C. bactrianus* and *C. dromedarius* and is smaller than *C. thomasi* from North Africa. It is probable that the Koobi Fora material is conspecific with other camelid remains from Omo, Olduvai and Marsabit Road.

Reference: J. M. Harris, in press.

GIRAFFIDAE

Sivatheriinae

Sivatherium maurusium

Material: cranium, mandibles, dentitions, post-cranial bones.

Collection units: 2–5; Kubi Algi Formation.

Remarks: The cranium is the only complete specimen yet known from Africa and serves as a model for orientation of other isolated *Sivatherium* ossicones (Harris, 1974). The teeth are of similar size to other specimens of this species but smaller than a Pliocene species of *Sivatherium* from South Africa.

Evolutionary changes: The species increases in size through time but the anterior limb becomes relatively shorter.

References: J. M. Harris, 1976c, f.

Giraffinae

Giraffa jumae

Material: ossicones, dentitions, postcranial elements.

Collection units: 2–5; Kubi Algi Formation.

Remarks: This is the largest of the three giraffine species from Koobi Fora and also the only species known from the Kubi Algi Formation.

References: J. M. Harris, 1976c, f.

Giraffa gracilis

Material: partial crania, ossicones, dentitions, postcranial bones.

Collection units: 3–5.

Remarks: The most complete cranial material and the only known associated dental and postcranial remains of this species are from the Koobi Fora Formation. It is the most common giraffine from this formation. The trivial name, although better known, is probably a junior synonym of *Giraffa stillei* from Laetolil.

References: J. M. Harris, 1976*c*, *f*.

Giraffa pygmaeus

Material: ossicones, dentitions.

Collection units: 2–5.

Remarks: This is the smallest and least common giraffine species from East Africa. Specimens from the Koobi Fora Formation, the Omo Shungura Formation, and Olduvai are smaller than those from the earlier localities of Hadar and Laetolil.

References: J. M. Harris, 1976*c*, *f*.

BOVIDAE
Tragelaphini
Tragelaphus strepsiceros

Material: crania, mandibles, horn cores, dentitions.

Collection units: 2–5.

Remarks: This species is rare in collection unit 2 but is common in the subsequent units. The species is known from Bed I at Olduvai but not until Shungura Member G at the Omo.

Evolutionary changes: Specimens from collection unit 3 are smaller and distinctly slighter than those from unit 4; those from unit 5 are correspondingly larger and more robust.

Reference: J. M. Harris, 1976*d*.

Tragelaphus nakuae

Material: crania, mandibles, horn cores, dentitions.

Collection units: 2–5; Kubi Algi Formation.

Remarks: This species is the predominant bovid from the Kubi Algi Formation and collection unit 2 but decreases sharply in relative abundance thereafter. It is known only from dentitions in unit 5.

Evolutionary changes: Horn cores from collection unit 4 are more arcuately curved and have a greater span, less torsion and a weaker anterior keel than in earlier representatives.

Reference: J. M. Harris, 1976*d*.

Bovini
Pelorovis oldowayensis

Material: fragmentary calvaria, horn cores.

Collection units: 4–5.

Remarks: A few specimens of comparable or slightly smaller size to specimens of this species from Olduvai Gorge are known from collection units 4–5.

Reference: J. M. Harris, 1976*d*.

Pelorovis sp.

Material: crania, calvariae, horn cores, dentitions.

Collection units: 2–5.

Remarks: Adult specimens of similar morphology to *P. oldowayensis* but distinctly smaller in size are not uncommon in collection units 4–5. There is no apparent intergradation in size between this form and *P. oldowayensis* and it seems likely that a separate species for the smaller form is warranted. A few specimens from collection units 2–3 are smaller and have strongly dorsoventrally compressed horn cores but have obvious close affinities with the unit 4 specimens.

Reference: J. M. Harris, 1976*d*.

Bovini gen. et sp. indet.

Material: calvaria with horn cores.

Collection unit: 3.

Remarks: A single specimen collected in 1975 bears no obvious close resemblances to the known *Pelorovis* taxa or to bovines from the Kubi Algi Formation but has yet to be studied in detail.

Reduncini
Kobus ancystrocera

Material: calvariae, frontlets, horn cores.

Collection units: 2–5; Kubi Algi Formation.

Remarks: This species differs from other *Kobus* species primarily in the orientation of its horn cores and is difficult to identify positively unless the intrafrontal sutures are preserved at the horn core bases. Although relatively common in collection unit 4, *K. ancystrocera* is known only from a handful of specimens in unit 3, and from single individuals from units 2 and 5.

Reference: J. M. Harris, 1976*d*.

Kobus sigmoidalis

Material: horn cores.

Collection units: 3–4; Kubi Algi Formation?

Remarks: Although previously recorded as absent (Harris, 1976*d*) a few specimens of this species are now known from Koobi Fora.

Kobus ellipsiprymnus

Material: crania, calvariae, horn cores, dentitions.

Collection units: 3–5.

Remarks: This is the most abundant bovid species and, appearing initially in collection unit 3, is thereafter represented by numerous crania and horn cores. It does not occur at Omo until Shungura Member G.

Evolutionary changes: Specimens from collection unit 3 tend to be smaller and to have more laterally compressed horn cores than those from

collection unit 4 but the degree of lateral compression never matches that of the *K. sigmoidalis* specimens from unit 4. Horn cores from collection unit 5 tend to be larger and even more rounded in transverse section.
Reference: J. M. Harris, 1976*d*.

Kobus cf. kob
Material: calvariae, horn cores.
Collection units: 2, 4, and 5.
Remarks: A species of *Kobus*, closely allied to but larger than the extant *kob*, is common in collection units 4–5. It is absent from unit 3 and represented by a single specimen from unit 2. *Kobus* cf. *kob* is perhaps related to a smaller species of *Kobus* from the Kubi Algi Formation. Kobs are uncommon earlier than Member H in the Omo Shungura sequence (Gentry, 1976).
Reference: J. M. Harris, 1976*d*.

Kobus sp.
Material: frontlets, horn cores.
Collection unit 2; Kubi Algi Formation.
Remarks: A small species of *Kobus* differing from those listed above is common in the Kubi Algi Formation and occurs also in unit 2 but has yet to be studied in detail.

Redunca sp.
Material: horn core, dentitions.
Collection unit 3; Kubi Algi Formation.
Remarks: A single horn core from collection unit 3 is very similar to that of the extant *Redunca redunca*. Reduncine dentitions small enough to belong to *Redunca* are known from the Kubi Algi Formation.

Menelikia cf. lyrocera
Material: crania, calvariae, horn cores, dentitions.
Collection units: 3–5.
Remarks: As in the upper part of the Omo Shungura sequence (Gentry, 1976) two morphs of *Menelikia* are known. A form with shorter lyrate horns than that of the pre-Shungura Member H morph predominates in collection unit 3. This is replaced by a short and straight-horned form in unit 4, which persists into unit 5. A similar change from lyrate to straight horns occurs in Shungura Member H.
Evolutionary changes: The change in horn shape and insertion has been interpreted as evolutionary by Gentry (1976). Although the 'advanced' forms of *M. lyrocera* are similar, the earlier forms from Omo and Koobi Fora differ somewhat in morphology. It is possible that the different morphs of *Menelikia lyrocera* are subspecies (cf. those of *Alcelaphus*

buselaphus) and that the story is one of replacement rather than evolution.
Reference: J. M. Harris, 1976*d*.

Menelikia sp.
Material: calvariae, horn cores.
Collection unit 2; Kubi Algi Formation.
Remarks: Long, mediolaterally compressed horn cores with deep longitudinal grooves on the anterior surface, similar to those from Omo Shungura Members C and D but rather smaller are known from the Kubi Algi Formation and lower portion of the Koobi Fora Formation.

Hippotragini
Hippotragus gigas
Material: calvaria, horn cores.
Collection units: 3–4.
Remarks: An isolated right horn core from collection unit 3 and a partial calvarium plus horn core from unit 4 are the sole representatives of this species from east of Lake Turkana. The calvaria is male but a little smaller than male representatives of this species recorded from Olduvai.
Reference: J. M. Harris, 1976*d*.

Oryx sp.
Material: calvariae, horn core.
Collection unit: 4.
Remarks: An undetermined species of *Oryx* is represented by two partial calvariae with incomplete both cores and a third isolated horn core in collection unit 4. Larger hippotragines with oryx-like horn cores are known also from the Kubi Algi Formation.
Reference: J. M. Harris, 1976*d*.

Alcelaphini
Megalotragus kattwinkeli
Material: cranium, calvariae, horn cores, dentitions.
Collection units: 2–5; Kubi Algi Formation.
Remarks: The largest alcelaphine from Koobi Fora is represented throughout the Koobi Fora Formation but is rare in collection unit 2. The horn cores of this species appear to vary greatly in size. A cranium from unit 4 is seen to be identical in morphology with the now destroyed holotype of *Rhynchotragus semiticus* (Reck, 1935).
Reference: J. M. Harris, 1976*d*.

Parmularius angusticornis
Material: horn core.
Collection unit: 4.
Remarks: This species, though common at Olduvai, is rare at Koobi Fora and absent from Omo.

49

Parmularius altidens
Material: cranium, mandibles.
Collection unit: 4.
Remarks: The smallest alcelaphine from Koobi Fora is represented by only three specimens from collection unit 4. Similar-sized alcelaphine teeth are known from the Kubi Algi Formation. Koobi Fora representatives of this species are smaller than those from Bed I at Olduvai and the cranium is, in many features, reminiscent of the species of *Damaliscus* comprising the Olduvai VFK herd from Bed II (which is also known from Bed I).
Reference: J. M. Harris, 1976d.

Parmularius sp. nov.
Material: calvariae, horn cores, dentitions.
Collection units: 2–5.
Remarks: The most abundant alcelaphine species is present throughout the Koobi Fora Formation but is rare in collection unit 2 and the Kubi Algi Formation. The horn cores are shorter and less stout than those of *P. altidens*. Similar horn cores from Olduvai have been tentatively identified as *Damaliscus niro* although they differ appreciably from typical *D. niro* morphology. A not dissimilar species of *Parmularius* is known from Makapansgat.
Reference: J. M. Harris, 1976d.

Connochaetes sp.
Material: cranium, horn cores, dentitions.
Collection units: 2–5.
Remarks: This species is present throughout the Koobi Fora Formation but is absent from the Kubi Algi Formation. It differs from the extant *C. taurinus* by the slenderness of its horn cores and by its backwardly protruding cranial region. The differences between the Koobi Fora specimens and those of *C. africanus* from Olduvai are consistent with *C. africanus* being ancestral to the extant *C. gnou* and the Koobi Fora specimens to *C. taurinus* (A. W. Gentry, pers. comm.).
Reference: J. M. Harris, 1976d.

Beatragus cf. antiquus
Material: incomplete horn cores.
Collection units: 5–6.
Remarks: This species is represented by only three specimens from Koobi Fora. *B. antiquus* is known also from Bed II at Olduvai and the uppermost part of the Omo Shungura sequence.

Rabaticeras sp.
Material: partial calvaria.
Collection unit: 4.

Remarks: This genus is represented by only a single weathered calvaria. It cannot at present be assigned to any of the East or South African species.

Aepyceros sp.
Material: male and female crania, calvariae, horn cores, dentitions.
Collection units: 2–5; Kubi Algi Formation.
Remarks: A species of impala is common throughout the Koobi Fora Formation but is known only from collection unit A of the Kubi Algi Formation. The species is probably conspecific with that from the Omo and is somewhat smaller than the extant *A. melampus*.
Evolutionary changes: Specimens from collection units 2–3 are distinctly smaller and slighter than those from unit 4. The contrast between the unit 4 and unit 5 specimens is less striking.
Reference: J. M. Harris, 1976d.

Antilopini
Antidorcas recki
Material: calvariae, horn cores, dentitions.
Collection units: 3–5; Kubi Algi Formation.
Remarks: This species was apparently absent from collection unit 2 although present throughout the remainder of the Koobi Fora Formation. It is known also from collection unit B. The horn cores are extremely variable but it is possible that a second species (not *A. bondi*) is present in the fauna.
Reference: J. M. Harris, 1976d.

Gazella spp.
Material: horn cores.
Collection units: 3–5.
Remarks: Three species of *Gazella* appear to be present in the Koobi Fora Formation. One species has severely laterally compressed horn cores and is represented in collection units 3–5. A second species has shorter and more rounded horn cores and is restricted to units 3–4. A third species from unit 4 is similar to but larger than the second species.
Reference: J. M. Harris, 1976d.

Neotragini
Madoqua sp.
Material: maxilla.
Collection unit: 4.
Remarks: Neotragines are rare at Koobi Fora and only one maxilla has been recovered to date.
Reference: J. M. Harris, 1976d.

LOWER VERTEBRATES

The lower vertebrate material has received little attention to date and is certainly under-represented in the collections. Fish, chelonian, and crocodilian remains are, however, abundant in the Koobi Fora Formation and may eventually provide important palaeoecological information in addition to recording the presence and development of various lower vertebrate taxa.

PISCES

No systematic attempt has yet been made to collect fish remains *per se* although records have been kept of the specimens encountered in palaeotaphonomic studies (A. K. Behrensmeyer, pers. comm.) and a few relatively complete specimens have been recovered by various personnel of the Koobi Fora Research Project.

An unpublished report prepared by McEnroe and Behrensmeyer states that the following taxa have been recorded during palaeotaphonomic studies: *Bagrus* sp., *?Barbus* sp., *Clarias* sp., *Hydrocynus* sp., *Lates* sp., *Synodontis* sp., *Tilapia* sp., *Polypterus* sp., *Protopterus* sp., Ariidae gen. et spp. indet., Myliobatiformes gen. et sp. indet.

The sampling programme, which was not specifically designed to assess piscine evidence, encountered the greatest number of specimens in collection unit 4. The variety of different fish taxa was best represented in the lake margin facies. Differences in fish assemblages from the lake margin, channel, and floodplain facies were reflected by the relative abundance of individual fish taxa rather than by presence or absence of species. *Clarias* is the most common genus although *Synodontis* predominates in the channel deposits. *Bagrus* sp. and ariid specimens were more common in collection unit 3 than in units 4–5. *Bagrus* sp. has been doubtfully recorded only from unit 3 while *Tilapia* was apparently restricted to unit 5. The unit 2 piscine faunas have yet to be sampled.

Material collected so far provides an interesting insight into the potential variety of the piscine fauna from the Koobi Fora Formation and indicates that further and more detailed investigation is warranted.

AMPHIBIA

A few amphibian limb bones have been retrieved from collection unit 3 during the microfaunal excavations but have not yet been studied in detail.

REPTILIA

CROCODYLIDAE

Crocodilian remains from the Koobi Fora Formation have been studied by Dr. E. Tchernov (Hebrew University, Jerusalem). Dr. Tchernov spent a short time in the field in 1972 but the crocodilian remains have been largely neglected in other seasons, only a few of the more complete specimens having been collected.

Three crocodilian taxa are known from the Koobi Fora Formation. *Crocodylus cataphractus*, a species now restricted to lakes of the western Rift Valley, is known from a single complete skull. A species of brevirostrine crocodile predominates throughout the formation. A number of relatively complete crania and mandibles of this new species have been retrieved and, if the skull length : body length ratio was similar to that of extant species, several individuals must have exceeded 10 metres in length. The slender-snouted and piscivorous *Euthecodon brumpti* occurs frequently throughout the formation and is known from several complete crania and mandibles.

The brevirostrine crocodile species predominates at African localities from the early Miocene onwards, but became extinct in the middle Pleistocene. *C. cataphractus* is known also from Omo and Kanapoi. *Euthecodon brumpti* was presumably derived from the North African Neogene *E. nitriae* but is currently known only from Omo and Koobi Fora. The extant *Crocodylus niloticus* was apparently a rare element of African faunas prior to the Middle Pleistocene. It is certainly absent from the Koobi Fora Formation and only a few undoubted specimens of the extant species have been recorded from Omo and Olduvai (Tchernov, 1976).

CHELONIA

Chelonian material is not uncommon in the Koobi Fora Formation but owing to the mammal-orientated nature of the faunal collecting programmes only a few of the more complete and easily portable specimens have been retrieved. At least three chelonian families—Testudinidae, Trionychidae, and Pelomedusidae—were present in the succession. The soft-shelled turtles include *Trionyx triunguis* and *Cycloderma* cf. *frenatum* and the side-necked turtles are *Pelusios sinuatus* and *P.* aff. *sinuatus* (F. de Broin, pers. comm.). Gigantic but as yet unidentified chelonians, similar or larger in size than the extant forms from Aldabra and Galapagos, were present in collection unit 2 and the Kubi Algi Formation.

SQUAMATA

This group is poorly known at present. A number of snake vertebrae, including a virtually complete vertebral column, and a few lizard vertebrae have been collected but have not yet been studied.

AVES

A small number of avian postcranial elements have been collected but have not yet been studied.

INVERTEBRATES

The majority of invertebrate taxa from east of Lake Turkana are molluscan although a few fossil millipedes have also been collected from the Koobi Fora Formation. Preliminary work on the molluscan faunas has been undertaken by P. G. Williamson (University of Bristol), who has identified 18 genera and 35 species in the Plio–Pleistocene part of the sequence. *Etheria* reefs occur in fluviatile facies but the majority of the molluscan taxa are from lacustrine sediments. Out of a molluscan sample of more than 1 million only two specimens of terrestrial molluscs have so far been collected.

Williamson recognizes seven distinct lacustrine mollusc zones, two from the Kubi Algi Formation and five from the Koobi Fora Formation (Table 3.2). Zone 1 occurs below the Hasuma Tuff and comprises some half-dozen mollusc species, most of which are indistinguishable from extant forms. These evolutionary conservative molluscan taxa, which were as widespread geographically in the past as they are at present, Williamson terms 'cosmospolitan species'.

Zone 2, occurring above the Hasuma Tuff, consists solely of species endemic to the Lake Turkana basin but clearly derived from cosmopolitan species. Williamson calls such taxa 'phyletic endemics'. The presence of the phyletic endemics suggests long-term stability of the lake during late Kubi Algi times but also isolation from adjacent aquatic regimes due, perhaps, to climatic or tectonic change. Zone 2 faunas are of interest also in that they include the earliest African examples of *Corbicula* and *Bulinus*.

Zone 3 begins at the base of the Koobi Fora Formation and extends above 117/T VI. Molluscs from this zone record a sudden return to generalized cosmopolitan forms which entirely replace the phyletic endemics of Zone 2. The immigration of extra-basinal taxa indicates re-establishment of communication with surrounding aquatic regimes and is perhaps correlative with increased climatic

humidity and concommitant with increase in lake size. Zone 3 includes the earliest African examples of *Burnupia* and *Lymnaea*. It also includes a species of *Valvata* and is the earliest and most southerly record of this genus. *Valvata* is an essentially holarctic genus and Williamson refers to it as 'exotic'.

All the cosmopolitan species of Zone 3 persist in Zone 4. In addition the bivalve *Pliodon*, primarily a West African (and Western Rift Valley) form and hence also termed 'exotic' by Williamson, makes its initial appearance in the Zone 4 fauna.

All the taxa of Zone 4 persist in Zone 5. In addition a new species each of *Coelotura* and *Melanoides* are present. These two species are endemic to the basin and are clearly derived from cosmopolitan forms present in the subjacent zones. Williamson calls these species 'radiative endemics' and interprets their presence to suggest a fairly deep, environmentally stable lake with a variety of facies exploitable by mollusca.

The fauna of Zone 5 continues into Zone 6 with the addition of a further cosmopolitan species of *Gyraulus* and additional radiative endemic forms of *Melanoides* and *Valvata*.

Zone 7, originating just above the putative level of the post-KBS erosion surface, and including the remainder of the upper member, is populated solely by cosmopolitan taxa. The disappearance of exotic and radiative endemic taxa at the top of Zone 6 is interpreted by Williamson to suggest a fundamental change from a relatively deep, environmentally stable, meromict lake to a shallower, environmentally unstable, holomict/polymict lake that perhaps was affected by periodic fluctuations in salinity or alkalinity.[1]

The limited molluscan evidence currently available from the Omo Shungura Formation suggests a molluscan sequence similar to that from east of Lake Turkana. Initial molluscan correlation of the Shungura and Koobi Fora Formations, on the assumption that both were deposited on the fringes of the same lake, is at odds with correlative evidence suggested by suid and elephantid taxa for the lower portion of both successions (M. Beden and P. G. Williamson, pers. comm.). More molluscan samples are needed from Koobi Fora areas that yield prolific vertebrate faunas before this apparent discrepancy can be pursued further.

The Plio–Pleistocene molluscan faunas from the

[1] *Meromict*: only the top layer of lake water mixed. *Holomict*: all levels of water fully mixed. *Polymict*: many turnovers of the water during the year.

Kaiso region of the Edward–Albert Rift are of similar antiquity to those from the Kubi Algi and Koobi Fora Formations. As in the latter, a diverse mollusc fauna including radiative endemic taxa is developed in the Kaiso Basin and is later succeeded by purely cosmopolitan forms. The two extinction events may represent a potentially important biologic and climatic datum between the Eastern and Western Rift Systems (Williamson, in prepn.).

PALAEOFLORA

Little attention has so far been paid to the palaeobotanical potential of the Koobi Fora Formation. An impression of a *Ficus* leaf was providentially recovered from the KBS Tool Site in area 105 (G. L. Isaac, pers. comm.), but no consistent efforts have been made to sample the macro-elements of the palaeoflora. Palynological investigations have been pursued by Dr. Raymonde Bonnefille (C.N.R.S., Paris) but only a single sample from collection unit 4 in area 12 has so far yielded a concentration of pollen sufficient for detailed analysis.

Of the 47 pollen taxa recorded from the area 12 sample, more than half (25) are not present in the contemporary vegetation to the east of Lake Turkana. Nine of the genera occur today in riverine communities along the Omo River and in the Omo delta. The other 16 are not now found nearer than the montane forests of southwest Ethiopia (some 150 to 200 km north-east of Ileret). The prominence of montane forest elements is particularly striking. This cannot be explained entirely by long-distance wind or water transport and it seems clear that highland forest-type vegetation must have existed close to the basin margins. The contrast between recent pollen assemblages of the region and the fossil one cannot be due simply to recent de-afforestation by human agency and thus the climate at the time represented by the area 12 sample must have been cooler or wetter than at present. The vegetation in the vicinity of the sample site was dominated by *Graminaea* and *Chenopodiaceae*, both of which are appropriate to the margins of a slightly saline or alkaline lake. The unusually good representation of *Acacia*, *Commiphora*, and *Salvadora* implies a tree and shrub cover more dense than that prevalent in the basin today. Altogether the indications are of a climate that was neither excessively humid nor semi-arid (Bonnefille, 1976*b*).

It is unfortunate that only one sample has so far proved fruitful as one cannot therefore assess the extent to which the observed vegetation assemblage was typical, stable, fluctuating, or subject to persistent long-term trends (R. Bonnefille, pers. comm.). Similar pollen analysis has been undertaken in the near-by Omo Shungura Formation (Bonnefille, 1976*a*) with good results from four levels (C7, C8, C9, and E4). Observed changes in the fossil pollen spectra are sufficient to suggest that the wooded savanna typical of the early part of the Omo Shungura Formation was replaced by extensive grassland about two million years ago (Bonnefille, 1976). Comparison of the Omo fossil pollen spectra with that from area 12 shows that the highland versus riverine versus savanna proportions of the area 12 sample are intermediate between those of Omo Shungura Members C and E (Bonnefille, 1976*b*). Further samples from the Koobi Fora Formation are, however, necessary before one can attach any significance to this apparent floral correlation.

TABLE 3.1. *Distribution of fossil mammal taxa in the Koobi Fora Formation (excluding micromammals)*

	Collection units			
	2	3	4	5
Australopithecus boisei	?	X	X	X
Homo sp.	?	X	X	X
Hominidae gen. et sp. indet.	?	X	X	X
Theropithecus oswaldi		X	X	X
Theropithecus brumpti	X			
Papio sp.		X	X	
Papionini gen. indet.		X		
Cercopithecinae gen. indet.	X			
Cercocebus sp.			X	X
Cercopithecus sp.			X	
Colobus sp.			X	X
Cercopithecoides sp. nov.			X	X
Colobinae gen. et. sp. nov.	X	X		
Colobinae gen. indet.		X		
Canis cf. *mesomalus*			X	X
cf. *Lycaon* sp.			X	X
Lutra sp. nov.	X	X	X	
Enhydriodon sp. nov.	X	X		
Mellivorinae gen. et sp. indet.		X		
Genetta cf. *genetta*			X	X
Pseudocivetta ingens			X	X
Hyaena hyaena		X	X	X
Crocuta crocuta		X	X	X
Hyaenidae gen. et. sp. indet.	X	X		
Panthera cf. *leo*			X	
Panthera pardus		X		
Panthera cf. *crassidens*	X	X	X	
Felis sp.		X		
Homotherium sp.	X	X	X	X
Megantereon eurynodon			X	
Dinofelis barlowi		X		
Dinofelis piveteaui			X	X
Deinotherium bozasi	X	X	X	
Elephas recki	X	X	X	X
Loxodonta adaurora	X			
Loxodonta sp. indet.			X	
Orycteropus afer crassidens		X	X	X
Hipparion sp.	X			
Hipparion cf. *ethiopicum*		X	X	X
Equus cf. *numidicus*		X	X	
Equus sp. A		X	X	
Equus sp. indet.			X	X
Ceratotherium simum germanoafricanum	X	X	X	X
Diceros bicornis		X	X	X
Nyanzachoerus cf. *kanamensis*	X			
Mesochoerus limnetes		X	X	X
Potamochoerus sp.	X			
Notochoerus euilus	X			
Notochoerus scotti		X		
Metridiochoerus andrewsi		X	X	X
Metridiochoerus modestus			X	

Table 3.1—continued

	Collection units			
	2	3	4	5
Metridiochoerus hopwoodi			X	X
Metridiochoerus compactus				X
Hexaprotodon karumensis	X	X	X	
Hippopotamus gorgops	X	X	X	X
Hippopotamus aethiopicus	X	X	X	X
Hippopotamidae gen. indet.	X			
Camelus sp.	X		X	
Sivatherium maurusium	X	X	X	X
Giraffa jumae	X	X	X	X
Giraffa gracilis		X	X	X
Giraffa pygmaeus	X	X	X	X
Tragelaphus strepsiceros	X	X	X	X
Tregalaphus nakuae	X	X	X	X
Pelorovis oldowayensis			X	X
Pelorovis sp. nov.	X	X	X	X
Bovini gen. et sp. indet.		X		
Kobus ancystrocera	X	X	X	X
Kobus sigmoidalis		X	X	
Kobus ellipsiprymnus		X	X	X
Kobus cf. *kob*	X		X	X
Kobus sp.	X			
Redunca sp.		X		
Menelikia cf. *lyrocera*		X	X	X
Menelikia sp.	X			
Hippotragus gigas		X	X	
Oryx sp.			X	
Megalotragus kattwinkeli	X	X	X	X
Parmularius angusticornis			X	
Parmularius altidens			X	
Parmularius sp. nov.	X	X	X	X
Connochaetes sp.	X	X	X	X
Beatragus cf. *antiquus*				X
Rabaticeras sp.			X	
Aepyceros sp.	X	X	X	X
Antidorcas recki		X	X	X
Gazella sp. A		X	X	X
Gazella sp. B		X	X	
Gazella sp. C			X	
Madoqua sp.			X	

TABLE 3.2. *Mollusc concurrent range zones in the Kubi Algi and Koobi Fora Formations*
(after Williamson)

FAUNAL CATEGORIES												
PHYLETIC ENDEMICS	Bellamya sp. nov.											
	Cleopatra sp. nov.											
	Gabbiella sp. nov.											
	Melanoides sp. nov.											
	Caelatura sp. nov. A											
	Caelatura sp. nov. B											
	Pseudobovaria sp. nov.											
	Corbicula sp. nov.											
	Mutela sp.											
	Bulinus sp.											
COSMOPOLITANS	Bellamya unicolor											
	Cleopatra ? dubia											
	Gabiella senaariensis											
	Melanoides tuberculata											
	Bulinus truncatus											
	Lymnaea natalensis											
	Pila ovata											
	Gyraulus costulatus											
	Caelatura rothschildi											
	Caelatura chefneuxi											
	Pseudobovaria mwayana											
	Corbicula consobrina											
	Mutela nilotica											
	Aspatharia wissmanni											
	Etheria elliptica											
	Eupera parasitica											
EXOTICS	Pliodon sp.											
	Valvata sp.											
RADIATIVE ENDEMICS	Caelatura sp. nov.											
	Melanoides sp. nov. A											
	Melanoides sp. nov. B											
	Valvata sp. nov.											
INDET.	Burnupia sp.											
	Gastropoda gen. et sp. indet.											
ZONES		1		2	3	4	5	6	7			
TUFFS		Hasuma		Suregei	Tulu Bor			KBS		Koobi Fora			
FORMATIONS		Kubi Algi		Koobi Fora									

DISCUSSION

Of the primate species, those of *Theropithecus* show evolutionary changes that should be quantifiable and may in future be of use for both internal and external correlation. *T. oswaldi* appears to show progressive specialization of the dentition; *T. brumpti* exhibits specialization in both dental and cranial morphology. Owing to the small sample of the latter from Koobi Fora, evaluation of such changes necessitates examination of Omo specimens as well. *T. brumpti* was more common at the Omo and perhaps indicates that collection unit 2 and earlier units were more heavily forested than later units. However the Cercopithecoidea also tend to be habitat-specific and *Cercocebus* and *Colobus* sp. were presumably from (gallery?) forest habitats. The large colobines from collection unit 3 may also have some ecologic significance. In the modern fauna of the region *T. oswaldi* has been replaced by *Papio*—the only primate regularly recorded, although occasional sightings of *Cercopithecus aethiops* have occurred.

The carnivores are generally too incomplete and represented by too few specimens to demonstrate evolutionary changes. *Dinofelis* provides the one exception in that differences may be observed between the lower and upper member material and can be correlated with specimens from other sites. The extant terrestrial carnivores are widespread and not very habitat-specific and the same appears to have been true in the Plio–Pleistocene. It is possible that the large *Lutra* was adapted to the deltaic environments along the shores of the lake. Among the Felidae of the Koobi Fora Formation the sabretooths and *Dinofelis* were the common large cats. These have now been completely replaced by the true cats—*Panthera leo*, *P. pardus*, and *Acinonyx*. Whether this was due to changing ecologic conditions or the impact of human activity cannot at present be determined.

Only a single African deinothere species is known from the Pliocene and Pleistocene. The changes in cranial anatomy from the Miocene *Prodeinotherium* suggest that the East African deinotheres evolved in isolation from their Eurasian relatives, but no crania are known from the African Pliocene and the few known postcranial specimens from East African Plio–Pleistocene sites have yet to be studied in detail. Though often thought of as peri-aquatic and paludinal mammals, the paucity of fossil remains has so far precluded any detailed investigation of the morphologic adaptations of the East African Plio–Pleistocene deinotheres. The family lasted longer in Africa than elsewhere but the causes of its extinction at about 1.5 million years B.P. are at present unknown.

Of the elephantids only *Elephas recki* is common in the Koobi Fora Formation although two different species of *Loxodonta* have also been recorded. Different stages of *E. recki* occur in different parts of the sequence and it is interesting that *E. recki* stage II_A of collection unit 3 is at Omo confined to Shungura Members B–E inclusive (Coppens and Howell, 1974). Recent studies of Plio–Pleistocene elephantid material have indicated that, although the evolutionary scheme proposed by Maglio (1973) is essentially correct, the material now available necessitates some revision of earlier ideas. Not until the hypodigm has been considerably augmented, particularly with relatively complete cranial material, will the elephantids fulfil their original promise (Cooke and Maglio, 1972) for precise chronological correlation.

Orycteropid remains are rare. Few isolated specimens have been retrieved and it seems likely that most of the specimens so far collected had been fortuitously preserved in pairs in their burrows. The Koobi Fora specimens furnish important potential information concerning the differences, if any, from extant representatives of this unique family but such information is unlikely to be of momentous chronological or ecological significance.

Two species of *Hipparion* have been collected from the Koobi Fora Formation and a possible third (*H. sitifense?*) is tentatively recorded from earlier levels. *Hipparion* cf. *ethiopicum* is common in all but the earliest unit and is similar to Omo specimens of this species. A few teeth from collection unit 2 and the southern units represent a species of *Hipparion* similar to that from the Chemeron Formation, which is probably not *H. primigenium* as recorded by Hooijer (1975) (V. Eisenmann, pers. comm.). *Equus* is common in collection units 3–5. The largest form may possibly be ancestral to *E. oldowayensis/numidicus* (V. Eisenmann, pers. comm.). A third, asinine, *Equus* species forms a rare constituent of the faunas of units 4–5. Isolated examples of *Equus* teeth are known from areas that have yielded unit 2 or older local faunas but no specimens have been collected *in situ* from such earlier levels. There is an apparent decrease in size of both *Equus* and *Hipparion* specimens through the sequence. It is possible that all five equid taxa recorded from the Koobi Fora Formation could have evolved locally (V. Eisenmann, pers. comm.).

The Koobi Fora Formation rhinoceroses differ very little from their modern counterparts although the latter have more hypsodont teeth. The low frequency of the rhinoceros specimens and the minor changes in morphology preclude their use for internal or external correlation. The white rhino is more common than the black in the Koobi Fora Formation and at other localities of similar age. It is probable that the white rhino had not then fully developed the grazing habit of its living descendants but the relative frequency of white versus black rhino tends to confirm the nearby presence of grassland. Only the black rhinoceros has been recorded from the Koobi Fora region in historic times.

The larger bunodont and hypsodont suid taxa all show parallel tendencies for increase in length, height, and complexity of the third molar to the extent that the terminal stages of several different lineages exhibit a remarkable degree of convergence. Relatives of all three extant African genera were present in the Koobi Fora Formation but the majority of species belonged to independent extinct lineages and gigantism was rife. Although nine suid species are recognized, only four at most occur in any one unit. It is likely that the known assemblages represent mixed accumulations of taxa with different habitat preferences, each faunal unit contributing representatives of both open and closed habitats. The warthog is the only extant suid known from the region.

The hexaprotodont hippos from the Kubi Algi Formation are very similar to *Hexaprotodon harvardi,* the common East African Miocene and Pliocene species. Several robust astragali from this part of the sequence demonstrate the presence of an additional species which may be an early form of *Hippopotamus gorgops* or of the closely allied *Hip. kaisensis*. At least three distinct hippo species occur in collection units 2–3 of the Koobi Fora Formation: *Hip. gorgops*, *Hip. aethiopicus*, and *Hexaprotodon karumensis*. An early tetraprotodont form of the latter was initially identified as *Hexaprotodon protamphibius* (Maglio, 1971) but subsequent study has shown that such specimens are unspecialized examples of *Hex. karumensis*. The three species from collection units 2–3 persist into unit 4 but *Hex. karumensis* has not been retrieved from unit 5. The differences in dental morphology and body proportions between *Hex. karumensis* and *Hip. gorgops* suggest that the two species must have utilized quite different habitats. The origin of the pygmy form *Hip. aethiopicus* is obscure. It is clearly unrelated to the extant *Choeropsis* but may conceivably be ancestral to some Mediterranean pygmy forms (Coryndon and Coppens, 1975). It is interesting that *Hex. protamphibius* is apparently unrepresented east of Lake Turkana and the related *Hex. karumensis* is rare at Omo.

Fossil camelid remains are rare in East Africa and are only poorly represented at North African sites. Probably only one species is represented at the East African localities but its phylogenentic relationship to other known fossil and extant camelid taxa is unclear. The ecologic significance of camelids in the Koobi Fora Formation is unknown but domestic camels today thrive in the general vicinity of Lake Turkana.

Among the giraffids, *Sivatherium maurusium* is a relatively conservative species that is first known from the late Pliocene and may have lingered on after the Pleistocene. Meladze (1964) suggested that sivatheres were adapted to life in the savannahs but Hamilton (1973) suggested that they were woodland or forest forms feeding on low vegetation or grasses of the woodland floor. The three Koobi Fora giraffine species are also first known from the late Pliocene. The largest, *Giraffa jumae*, appears to have been stable throughout its known history and a similar large giraffe is recorded from the early Pliocene of South Africa. There is some evidence to suggest that the two smaller species shared a common ancestry in the late Pliocene. It is possible that the three giraffine species were habitat-specific. Only one extant species is recognized, the reticulated variety of which occurs today in the Koobi Fora region, but there is no obvious close relationship between the three Pleistocene species and the extant representative.

Few unequivocal evolutionary trends are exhibited by the bovid species although several taxa apparently increase in size through the sequence. It is probable that, when studied in detail, the bovids will provide a wealth of ecological information reflecting changes in environment. In recent years the collection of new bovid material has, however, far outstripped any time available for its examination. In all units the bovid faunas include a mixture of grassland and closed habitat forms and the latter predominate in all save collection unit 4. Many of the bovid species from unit 2 are unrepresented in units 3–5. Other elements achieve prominence for the first time in collection unit 3 and are common thereafter. This change in emphasis of the bovid taxa is also seen in the suids, elephants, equids, and primates. It may possibly represent a rather dramatic change in environmental conditions although, as far as can be determined, grassland and closed habitat bovid taxa are present in both the earlier and later faunas. It may alternatively represent a biogeographic change, in the sense of a shifting faunal province boundary, or an appreciable gap in time between the samples from collection units 2 and 3. Current evidence suggests the last alternative is the most likely one.

The lacustrine sediments from east of Lake Turkana have yielded the best-preserved, most numerous, and one of the longest series of molluscan assemblages known from the Cenozoic of Africa (P. G. Williamson, pers. comm.). The molluscs are proving valuable environmental indicators, reflecting physical and chemical changes in the past history of the lake. They are providing important insights into the type of evolutionary mechanisms responsible for the unique diversity of East African rift valley lacustrine mollusc faunas, past and present. They are also of great potential value for intra- and extra-basinal correlation. The molluscan assemblages confirm evidence from aquatic vertebrates both that Lake Turkana had, in the past, faunal links with the Western Rift Valley (*Crocodylus cataphractus*) and North Africa (*Lates nilotica*) and that at time it was isolated from nearby aquatic regimes.

Radiometric dates have been obtained for four major tuff units of the Koobi Fora Formation (Findlater, this volume; Fitch *et al.* 1974). Some controversy has arisen over the apparent age of the KBS Tuff (Curtis *et al.* 1975; Behrensmeyer *et al.* 1978; White and Harris, 1977). When investigating different localities of approximately similar age, the relevance of overall faunal composition for their correlation is equivocal because faunal differences may be due to ecological rather than chronological factors. The most valuable criteria for correlation by faunal evidence are different stages of single evolving lineages. Many of the elements of the East African Plio–Pleistocene mammalian faunas have not yet been studied in sufficient detail for such comparisons to be made. Current work on various taxa has suggested that the Tulu Bor Tuff has been correctly dated by radiometric methods, that the fauna of collection unit 3 may be equivalent in time range to Omo Shungura Members F through G (equivalent to Bed I at Olduvai) and that the fauna of unit 5 perhaps predates Upper Bed II at Olduvai (White and Harris, 1977).

Monographic treatment of the faunal elements from the Koobi Fora Formation is currently being undertaken by various members of the Koobi Fora Research Project. Evidence from individual faunal elements and from the changing composition of the local faunas through the sequence augurs well for detailed palaeoecological analysis in due course. Having established controls for the biogeographic, evolutionary, and chronological variables it should be possible to isolate ecological and environmental changes. These are both important in their own right and of interest from other points of view. Indeed it is possible that the documentation of fluctuating faunal assemblages, which reflect changing ecological conditions, will be one of the more important pieces of information to emerge from the study of the Koobi Fora faunas. This objective will be striven for through closely integrated geological, taphonomic, and palaeontological investigations.

The Kubi Algi Formation has so far been less intensively investigated. No hominid material has yet been retrieved from this part of the succession but the hominid-bearing potential of the Kubi Algi Formation cannot be evaluated on the limited information currently available. Greater emphasis is planned for this portion of the succession in future. Palaeontological investigation of the region to the east of Lake Turkana has so far been logistically confined to about 1000 km² on the north-eastern edge of the lake. It is evident from preliminary prospecting in recent years that the fossiliferous sediments of the Kubi Algi Formation extend southwards and that a considerable expanse of potentially fossiliferous sediments extends northwards from the Il Erriet River to the Ethiopian border. In future years attention will be paid to the periphery of the current region as well as to the less intensively investigated parts of the succession (Kubi Algi Formation, Guomde Formation, Galani Boi beds) within it.

ACKNOWLEDGEMENTS

Precise field documentation of the faunal remains from the Koobi Fora Formation was initiated in 1971 by Dr. V. J. Maglio and his established field procedure has been very little modified subsequently. Nearly all of the participants in various disciplines of the Koobi Fora Research Project have assisted in the faunal collecting programmes.

I am particularly indebted to the following people for unpublished information on various aspects of the Koobi Fora faunas: Dr. M. G. Leakey (Primates and Carnivora), Dr. M. Beden (Elephantidae), Mme. Vera Eisenmann (Equidae), the late Mrs. S. C. Savage (Hippopotamidae), Dr. T. D. White (Suidae), Drs. C. C. Black, L. Krishtalka, J. F. Sutton, and D. Womochel (microfauna), Dr. E. Tchernov (Crocodylidae), Dr. R. Wood, and Mme. F. de Broin (Chelonia), Mr. P. G. Williamson (invertebrates), and Dr. R. Bonnefille (palaeoflora).

For stimulation and assistance in the field much credit is due to Richard and Meave Leakey, Tim White, and, especially, Kamoya Kimeu and his crew of 'hominid hunters'.

REFERENCES

BEDEN, M. 1976. Proboscideans from Omo Group Formations. In Coppens et al. (1976), pp. 193–208.

BEHRENSMEYER, A. K. 1975. The taphonomy and paleoecology of Plio–Pleistocene vertebrate assemblages east of Lake Rudolf, Kenya. Bull. Mus. Comp. Zool. 146, 473–578.

——. 1976. Fossil assemblages in relation to sedimentary environments in the East Rudolf succession. In Coppens et al. (1976), pp. 383–401.

——. (in press), a. The habitat of Plio–Pleistocene hominids in East Africa. In African Hominidae of the Plio–Pleistocene: evidence, problems and strategies (ed. C. Jolly).

——. (in press), b. Taphonomy and paleoecology in the hominid fossil record. In Yearbook of Physical Anthropology, Am. Assoc. Phys. Anthrop. (ed. J. Buettner-Janusch).

——, BISHOP, W. W., and HOWELL, F. C. 1978. Correlation in Plio–Pleistocene sequences of the northern Lake Turkana basin: a summary of evidence and issues. In Geological background to fossil man (ed. W. W. Bishop). Geol. Soc. Lond. Special Publ. No. 6. Scottish Academic Press, Edinburgh.

BONNEFILLE, R. 1976a. Palynological evidence for an important change in the vegetation of the Omo basin between 2.5 and 2 million years. In Coppens et al. (1976), pp. 421–31.

—— 1976b. Implications of pollen assemblages from the Koobi Fora Formation, East Rudolf, Kenya. Nature, Lond. 264, 403–7.

BOWEN, B. E. and VONDRA, C. F. 1973. Stratigraphical relationships of the Plio–Pleistocene deposits, East Rudolf, Kenya. Nature, Lond. 242, 391–3.

Coppens, Y. and Howell, F. C. 1974. Les faunes de mammifères fossiles des formations Plio–Pléistocènes de l'Omo en Ethiopie (Proboscidea, Perissodactyla, Artiodactyla). *C.R. Acad. Sci.* Paris, **278** D, 2275–8.

——, Howell, F. C., Isaac, G. L., and Leakey, R. E. (eds.). 1976. *Earliest man and environments in the Lake Rudolf Basin: Stratigraphy, paleoecology and evolution*, University Press of Chicago.

Cooke, H. B. S. and Maglio, V. J. 1972. Plio–Pleistocene stratigraphy in East Africa in relation to proboscidean and suid evolution. In *Calibration of hominid evolution* (ed. W. W. Bishop and J. A. Miller), pp. 303–29. Scottish Academic Press, Edinburgh.

Coryndon, S. C. 1976. Fossil Hippopotamidae from Pliocene/Pleistocene successions of the Rudolf Basin. In Coppens *et al.* (1976), pp. 238–50.

—— and Coppens, Y. 1975. Une éspece nouvelle d'Hippopotame nain due Plio–pleistocène du bassin du lac Rudolphe (Ethiopie, Kenya). *C.R. Acad. Sci. Paris*, **280**, 1777–80.

Curtis, G. H., Drake, R., Cerling, T. E., and Hampel, J. H. 1975. Age of KBS Tuff in Koobi Fora Formation, East Rudolf, Kenya. *Nature, Lond.* **258**, 395–8.

Eck, G. G. 1976. Cercopithecoidea from Omo Group deposits. In Coppens *et al.* (1976), pp. 332–44.

—— and Howell, F. C. 1972. New fossil *Cercopithecus* material from the lower Omo Basin, Ethiopia. *Folia Primat.* **18**, 325–55.

Eisenmann, V. 1976. A preliminary note on Equidae from the Koobi Fora Formation, Kenya. In Coppens *et al.* (1976), pp. 234–7.

Findlater, I. C. 1978. Isochronous surfaces within the Plio/Pleistocene sediments east of Lake Turkana, Kenya. In *Geological background to early man* (ed. W. W. Bishop). Geol. Soc. Lond. Special Publ. No. 6. Scottish Academic Press, Edinburgh.

Fitch, F. J. *et al.* 1974. Dating of the rock succession contributing fossil hominids at East Rudolf, Kenya. *Nature, Lond.* **251**, 213–5.

Gentry, A. W. 1976. Bovidae of the Omo Group deposits. In Coppens *et al.* (1976), pp. 275–92.

Hamilton, R. W. 1973. The Lower Miocene ruminants of Gebel Zelten, Libya. *Bul. Brit. Mus. (Nat. Hist.), Geol.* **21**, 75–150.

Harris, J. M. 1976a. Cranial and dental remains of *Deinotherium bozasi* (Mammalia, Probo-scidea) from East Rudolf, Kenya. *J. Zool.* **178**, 57–75.

——. 1976b. Rhinocerotidae from the East Rudolf succession. In Coppens *et al.* (1976), pp. 222–4.

——. 1976c. Giraffidae from the East Rudolf Succession. In Coppens *et al.* (1976), 264–7.

——. 1976d. Bovidae from the East Rudolf Succession. In Coppens *et al.* (1976), 293–301.

——. 1976e. Fossil Rhinocerotidae (Mammalia, Perissodactyla) from East Rudolf, Kenya. *Fossil Vertebrates Afr.* **4**, 147–72.

——. 1976f. Pleistocene Giraffidae (Mammalia, Artiodactyla) from East Rudolf, Kenya. *Fossil Vertebrates Afr.* **4**, 283–332.

——. (in press). Fossil Camelidae (Mammalia, Artiodactyla) from the Koobi Fora Formation, northern Kenya. *Origins* **1**.

—— and White, T. D. (in press). Evolution of Plio–Pleistocene Suidae from sub-Saharan Africa. *Trans-Amer. Phil. Soc.*

Hooijer, D. A. 1973. Additional Miocene to Pleistocene Rhinoceroses of Africa. *Zool. Med.* **46**, 149–78.

Howell, F. C. and Petter, G. 1976. Carnivora from Omo Group Formations, southern Ethiopia. In Coppens *et al.* (1976), pp. 314–31.

Leakey, M. G. 1976a. Cercopithecoidea of the East Rudolf Succession. In Coppens *et al.* (1976), 345–50.

——. 1976b. Carnivora of the East Rudolf Succession. In Coppens *et al.* (1976), 302–11.

—— and Leakey, R. E. 1973. New large Pleistocene Colobinae (Mammalia, Primates) from East Africa. *Fossil Vertebrates Afr.* **3**, 121–38.

—— and Leakey, R. E. 1976. Further Cercopithecinae (Mammalia, Primates) from the Plio/Pleistocene of East Africa. *Fossil Vertebrates Afr.* **4**, 212–46.

Maglio, V. J. 1970. Early Elephantidae of Africa and a tentative correlation of African Plio–Pleistocene deposits. *Nature, Lond.* **225**, 328–32.

——. 1971. Vertebrate faunas from the Kubi Algi, Koobi Fora and Ileret areas, East Rudolf, Kenya. *Nature, Lond.* **231**, 248–9.

——. 1972. Vertebrate faunas and chronology of hominid bearing sediments East of Lake Rudolf, Kenya. *Nature, Lond.* **239**, 379–85.

——. 1973. Origin and evolution of the Elephantidae. *Trans. Amer. Phil. Soc.* (n.s.) **63**, 1–149.

Meladze, G. K. 1964. On the phylogeny of the

Sivatheriinae. *Int. Geol. Congress*, **22**, 47–50 (in Russian).

PETTER, G. 1973. Carnivores Pléistocènes du Ravin d'Olduvai (Tanzanie). *Fossil Vertebrates Afr.* **3**, 43–100.

PICKFORD, M. 1975. New fossil Orycteropodidae (Mammalia, Tubilidentata) from East Africa. *Netherlands J. Zool.* **25**, 57–88.

RECK, H. 1935. Neue Genera aus der Oldoway-Fauna. *Zentbl. Miner. Geol. Palaeont.* B. **6**, 215–18.

TCHERNOV, E. 1976. Crocodilians from the late Cenozoic of the East Rudolf Basin. In Coppens *et al.* (1976), pp. 370–8.

VONDRA, C. F. and BOWEN, B. E. 1976. Plio–Pleistocene deposits and environments, East Rudolf, Kenya. In Coppens *et al.* (1976), pp. 79–93.

WHITE, T. D. and HARRIS, J. M. 1977. Suid evolution and correlation of African hominid-bearing localities. *Science*, **198**, 13–21.

WILLIAMSON, P. G. (in prepn.). Plio-Pleistocene mollusc assemblages from East Rudolf, North Kenya.

4

ARCHAEOLOGY

GLYNN LL. ISAAC AND JOHN W. K. HARRIS

ARCHAEOLOGICAL enquiry into traces[1] of hominid behaviour and the study of the skeletal anatomy of early hominids are complementary. It can fairly be said that the archaeological information is part of the context of the fossils and *vice versa*. All that can be offered here is a brief summary of the insights being contributed by archaeological methods into the technological capabilities and mode of life of some of the hominid populations whose bones are the principal subject of this volume. A subsequent monograph in this series will provide full details of the sites and the archaeological finds. Previously published preliminary reports are listed in the Koobi Fora Research Project bibliography p. 180 (Nos. 4, 9, 38, 72, 73, and 80). General reviews of the relationships between the Koobi Fora evidence and that from other sites can be found in Harris and Herbich (1978), and Isaac 1976*b*, *c*.

The Koobi Fora region yields archaeological traces that span a time range extending from historic times back to those of the remote Plio–Pleistocene period. The most recent remains include such items as stone fortifications, burial cairns, and traces of pastoralists' encampments. From a slightly earlier period are Neolithic settlements and hunter–gatherer camp sites belonging to the late Pleistocene and Holocene. The early Holocene lakeside sites commonly yield barbed bone points ('harpoons'), and stone artefact assemblages that include microliths. Many of them also contain pottery. This late Pleistocene and early Holocene material is currently being investigated by John Barthelme. However, while the material is of great intrinsic interest, it is not part of the context of the hominid fossils catalogued in this volume.

Upper Pleistocene so-called 'Middle Stone Age' artefact-scatters have been identified in various localities, but these have not yet been studied and no hominid fossils of this age have yet been recovered. By contrast, Middle Pleistocene archaeological manifestations are rare. Sediments of this age are poorly represented.[2] However, the late Pliocene and early Pleistocene sediments of the Koobi Fora Formation contain a rich archaeological record to which the remainder of this chapter is devoted.

---

[1] 'Traces' is used to mean the diverse totality of archaeological remains: sites, isolated artefacts, bone food refuse, and so on.

[2] The Guomde Formation, which may be of late Lower or early Middle Pleistocene age, has yielded one minor scatter of artefacts (FwJi 1) associated with the hominid femur KNM-ER 999.

ARCHAEOLOGICAL TRACES IN THE KOOBI FORA FORMATION

The principal archaeological materials recovered from the Koobi Fora Formation are stone artefacts, but our archaeological studies are no longer mere studies of tool types. In modern research the artefacts are most important as markers of the loci of the activities of early tool-making hominids and as the means whereby hominid food-refuse can be recognized. All in all, information on the field context and spatial configurations of artefacts are regarded as being quite as important as technical data on the morphology of the objects themselves.

The traces of early hominid activities form a web over the ancient landscape. Archaeological research in the Koobi Fora Formation includes investigation of the following topics:

Tool-making skill: inferred from the technical features of the artefacts themselves.
Cultural habits and tradition: inferred from the design and technique of manufacture of artefacts.
Tool usage: inferred from the morphology of artefacts, damage patterns, and context.
Aspects of diet and subsistence: inferred from refuse at camps and butchery sites.
Aspects of socio-economic organization: inferred from the size, contents, and internal arrangements of sites.
Aspects of land use: inferred from the distribution of traces through a mosaic of different topographic settings and habitats.

Table 4.2 provides a list of the sites, which have been catalogued according to the Standard African Site Enumeration System (SASES). Under this system all of Africa is divided into a series of squares $\frac{1}{4}°$ of latitude by $\frac{1}{4}°$ longitude. Each square has a coded, hierarchic four-letter designation. The squares covering the Koobi Fora

TABLE 4.1. *The archaeological sites shown in relation to the stratigraphic subdivisions of the Koobi Fora Formation*

	Ileret	Karari escarpment				KBS Ridge
	Area 8	130 East	130	131	118	105
	CHARI TUFF	← KARARI TUFF →				
Faunal collection units 5	FwJj 1	FxJj 23	FxJj 17 FxJj 16 FxJj 18	FxJj 21 FxJj 20		
	Base of L/M Tuff	← Base of Okote Tuff beds				
4			FxJj 11 FxJj 38 130/T III 130/T II FxJj 15 130/T I	131/T I	FxJj 10 118/T II	KBS Tuff [FxJj 1 [FxJj 3
3					118/T I	FxJj 13 105/T I

Probable lateral time-stratigraphic relationships are suggested by alignments but the correlations are not yet confirmed. Tuff names are used only in the areas containing the type section or immediately adjacent areas where the correlation is certain; otherwise the tuff index number is used (e.g. 130/T I).

TABLE 4.2. *List of catalogued sites in the Koobi Fora and Guomde Formations*

SASES reference	Other labels	Area No.	Stratigraphy	Archaeological classification	Site type (see Table 4.4)
			Grid square FwJi (4° 15–30′ N/36° 0–15′ E)		
FwJi 1	GFS	6A	Guomde Formation	Industry undetermined (sample inadequate)	D
			Grid square FwJj (4° 15–30′ N/36° 15–30′ E)		
FwJj 1	NAS	8	Stratified in Lower/Middle Tuff	Karari Industry?	A
			Grid square FxJj (4° 0–15′ N/36° 15–30′ E)		
FxJj 1	KBS	105	Stratified in KBS Tuff (type locality)	KBS Industry	C
2	—	105	Surface and superficial Pleistocene beds	Includes MSA elements	Surface*
3	HAS	105	Excavation into KBS Tuff	KBS Industry	B
4	PBS	105			Surface
5	—	105			Surface
6	—	105	Surface indications of site in KBS Tuff	KBS Industry	Surface
7	—	105			Surface
8		105			Surface
9	—	105			Surface
10	NMS	118	Excavation in tuff 118/T II or a tuffaceous sand above it	KBS Industry	A
11	BBS	130	Excavation into horizon just below base of Okote Tuff	Karari Industry	D
12	—	105	Excavations in Galana Boi beds	Later Stone Age	C/G†
13	CPH	105 East	Excavation in sediments of KBS Tuff	KBS Industry	G
14	—	130	Surface indication of site in tuff 130/T I	?KBS Industry	Surface
FxJj 15	—	130	Excavation in channel which cuts into tuff 130/T I and was filled with tuffaceous silt	Industrial classification undeterminable (sample inadequate)	G
16	—	130	Excavation in channel within Okote Tuff beds		G
17	—	130	Excavation in Okote Tuff beds		D?
18 GS (LH)	Lower Horizon	130	Excavation into surface of coarse gravels of channel at base of Okote Tuff beds		A
18 GS (UH)	Upper Horizon	130	Excavation in sands of channel complex at base of Okote Tuff beds		A
18 NS	North Site	130	Excavation in sand/silt interface at base of Okote Tuff beds	Karari Industry	A
18 IHS	—	130	Excavation of horizon within a tuff lens in the Okote Tuff beds		C
19	—	130	Surface indications of site in channel lateral to Okote Tuff beds		Surface
20 M	Main site	131			C
20 E	East site	131	Excavation in floodplain silts within the Okote Tuff beds		C
20 AB	—	131			C
21	—	131	Surface indications of site in Okote Tuff beds	Acheulian?	Surface

Table 4.2—continued

SASES reference	Other labels	Area No.	Stratigraphy	Archaeological classification	Site type (see Table 4.4)
23	—	East of 130	Excavation in sands of channel. Overlying silts thought to be part of Okote Tuff beds		A/G
24	—	East of 130			Surface
FxJj 25	—	East of 130			Surface
26	—	East of 130			Surface
27	—	East of 130	Surface indications of site in sands; thought to be lateral equivalent of Okote Tuff beds	Karari Industry	Surface
28	—	East of 130			Surface
29	—	East of 130			Surface
30	—	129			Surface
31	—	129			Surface
32	—	129	Surface indications of site in Okote Tuff beds		Surface
34	—	129			Surface
35	—	129			Surface
38 NW	North-west site	130	Excavation in consolidated sands and caliche between tuff 130/T II and Okote Tuff	KBS Industry	A/G
38 E	East site	130	Excavation in caliche; same stratigraphic level as 38 NW. Hominid KNM-ER 1806 found on surface	Industry indeterminate (sample inadequate)	D
38 SE	South-east site	130	Excavation in caliche; same stratigraphic horizon as 28 NW. Hominid KNM-ER 1805 recovered *in situ*	Industry indeterminate (sample inadequate)	D
40	—	130	Surface indications of site in sandstone conglomerate of Okote Tuff beds	Karari Industry	Surface
41	—	130			Surface
44	—	118		Acheulian?	Surface
			Surface indications of site in sands/ gravels. Lateral equivalent of Okote Tuff beds		
FxJj 45	—	118			Surface
46	—	118		Karari Industry	Surface
50	—	131	Surface indications of site in floodplain silts of Okote Tuff beds		Surface

* Surface denotes a site identified by surface traces which has not yet been excavated. Such sites cannot be classified reliably.

† G denotes disturbed 'geological' context.

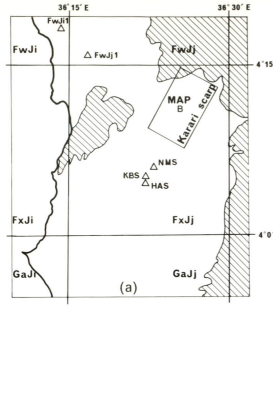

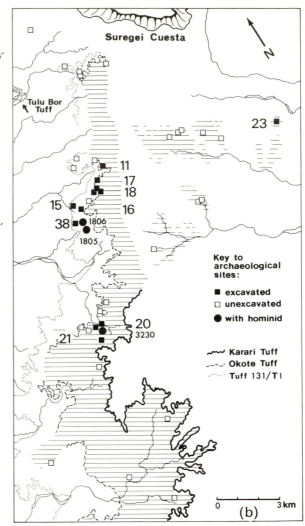

FIG. 4.1. (a) Map showing the grid squares used to catalogue the sites (FwJi, FxJj, etc.) and the relative position of the main sites. Diagonal lines indicate volcanics. (b) Detail of sites along the Karari escarpment (Areas 129–31). Horizontal lines indicate strata below the Karari Tuff.

region are FwJi, FwJj, FxJi, and FxJj (Fig. 4.1). Within each of these squares, localities of all ages are simply catalogued sequentially. No Plio–Pleistocene sites have yet been recorded for square FxJi but those catalogued for the other squares are shown in Table 4.2.

The location of some of the Karari sites is shown on the map of the Karari area in Fig. 4.1. Table 4.1 provides a summary of the stratigraphic relationships among archaeological sites hitherto investigated. Patterns of spatial relationships between archaeological and hominid fossil finds are shown diagrammatically for a series of specified stratigraphic intervals (Fig. 4.2). It can be seen that the distribution of occurrences of these two classes of palaeo-anthropological evidence are significantly different, though they do overlap.

The main cluster of hominid fossils in the lower member is in area 131, where the specimens are preserved in beds deposited in various lake margin-environments, but where archaeological sites have not yet been found. Discoveries of lower member

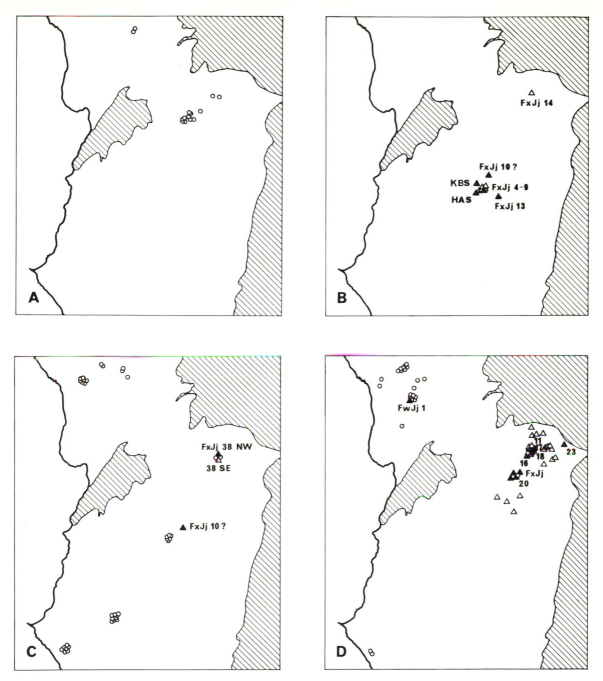

FIG. 4.2. Diagrammatic representation of the relationship between the location of hominid fossil sites (circles) and archaeological sites (triangles) for each of four stratigraphic intervals. A, Faunal collection unit 3; B, The base of faunal collection unit 4 (KBS Tuff and 130/T I); C, Faunal collection unit 4; D, Faunal collection unit 5. Each frame represents finds from a stratigraphic interval, *not* from a horizon. Clearly hominid fossils and archaeological sites do not tend to be found in the same areas, though the distributions do overlap. Because of the high density of individual clusters, the plot is schematic. For details of the hominid finds see Fig. 2.5; for the archaeological sites, see Fig. 4.1.

archaeological sites have hitherto been confined to the top of the member, and they occur in beds that represent the encroachment of alluvial-deltaic and alluvial floodplain conditions over the area formerly occupied by the lake margins. Area 105 and the adjoining part of Area 118 have proved archaeologically the most productive sector for these sites. Three concentrations of material have been excavated: KBS (FxJj 1), HAS (FxJj 3), and NMS (FxJj 10). A further six minor artefact patches have been identified in the KBS Tuff itself. One very minor occurrence of abraded artefacts has been excavated at FxJj 13, where the pieces derive from a channel deposit below the KBS Tuff. The artefact-bearing channel deposits represent the first extension of alluvial conditions into area 105 in late lower member times. Further north the very top of the lower member includes fluvial-deltaic environments, but so far only rare stray artefacts and one very small patch of material have been located (FxJj 14) in area 130.

In the upper member, and the Ileret Member, there are several clusters of hominid finds, the three most notable of which are (1) the finds from around Ileret, (2) those from area 105, and (3) those from area 104. At Ileret in area 8 one archaeological site is interstratified in close proximity to the hominid fossils, but in the other two clusters hominid specimens occur in the absence of any detectable concentration of artefacts.

The upper member archaeological finds themselves show strong clustering; they occur in profusion along the Karari escarpment from area 129 southwards into areas 130 and 131. They are especially frequent in the beds at and just above the stratigraphic level of the base at the Okote Tuff. During the initial survey we have identified more than forty sites and this number will surely be increased as the work proceeds (Fig. 4.2). In addition to the clusters of specimens that constitute 'sites', artefacts occur as a diffuse scatter through the deposits. The beds which contain this rich and varied archaeological record consist of the 'cut-and-fill' deposits of an aggrading alluvial plain. Conglomerates and sands represent the deposits of shifting channels, which were lateral to expanses of sandy floodplain silts. The bed load of many channels included lava cobbles and boulders of a size suitable for stone artefact manufacture. The sites occur both in close association with the channels and on flat featureless portions of the interfluves, which were, however, never very far from the stream beds. As the outcrop of the upper member is traced south from areas 130 and 131, the frequency of channel conglomerates decreases and so does the incidence of sites. As yet hominid fossils have been found at only two localities along the Karari escarpment in the upper member.

Although beds which are probably contemporaneous with the Okote Tuff occur along the Koobi Fora Ridge, in areas 104, 102, and 103, they do not contain archaeological sites equivalent to those of the Karari. Equally, while one site and a scatter of artefacts is known from those beds at Ileret which are presumed to be laterally equivalent (Lower/Middle Tuff), archaeological traces are rare by comparison with the Karari area. This is so in spite of the fact that numerous hominid fossils attest that hominids did range over the Koobi Fora and Ileret areas.

The disparity between the distribution of artefacts and the distribution of hominid fossils deserves continued study. More intensive searches need to be made in areas where hominids occur but where cultural traces have not yet been found. One factor that can be suggested as having helped to produce the observed pattern is proximity to raw material (Harris and Herbich, 1978). The upper member sites in areas 130–1 were in terrain where lava cobbles were always available within a radius of not more than a few hundred metres. There may well also have been conglomerates within a few kilometres of the KBS Industry sites of area 105, though this has yet to be verified. By contrast the beds of Ileret and Koobi Fora are virtually devoid of conglomerates and the nearest coarse conglomerates may well have been 10 to 15 km away. If this was a major factor in determining the observed patterns, then one could make certain tentative inferences with regard to hominid behaviour. The following alternative explanations are offered:

(1) The stone-tool carrying habit was only weakly established and the early stone artefacts that we have been able to find were made, used, and discarded only within a few kilometres of stone sources.
(2) Those hominids operating in environments lacking suitable stone conserved their implements extremely carefully, so that stone artefacts were seldom discarded. By contrast, perhaps hominids in stone-rich environments were more prodigal with their manufacture, thereby creating a locally prolific record.
(3) Activities occurring in the areas close to the lake may have been such that they did not lead to the use and discarding of concentrated patches of stone-tools. (For instance hominids may have ranged in these areas without establishing home-bases: see below.)
(4) Territoriality may have excluded some hominids from access to raw material. If this was the case, they presumably had to manufacture cutting tools from such alternative materials as would be universally available, for instance bone, tusk, shell, or hard wood. Simple utensils of these materials would be difficult to detect.

At only three sites do archaeological and hominid fossil materials occur in very close proximity to each other. These instances are marked in Fig. 4.2. They are as follows:

(a) At FxJj 20 East, in the beds above the Okote Tuff, the hominid mandible specimen KNM-ER 3230 was recovered during the archaeological excavation. It lay encased in floodplain silts about 10–15 cm above the major archaeological horizon which was being uncovered by excavation. About fifty scattered artefacts and some bone occurred at the same level as the mandible itself (Harris and Isaac, 1976). The artefacts from the site are clear-cut representatives of the Karari Industry (see below). There is no way to tell whether the mandible represents the remains of a tool-maker, an item of the tool-makers' diet, or a specimen which was fortuitously preserved at the site after the camp had been abandoned.
(b) Site FwJj 1 was found by Peter Nzube in the Ileret Lower/Middle Tuff beds of Area 8 close by a clustered series of hominid fossil finds (as shown in Fig. 4.2 and in Findlater, 1976, Fig. 3). Excavations at the site itself did not yield any hominid remains, but a few flakes were found washing out from beds at the near-by site which yielded associated skeletal remains (KNM-ER 803). The artefacts are consistent with inclusion in the Karari Industry category, but the sample lacks sufficient diagnostic elements to make this certain. This instance represents close conjunction, but *not* direct association.

71

(c) Site FxJj 38 NW, which is stratified just below the Okote Tuff beds, was discovered and excavated by J. W. K. Harris very close to the find spot of KNM-ER 1805 and 1806 (Fig. 4.2). These fossils were themselves found only 10–15 m apart. The site is at the same horizon as that in which 1805 was embedded and some scattered flakes were found in the layer that encased the fossil. The industry from FxJj 38 NW has hitherto been treated as a part of the Karari Industry, but it is dominated by choppers and has been reclassified as belonging to the KBS Industry. The assemblage is also very like some of the Olduvai Bed 1 assemblages (see below). This is another instance in which there is close conjunction without direct association.

ASSEMBLAGE CHARACTERISTICS AND NOMENCLATURE

The archaeological assemblages from the two main artefact-bearing stratigraphic intervals show partly contrasting characteristics, and it is convenient to designate each of these sets as a separate archaeological entity or industry (Bishop and Clark, 1967):

Karari Industry, represented by samples derived from the Okote Tuff beds (Harris and Isaac, 1976).
KBS Industry, represented by samples derived from KBS Tuff (Isaac, Harris, and Crader, 1976).

Table 4.3 summarizes assemblage composition showing the contrasts in the typological data for each industry. In addition the series of Karari Industry sites has been subdivided internally to allow comparison between those assemblages that come from the context of stream-channel deposits and those from floodplain settings.

The Karari Industry has been given the following formal definition by Harris and Isaac (1976).

The 'Karari Industry' is a set of early Pleistocene artefact assemblages that shares broad, generalized features with other near-contemporary industries such as the Developed Oldowan Industry from Bed II at Olduvai, but which also shows distinctive patterns of differences from them. Generalized features held in common include the preponderance of opportunistic flaking technology in which highly organized, fixed patterns of core preparations are rare or lacking. Choppers, polyhedrons and discoids are important components of the Karari Industry as in many other generalized industries. Handaxes and cleavers seem to have been a rare but significant part of the total artefact repertoire, as in the case of the Developed Oldowan B. The Karari Industry, however, is distinguishable from all other near contemporaneous industries by the tendency of its component assemblages to include a conspicuous series of core-scrapers. The percentage incidence of these is variable. A few assemblages, that clearly formed part of the material culture system that we are designating as the Karari Industry, show a low or negligible incidence of the key forms, but in the majority, where the sample is large enough, they are present in proportions well outside the range observed in other contemporary industries. In the Karari Industry even the scrapers that are not specifically core-scrapers, are distinct from those of most Oldowan assemblages by their tendency to be more massive.

If an associated set of excavated artefacts is needed as a type-sample of the newly defined industry, we would nominate the archaeological material from the FxJj 18 site complex as suitable.

Fig. 4.3 provides illustrations of a series of distinctive Karari Industry artefacts. The material includes a wide diversity of forms.

TABLE 4.3. *The percentage composition of the main excavated assemblages*

	Sites	Overall composition				Percentage representation of tool categories relative to the total of shaped tools*									
		No. of artefacts	Debitage (%)	Tools (%)	No. of tools	Core scrapers	Flake scrapers +	Choppers	Protobifaces	Bifaces	Discoids	Polyhedra	Sundry tools	Other tools	RCCF†
	Karari Scarp assemblages from floodplain silts														
KARARI INDUSTRY	FxJj 11 (BBS)	337	95·9	3·6	12			(33)			(8)	(17)		(25)	(17)
	17	263	98·9	0·4	1						(100)				
	18 IHS	3267	96·2	3·5	114	21	17	2	3		25	21	6		5
	20 M	2497	97·5	1·7	42	2	31	12	5		19	7		2	21
	20 E	1205	96·6	2·7	33	9	18	33			24	9		3	3
	20 AB	3462	98·7	0·7	25	20	20	16			4	8			32
	Karari Scarp assemblages from channel sands and gravels														
	FxJj 16	173	57·8	26·0	45	18	18	27	4		9	16			9
	18 GSL	1556	87·2	10·9	169	20	17	19	2		15	19	3		5
	18 GSU	216	86·1	11·6	23	20	36	16			4	16	8		
	18 NS	993	91·0	5·8	58	14	29	10	3		14	19		5	5
	21 surface	54	85·2	11·1	6			(17)		(67)				(17)	
	23	73	97·3	1·4	1			(100)							
KBS INDUSTRY	38	117	57·3	34·2	40		2	72			5		2		18
	Ileret assemblage from lake margin floodplain silts														
	FwJj 1	320	99·4	0·3	1			(100)							
	Delta floodplain assemblages from areas 105 and 118														
	FxJj 1 (KBS)	139	93·0	5·0	7	(14)		(43)			(29)	(14)			
	3 (HAS)	118	96·7	2·5	3			(33)				(33)	(33)		
	10 (NMS)	306	93·1	4·9	15		(13)	(53)	(7)		(7)		(7)	(13)	

* The percentages are given to the nearest whole number to facilitate reading the table. Values for sets where the total number of tools is less than 30 are shown in parentheses to draw attention to the fact that they are very uncertain indices.

† RCCF Retouched core and cobble fragments.

Based on Isaac (1976*a*), Harris and Isaac (1976), Harris (unpublished), plus previously unpublished analyses of FxJj 10 made by Barthelme and Isaac.

Some of the core-scrapers have a surprisingly neat and 'fancy' aspect considering the early date of the assemblages. Several sites have yielded boulder-cores which weigh 4 to 5 kg. It is quite clear from this and from the large volume of discarded material that the makers of the Karari Industry were deft tool-makers possessed of considerable muscular strength. Stone-knapping had become an habitual behaviour pattern.

At several points on the outcrops of the upper part of the upper member, along the entire Karari escarpment, handaxes and cleavers have been found as surface specimens. In some instances the circumstances of discovery are such that it is certain that the pieces in question did derive from the upper member. However, no specimens have yet been recovered from excavations and in fact the pattern of surface finds makes it appear that the bifaces occur primarily as isolated pieces or as very small clusters of bifaces without other artefacts. It is not yet clear whether they are inter-

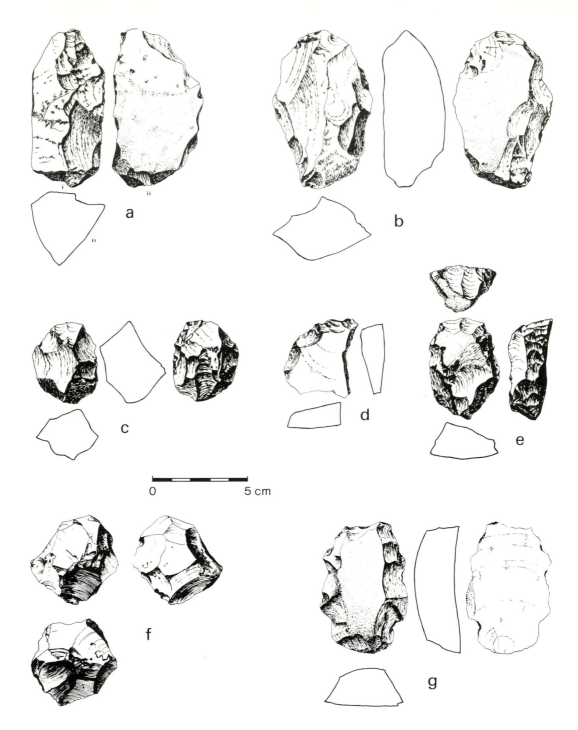

FIG. 4.3. A selected series of artefacts from the Karari Industry. (a), (b) proto-bifaces; (c) discoid; (d), (e) light-duty (flake) scrapers; (f) polyhedron; (g) denticulate scraper ('limace-like') on a flake. (d) and (e) are from FxJj 20; all others from FxJj 18 IHS.

stratified with the excavated sites in the Okote Tuff beds, or whether they come from beds at a slightly higher level. The bifaces are generally fairly thick heavy forms, shaped by the removal of relatively few, bold flake scars.

The term 'KBS Industry' has been introduced by Isaac (1976a) together with a description of the material, but without any formal definition. The 'KBS Industry' like various other early artefact series, is less distinctive than the Karari Industry and we intend to treat this entity as a tentative one, introduced for convenience in dealing with the Koobi Fora archaeological sequence. A brief, provisional definition is offered as follows:

'The "KBS Industry" is represented by a set of late Pliocene and/or early Pleistocene artefact assemblages that share broad generalized features with other early stone industries, especially those of the Oldowan Industry as represented in the samples from Bed I at Olduvai. The available samples of the KBS Industry differ from the type Oldowan Industry in these respects:

(1) Small scrapers and allied forms made on flake fragments are almost entirely lacking;
(2) Spheroids and subspheroids are not represented;
(3) The mean size of both core tools and flakes is slightly smaller. (This latter feature could easily be due to non-cultural limitations imposed by the available raw material).

'The KBS Industry differs from the Karari Industry by the lack of the characteristic scrapers, and of bifaces.'

The main differentiating features for the KBS Industry are negative and might be affected by the discovery of samples in which the artefact forms in question are present. If this occurs in the course of future research, the KBS Industry should be formally merged with the Oldowan industry from which it is only marginally distinct.

Fig. 4.4 provides illustrations of KBS Industry artefacts. They are smaller, rarer, and much less elaborate than the Karari specimens.

The setting up of these defined archaeological taxa for the classification of the archaeological material from the Koobi Fora Formation is not intended to denote the existence of culturally or ethnically distinct entities. These are divisions based on a combination of stratigraphy and artefact morphology. Interpretations of the meaning of the divisions in anthropological or other terms would be a separate step which is not being attempted here.

At the present time only two excavated artefact assemblages pose problems relating to inclusion in one or other of these entities. The samples in question are intermediate in stratigraphic position (Table 4.1). Site FxJj 38 is stratified just below the Okote Tuff complex and its assemblage is dominated by choppers, to the almost total exclusion of the distinctive scraper forms that characterize most of the Karari Industry samples. This assemblage was tentatively grouped in the Karari Industry (Harris and Isaac, 1976), but it has been reclassified as belonging to the KBS Industry (Harris, unpublished). Site FxJj 15 has yielded only a small and nondescript series of abraded flakes and perhaps one or two core-choppers (surface finds), (J. Barthelme, unpublished report). This material comes from a channel complex cut into one major bed of tuff (130/T I) and silted in with partially tuffaceous sediment.

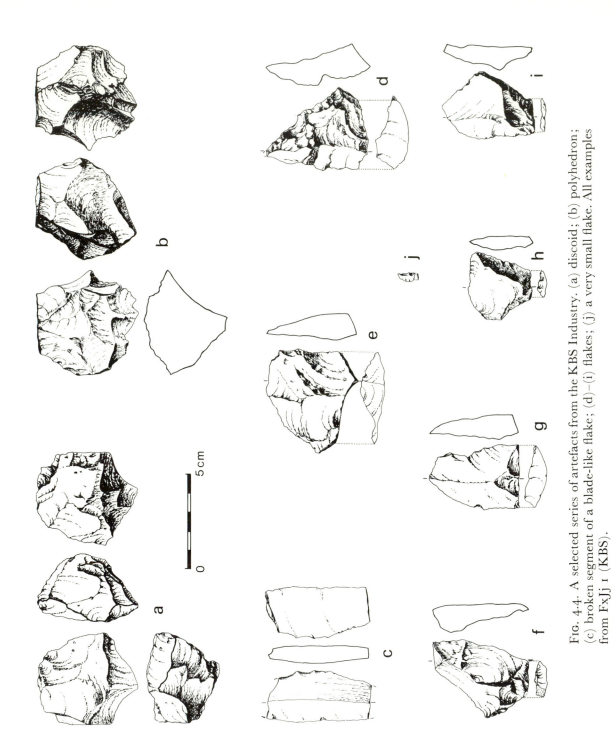

Fig. 4.4. A selected series of artefacts from the KBS Industry. (a) discoid; (b) polyhedron; (c) broken segment of a blade-like flake; (d)–(i) flakes; (j) a very small flake. All examples from FxJj 1 (KBS).

If the dating hypotheses of Fitch and Miller (1976), and of Hurford *et al.* (1976) prove to be the best approximations of the age of the KBS Tuff and of Tuff 130/T I, then this industry is half to three-quarters of a million years older than the known samples of Oldowan from Olduvai Bed I. However, if the dating hypothesis of Curtis *et al.* (1975) is later substantiated, then the available KBS samples are more or less contemporaneous with the Olduvai Bed I and Lower Bed II samples.

The Karari Industry is securely dated to the interval between about 1.2 and 1.5 million years and it is thus contemporaneous with parts of Middle and Upper Bed II at Olduvai (M. D. Leakey, 1975). Its taxonomic affinities are, however, a more complex matter, largely because archaeologists disagree over the conceptual framework involved in setting up an assemblage classification for a sample set which shows considerable internal variation (Table 4.3). While the series as a whole is distinctive, some of the variants within it may resemble Acheulian Industries (e.g. site FxJj 21).

The contrast between the KBS and the Karari Industries involves the particular features specified in the definitions of each, but there are also several general points of distinction that deserve comment. The number of distinguishable categories of tool types is noticeably greater in the Karari Industry. Further, the overall density of discarded material in the upper member of the Karari escarpment is far higher than that of even the most productive sector of the lower member that is yet known (Area 105). The incidence of Karari sites per unit area of outcrops is greater and the density of objects on the sites themselves is commonly much higher. It may be of interest to note that similar points of contrast have been recognized at Olduvai between the archaeological material characteristic of Bed I and that of Middle and Upper Bed II (M. D. Leakey, 1971). It is possible that in both sequences the changes represent an important rise in technological abilities, but in view of the fact that in each case the sedimentary facies yielding the successive phases are not fully comparable, more research will be needed to confirm or refute this interpretation.

The hominid fossils give evidence that more than one species occupied the basin during the time range represented by the archaeological traces. However, at present we lack direct evidence concerning which species made the stone implements. All that can be said with certainty is that there was at least one tool-making species present.

THE CHARACTERISTICS OF SITES

Currently we would recognize four different ways in which artefacts that have not been subjected to fluvial redeposition occur in the Koobi Fora Formation. The scheme which is set out below is an elaboration of one presented by M. D. Leakey (1971, p. 258).

Occurrence type A: Concentration of artefacts with little or no associated bone.
Occurrence type B: Modest numbers of artefacts associated with bones from the carcass of a single large animal.
Occurrence type C: A concentration of artefacts associated with a conspicuous patch of broken-up bones from the carcasses of several different animals, usually of different species.
Occurrence type D: Artefacts dispersed at very low density over ancient land surfaces, or through sediment beds.

Each of these manifestations leads to possible interpretation along a different line. Occurrences of type B are commonly taken to denote the cutting up of a carcass by the tool-makers and are then called butchery sites. Type C is ordinarily treated as representative of a camp or 'home base site'. Hitherto far less explicit attention has been devoted to the interpretation of occurrence types A and D. Some concentrations of artefacts without bone may be 'factory sites' but many clearly are not. It is possible that some of these type A sites are camps where plant foods rather than meat constituted the principal items of diet. Type A sites could, however, also result simply from the decay of bone at an occurrence that was of type B or C at the time of hominid occupation. At present it is often impossible to distinguish sites in which bone has largely decayed from those where it was never present.

TABLE 4.4. *The classification of artefact occurrences*

	A	B	C	D
	Artefacts + little or no bone	Artefacts + bone from one carcass	Artefacts + bones from several carcasses	Diffuse occurrences
KBS Industry	FxJj 10 (NMS) 38	FxJj 3 (HAS)	FxJj 1 (KBS)	Various in areas 105, 130, 131
Karari Industry	FxJj 16 FxJj 18 NS FxJj 18 GS (LH) FxJj 18 GS (UH) FxJj 23 FwJj 1		FxJj 18 IHS FxJj 20 M FxJj 20 E FxJj 20 AB	FxJj 11, 17, 21 and others in areas 129, 130, 131, 118, and some in Ileret

Table 4.4 shows the main excavated sites classified into the four categories. The three main excavations of KBS Industry occurrences represent site type B (butchery), site type C (home base), and site type A (in this case, a site which has very possibly been secondarily depleted of bone). The Karari Industry sites show the same broad range though a butchery site of this age has not yet been found. Conditions of bone preservation in the upper member sediments of areas 129–31 are comparatively poor and so the majority of sites are of type A. However, the floodplain sites, especially FxJj 20 M, E, and AB and FxJj 18 IHS, do contain varied bone remains in association with the artefacts and these are type C sites. For reference purposes there follows a brief introduction to the characteristics of the principal sites excavated prior to 1975. For most, more detailed accounts, together with plans and sections, are available (Isaac, Harris, and Crader, 1976; Harris, unpublished). Full monographic treatment will be undertaken in a future volume of this series.

KBS Industry sites

FxJj 1 KBS (Kay Behrensmeyer Site). This locality was discovered in 1969 by A. K. Behrensmeyer. Test excavations were undertaken immediately by R. E. Leakey and Kamoya Kimeu (R. E. Leakey, 1970; M. D. Leakey, 1970). Subsequently in 1970 Glynn Isaac was invited to direct research at the site, and with J. Barthelme as site supervisor a lengthy programme of careful excavations was undertaken spanning a cumulative total of five to six months, ending in 1972. Plans and sections have been published (Isaac, Leakey, and Behrensmeyer, 1971; Isaac, Harris, and Crader, 1976).

This site is associated with a prominent outcrop of pale altered volcanic ash, and it serves as the type locality for the KBS Tuff. The tuff bed is particularly thick and prominent at this spot, because the modern erosion surface intersects the bed of an ancient stream or distributary channel, which was choked with deposits of grey vitric tuff mixed with subordinate quantities of normal clastic sediment. The archaeological horizon occurs at the interface between two subdivisions of the tuff beds that fill the palaeo-channel. The material rests on an earlier set of sandy tuff deposits and was covered over by a later set of fine ash silt and dust. We can tell that the process of site burial took place after the channel had ceased to carry a current flow of any strength, because in places the horizon is entirely encased in the base of the upper layer of fine-grained, low-energy silt and dust. These silts also preserve the impression of tree leaves which evidently fell into puddles in the swamp left when the stream shifted away from this particular course. The tree growth along the banks of the stream may help to account for the suitability of the locale as a focus of hominid activity.

Excavations show that at this spot artefacts were discarded so as to form a patch about 12 to 15 m in diameter. Recent headward erosion of small gulleys has cut into and destroyed slightly more than half of the patch, but enough remained to provide a good estimate of the overall size of the site and a valid sample of its contents. We have recovered 139 objects from the trenches and a further 60 to 70 from the eroded surface. Altogether it can be safely estimated that the entire site probably contained between 300 and 500 discarded stone artefacts and manuports. Coincident with the patch of discarded artefacts is a scatter of broken-up animal bones. Many are so fragmentary as to be unidentifiable, but it is certain that a considerable variety is represented: *Kobus* cf. *ellypsiprymnus* (waterbuck); *Antidorcas recki* (a gazelle); *Hystrix* sp. (porcupine); *Metridiochoerus andrewsi* (a pig); and hippopotamus (J. M. Harris in Isaac, Harris, and Crader, 1976).

KBS is clearly an excellent example of occurrence type C, and there is good circumstantial evidence for regarding it as a fossilized remnant of a hominid home base.

FxJj 3 HAS (Hippo and Artefact Site). This locality was discovered in 1969 by R. E. Leakey. Erosion had exposed numerous fossilized bones from the carcass of a single hippopotamus and among the bones was a scatter of stone artefacts. The locality is about 1 km to the south of KBS and the remains derive from exactly the same stratigraphic level, namely the upper part of the KBS Tuff. In this case the source horizon is a palaeo-land surface within the tuff, on which very weak soil development was taking place.

Excavations were carried out from 1970 to 1972 with J. W. K. Harris and J. Onyango-Abuje acting as site supervisors. Trenches revealed a scatter of artefacts some 8–10 m in diameter. Well-preserved examples of whole bones are restricted to the north-west sector of the patch where erosion had already disinterred most of the material. Sloping gently up from the sector of the site with the unbroken hippo bones was a bank or mid-channel bar on which were recovered more artefacts and some very fragmented, badly weathered bone. Most of the bone is unidentifiable but it certainly includes small pieces of hippo tooth and tusk. Altogether 118 artefacts were recovered from the excavation, and about 50 more from the outcrop. At this site erosion damage is much less advanced than at KBS and it is reasonable to estimate that the entire site never contained more than about 200 artefacts.

The coincidence of the patch of artefacts and the remains of the hippopotamus carcass renders this a clear instance of a type B occurrence. The dead hippo probably lay in a small hollow or pool with the hominid activity occurring both at the carcass and on the adjacent bank. There is no way of knowing whether the tool-makers killed the hippo or found it dead, but the artefacts were presumably made in order to assist in cutting parts of it into pieces. Many stone implements were clearly made on the spot, since we have recovered both a hammerstone and very small waste flakes and splinters. This site carries the strong implication that periodically the tool-makers engaged in the butchery of a large carcass and the consumption of substantial quantities of meat.

FxJj 10 NMS (Nathaniel Mudoga Site). This locality was discovered in 1970 by N. Mudoga, J. Barthelme, and G. Isaac. In 1972, J. W. K. Harris and Isaac mapped it. Excavations were carried out in 1972 by D. Stiles and D. Crader and in 1973 by J. Barthelme.

The site is about 1 km east-north-east of KBS, in area 118. The locality consists of a large dissected outcrop of a tuff now designated 118/T II. Hitherto this tuff has been regarded as a correlative of the KBS Tuff, which it may well be, though the question is under scrutiny. The outcrop is bounded on one side by a fault and on the other by an area of cut-and-fill deposits representing a major river channel complex. Artefacts are scattered along the eroded margins of the upper part of the tuff beds.

Some 400 specimens have been identified and mapped. Two areas of relatively high artefact concentration were detected, and an excavation was carried out at one of these.

The trenches showed that the artefacts were scattered through a series of tuffaceous sands and sandy tuffs, with one level showing a concentration of the kind that could be designated as a 'floor'. Developed immediately above the archaeological stratum is a weathering horizon and a caliche. The lava artefacts are severely rotted and, presumably because of chemical alteration, hardly any bone is preserved.

The artefact-bearing tuffaceous sands are overbank deposits of the river-channel complex in the east, but it is not yet clear whether this upper tuffaceous sand in which the material occurs should be treated as part of 118/T II (?KBS) or as an entirely separate unit in the upper member.

The site is a clear instance of a type A occurrence, showing a focus of activity by tool-makers on the banks and floodplain of a large stream or river. Because the bone has been destroyed, no direct inferences regarding subsistence can be made.

Karari Industry Sites

FxJj 11 BBS (Bruce Bowen Site). This locality in area 130 was discovered in 1971 by R. E. Leakey and G. Ll. Isaac while they were examining one of Bowen's geological sections. Excavations were carried out by J. W. K. Harris in 1972. Erosion has exposed a scatter of artefacts along the outcrops of a dominantly sandy claystone horizon approximately 1 m below the base of the Okote Tuff.

Three hundred surface specimens have been identified and mapped and a small test excavation (6 m × 3 m) was carried out to find the location of the archaeological horizon. Artefacts were found dispersed through a clay-rich sedimentary unit, which showed pedogenic reworking (White in Harris, unpublished). Material was presumably discarded on a palaeo-land surface which developed on a river floodplain. This scattered material at a site with little associated bone can be regarded as being in part an occurrence of type D and in part one of type A.

Site FxJj 16. The site was discovered and excavated by J. W. K. Harris in 1972. Artefacts were found concentrated in the base of a large channel cut which was subsequently filled with sand. The margins of the channel are stratified within the base of the Okote Tuff. The assemblage which was recovered (Table 4.2) is dominated by large cores and core-tools, only comparatively few flakes being present. Small flakes and angular chips of stone are particularly rare. It seems clear that this material was swept along by the stream current and concentrated at this point in the channel. Very probably the smaller components of the original assemblage have been separated and deposited elsewhere.

FxJj 17. This locality is 400 m to the south-east of FxJj 11 in area 130 and was discovered by G. Ll. Isaac and J. W. K. Harris. It appeared to be an example of a discrete, low-density occurrence of stone artefacts and broken-up bone. In order to enlarge the sample of settlement types, excavations were commenced under the supervision of J. Gowlett in 1972 and continued in 1973 by J. W. K. Harris.

A small number of artefacts, comprising a high proportion of flakes and flaking debitage (98 per cent), and fragmentary bone debris were found scattered over an undulating surface in sandy floodplain silt deposits of the Okote Tuff. The low density may be indicative of one or more very brief occupation episodes, and the locality should perhaps be treated as an occurrence of Type D (i.e. dispersed).

FxJj 18. This site complex in area 130, one of the richest archaeological localities along the Karari escarpment, was discovered in 1972 by G. Ll. Isaac and J. W. K. Harris. The site complex measures approximately 75 m from north to south and 95 m from east to west and covers some 7200 m². Stratigraphically, the site complex occurs at the base of the Okote Tuff.

The local stratigraphic sequence, which attains a maximum thickness of 12 m, commences with gravelly sands which were deposited in the bed of a large stream channel. As the stream shifted its bed laterally, a sequence of layers was deposited that became finer grained upwards. Tuffaceous silts were deposited at the close of the local fluvial cycle, and a soil horizon and caliche developed on these silts before the commencement of the next fluvial cycle. Four archaeological occurrences were discovered stratified in several different rock-types. These show shifts in the spatial focus of occupation through the stratigraphic sequence.

(1) Gravel Site, Lower Horizon (FxJj 18 GS (LH)). A test trench was dug by J. W. K. Harris in 1973 and a large-scale excavation was carried out under the supervision of Ingrid Herbich in 1974. A large concentration of core-tools and flakes was found on a gravel bar; evidently the tool-makers used the spot as a source of raw materials, and perhaps also as a camp place. This site is an excellent example of occurrence type A and perhaps could be interpreted as a 'factory site'.

(2) Gravel Site, Upper Horizon (FxJj 18 GS(UH)). This site, a type A occurrence, was excavated in 1973 by J. W. K. Harris. The horizon of artefacts was found in silty sands that were deposited immediately above the Lower Horizon along the margin of the stream as the channel shifted. It is not entirely clear whether the lack of bone in both archaeological horizons at 18 GS is due to poor preservation or whether it is an original feature.

(3) North Site (FxJj 18 NS). The site, 35 m to the north of 18 GS, was excavated in 1972 by J. Gowlett and J. W. K. Harris. A dense patch of artefacts and a small number of comminuted bone fragments were recovered at the interface of gravelly sands and finer silty sands.

The focus of hominid activity was on the bank of a stream channel, and since bone remains are only sparsely represented it is classified as type A. The discrete, concentrated lens of artefacts is approximately 5 cm in thickness and may well represent a single occupation episode.

(4) Ingrid Herbich Site (FxJj 18 IHS). This site is the uppermost in the local stratigraphic sequence and was excavated in 1973 by Ingrid Herbich. An extraordinary dense, localized concentration of artefacts and broken-up bone fragments was located in a weathered silty tuffaceous unit which was deposited on a floodplain.

The material was concentrated in a heap which covered 2–3 m² of the total excavated area of the site. Artefacts totalling 3142 specimens were recovered in association with about 400 bone and tooth fragments, mostly in a finely comminuted state. The faunal remains comprise a wide variety of species which suggests that both riverine and savanna habitats were being exploited by the occupants. The taxa include Hippopotamidae, Tragelaphini, Reduncini, Elephantidae, Giraffidae, Suidae, and *Clarius* sp.

FxJj 18 IHS represents a sample of the material remains of an abandoned camp site situated on a floodplain close to a stream channel and associated with a palaeo-land surface stratified within the fluviatile sediments. Because a varied bone assemblage occurs with the artefacts, it is a good example of an occurrence of type C.

FxJj 20. This site complex is located approximately 500–600 m north-west of the Karari escarpment ridge in area 131 and was discovered by G. Ll. Isaac and J. W. K. Harris in 1972. Concentrations of stone artefacts in association with preserved faunal remains in stratified contexts of brown tuffaceous floodplain silts of the Okote Tuff have also been recovered by excavation from three adjacent sub-localities: FxJj 20 Main, FxJj 20 East, and FxJj 20 AB. Excavations were carried out under the supervision of J. W. K. Harris (1972–4), Ingrid Herbich (1973–4), and Simuyu Wandibba (1973).

The sites are located within 150 m of each other and are adjacent to the deposits of a large channel complex, which was probably in the same geographic position during the deposition of the tuffaceous silts in which the sites are found stratified. When traced in the direction of the channel, the lateral extensions of the silts containing the sites were found to have been truncated by the channel. However, on the assumption that the channel did occupy approximately the same position at the time of hominid usage, the sites can be said to have been within 200 m of the bank.

Bones are better preserved in these sites than in any other upper member site yet excavated, and since a variety of faunal remains are present, the sites are classifiable as being of type C. They seem to be clearly demonstrable examples of home-base sites. Detailed analysis of the configurations are currently in progress (Harris, unpublished).

At one of the sites, FxJj 20 East, discoloured patches were found in the substratum of the main occupation level which appeared to represent traces of camp fires. Preliminary tests have failed to confirm this, but it remains a possibility and research is continuing. At this site, in the silts 10–15 cm above the main artefact-bearing horizon, the mandible of a robust australopithecine (KNM-ER 3230) was recovered in conjunction with a low-density scatter of bone fragments and stone artefacts that are scattered through the silts at the same level.

FxJj 21. Five bifaces and a number of other artefacts, as well as fragmentary faunal remains, were discovered by J. W. K. Harris in 1973 on a small eroded area at the base of an outcrop of the Karari Tuff near FxJj 20. This surface locality is at a slightly higher stratigraphic level in the Okote Tuff beds than any of the other excavated Karari sites. A test trench failed to recover any further artefacts.

FxJj 23. This type A site is located on the plains which slope gently eastward from the crest of the Karari escarpment. It is 5 km to the east of the main cluster of Karari sites, which are situated on the face of the escarpment itself (Fig. 4.1). B. Bowen discovered the site in 1972 during geological reconnaissance of the area and it was excavated in 1973 under the supervision of J. W. K. Harris.

A small occurrence of artefacts and bone fragments was stratified in a sequence of medium-grained sands which became finer upwards. Precise correlation of this locality with sites on the western face of the Karari escarpment is made difficult by the discontinuous nature of the outcrops on the eastern backslope; however, the silts overlying the site closely resemble the floodplain silts of the Okote Tuff. After the excavation of this site, further surface localities were mapped so as to extend knowledge of the geographic range of Karari Industry sites. Additional sites were found in the vicinity of the Ol Bakate gap and at the base of the Suregei cuesta in area 129 (Fig. 4.1).

FwJj 1. In area 8, Peter Nzube found the only concentration of archaeological material known in the Ileret Member, though scattered specimens occur fairly widely. Excavations were supervised by D. Crader in 1973 (Isaac, Harris, and Crader, 1976) and by J. Barthelme in 1974. Erosion had exposed a small, fairly dense patch of artefacts which lay on the sandy bank of a small stream channel. Several of the flakes derive from successive blows to the same core and can be fitted back together, suggesting that the assemblage has not been transported or redistributed by stream currents. Bone is rare and in poor condition; this site is thus classified as a type A occurrence.

SUMMARY AND DISCUSSION

The available hominid fossils show that more than one species of upright bipedal creatures was moving about in the sedimentary basin, though there may have been specific differences in limb anatomy among them. As a complement to this palaeontological information, the archaeological evidence elucidates aspects of some adaptive patterns associated with the bipedal locomotion of at least one hominid species. First, the presence of discarded stone artefacts in the sediments shows that some hominids were making and using equipment with a degree of deliberateness far beyond anything yet observed in any non-human primate. Further, the locations of flaked stones show that the tool-makers were transporting materials to a degree beyond that recorded for any living ape or monkey. The combined distribution of hominid fossils and artefacts shows that the hominids ranged widely, covering many varied habitats on the basin floor, and very probably many parts of the bounding hills and plateaux. These findings are consistent with the view that bipedalism served in part to facilitate tool-making, mobility, and the ability to carry things over distances.

Specimens of fossil crania show that some, but not all, hominid species were undergoing an evolutionary trend towards enlargement of the brain. Viewed as a background to the palaeontological evidence, the pattern of the archaeological traces is indicative of ways in which brain function was being extended. It appears that meat was being consumed and that at times it was transported to particular places where a combined refuse of bone and discarded artefacts accumulated. The places where such material occurs were very probably home-base sites, and the pattern may well imply that the hominids who used them engaged in active sharing of meat. Although they are not as yet directly documented, it is possible that plant foods were also being gathered and shared at these sites. Such behavioural arrangements all depend in some degree on the use of tools and equipment, at the least sharp flakes for cutting up carcasses and some kind of bag or other receptacle for carrying food and stones. All these traits are fundamental to modern human behaviour but would have required evolutionary modifications and elaborations of the brain in order to become established.

In summary we have tentative evidence from Koobi Fora and elsewhere for recognizing a distinctive proto-human adaptive complex in which anatomical, neurophysiological, technological, and sociological developments were all intertwined. This system in turn very probably helped to establish selection pressures that favoured advances in communication and fine adjustment of social relations. (For fuller discussion of these questions see Isaac, 1971, 1976*b*, *c*, and references therein.)

This concluding section is in part speculative and the hypothesis offered in it is merely one of several that are possible. It is, however, based on existing evidence and can be tested in future research. The speculations show that in the Koobi Fora Project archaeology, palaeontology, and palaeo-ecology are merging so that each is losing its former clear-cut identity. These themes will be taken up in later volumes of this series.

REFERENCES

BISHOP, W. W. and CLARK, J. D. (eds.) 1967. *Background to evolution in Africa*. University of Chicago Press.

COPPENS, Y., HOWELL, F. C., ISAAC, G. L., and LEAKEY, R. E. (eds.). 1976. *Earliest man and environments in the Lake Rudolf Basin: Stratigraphy, paleoecology and evolution*. University of Chicago Press.

CURTIS, G. H., DRAKE, R., CERLING, T. E., and HAMPEL, J. H. 1975. Age of KBS Tuff in Koobi Fora Formation, East Rudolf, Kenya. *Nature, Lond.* **258**, 395–8.

FINDLATER, I. C. 1976. Tuffs and the recognition of isochronous mapping units in the East Rudolf succession. In Coppens *et al.* (1976), pp. 94–104.

FITCH, F. J. and MILLER, J. A. 1976. Conventional potassium–argon and argon 40/argon 39 dating of the volcanic rocks from East Rudolf. In Coppens *et al.* (1976), pp. 79–93.

HARRIS, J. W. K. (unpublished). Karari Industry: its place in African Prehistory. Ph.D. thesis. University of California, Berkeley.

——— and HERBICH, I. 1978. Aspects of early Pleistocene hominid behavior at East Rudolf, Kenya. In *Geological background to fossil man* (ed. W. W. Bishop). Geol. Soc. Lond. Special Publ. No. 6. Scottish Academic Press, Edinburgh.

——— and ISAAC, G. Ll. 1976. The Karari Industry: early Pleistocene archaeological evidence from the terrain east of Lake Turkana, Kenya. *Nature, Lond.* **262**, 102–7.

HURFORD, A. J., GLEADOW, A. J. W., and NAESER, C. W. 1976. Fission-track dating of pumice from the KBS Tuff, East Rudolf, Kenya. *Nature, Lond.* **263**, 738–40.

ISAAC, G. LL. 1969. Studies of early culture in East Africa. *World Archaeology* **1**, 1–28.

———. 1971. The diet of early man: aspects of archaeological evidence from Lower and Middle Pleistocene sites in Africa. *World Archaeology*, **2**, 278–98.

———. 1976*a*. Plio/Pleistocene artefact assemblages from East Rudolf, Kenya. In Coppens *et al.* (1976), pp. 552–64.

———. 1976*b*. The activities of early African hominids: a review of archaeological evidence from the time span two and a half to one million years ago. In *Human origins: Louis Leakey and the East African Evidence* (eds. G. Ll. Isaac and E. R. McCown). W. A. Benjamin Inc., Menlo Park, California.

———. 1976*c*. Early hominids in action: a commentary on the contribution of archaeology to understanding the fossil record in East Africa. In *Yearbook of Physical Anthropology for 1975* (ed. J. Buettner-Janusch), pp. 19–35. Amer. Assoc. of Phys. Anthropologists, Washington.

———, HARRIS, J. W. K., and CRADER, D. 1976. Archaeological evidence from the Koobi Fora Formation. In Coppens *et al.* (1976), pp. 533–551.

———, LEAKEY, R. E. F., and BEHRENSMEYER, A. K. 1971. Archaeological traces of early hominid activities, east of Lake Rudolf, Kenya. *Science* **173**, 1129–34.

LEAKEY, M. D. 1971. *Olduvai Gorge. Vol. 3. Excavations in Beds I and II, 1960–1963*. Cambridge University Press.

———. 1975. Cultural patterns in the Olduvai sequence. In *After the Australopithecines* (eds. K. W. Butzer and G. Ll. Isaac), pp. 477–93. Mouton, The Hague.

LEAKEY, R. E. F. 1970. Fauna and artefacts from a new Plio–Pleistocene locality near Lake Rudolf in Kenya. *Nature, Lond.* **226**, 223–4.

5

THE HOMINID CATALOGUE

RICHARD E. LEAKEY, MEAVE G. LEAKEY, AND
ANNA K. BEHRENSMEYER

THIS chapter presents the hominid specimens recovered from the Koobi Fora region between 1968 and 1974 in the form of a catalogue. Each specimen is described briefly and, except in the case of isolated teeth, is illustrated. The illustrations are intended to reduce the need for lengthy descriptions. The specimens are all surface finds except where indicated as *in situ* (**KNM-ER** 729, 732, 820, 1464, 1477, 1805, 1813, 1816, and 3230). A brief review of the taxonomy is given on p. 88.

The *stratigraphic position* is given as upper, lower, or Ileret Member (Bowen and Vondra, 1973) based on I. C. Findlater's provisional stratigraphic correlation (Fig. 2.5). Where possible the stratigraphic position is also related to a tuff identified according to the index of labels for the tuffs explained in Chapter 3 (p. 36; Fig. 3.1). The informal palaeontological collection unit, (also explained in Chapter 3, p. 36; Fig. 3.3) is also given. A. K. Behrensmeyer has compiled reference sections for the more important specimens, and their relative positions based on I. C. Findlater's provisional correlation are shown in the stratigraphic catalogue (Fig. 2.5). All the specimens are from the Koobi Fora Formation except KNM-ER 999 which is from the Guomde Formation.

The *environment of deposition* is based on the microstratigraphic interpretations of A. K. Behrensmeyer and the coarser divisions of the sedimentary environments of I. C. Findlater (p. 19; Fig. 2.8 and Table 2.1).

The *references* in most cases include only the initial preliminary report published in *Nature* (in which the discovery of the specimen was announced) and the subsequent description in the *American Journal of Physical Anthropology*. These are given as Koobi Fora Research Project Publication Numbers (K.F.R.P. Publ. Nos.) and the reference can be found in the Research Project bibliography (p. 180). Reference to papers by authors outside the project is given only in a few cases where this is considered relevant.

COMMENTS ON THE STRATIGRAPHIC REFERENCE SECTIONS

Microstratigraphic sections of the hominid sites show the sedimentary environment as well as the stratigraphic context of the most important specimens in the 1968–74 collections. Most of these specimens were found on the surface of eroding outcrops of the Koobi Fora Formation and in such cases determinations of both sedimentary provenance and original stratigraphic level are interpretive.

Dashed lines on the sections show the range of most probable source horizons for each specimen. The assignment of the hominids to this interval is based on the following lines of evidence: (1) similarity between matrix on the fossil and sedimentary rocks *in situ*; (2) limitations of the local outcrop topography, e.g. area of drainage, slope morphology, etc.; (3) level of distinct fossil-producing horizons (if any) in the vicinity of the site; (4) condition of the fossil, whether obviously weathered from a long period on the surface or fresh due to relatively recent exposure by erosion; (5) spatial proximity of fragments of the same specimen or parts of associated skeletal material. Lithological similarity between matrix and outcrop is the most valuable key to source horizon. Further work using petrography to match matrix with associated rock types could allow virtually certain identification of the source of the most important surface finds.

Many of the hominids can be placed between well-defined levels in the local rock sequence; others (especially very weathered specimens) can be assigned only to a rather large stratigraphic interval. In addition, assignment to stratigraphic level within generalized sections (Fig. 2.5) of the Koobi Fora Formation is complicated by the lateral variation in thickness of lithostratigraphic units and the lack of lateral continuity of critical marker horizons.

The combined possible stratigraphic source interval for each hominid is given with the description of the specimen (e.g., 4–6 m below the base of the Chari Tuff), and this can be regarded as the best information currently available. When the regional palaeogeography and stratigraphy of the Koobi Fora Formation are worked out in greater detail, many of the hominids will be more precisely placed in relation to each other and to the generalized sections given in the correlation chart (Fig. 2.5).

Correct assignment of surface fossils to an environment of deposition is also somewhat dependent on the types of evidence listed above. However, designation of the local sections as either fluvial or lake margin is generally unambiguous, allowing most hominid fossils to be related to one of these broad environmental categories. Greater resolution as to environment of burial is possible in some cases, e.g. fluvial channel, interdistributary, etc.

The microstratigraphic sections provide the basic evidence for differences in the burial environment and hence the palaeoecology of the different hominid taxa (Behrensmeyer, in press). Specimens identified as *Homo* sp. appear to be significantly more common in lake margin than in fluvial deposits, whereas specimens of *Australopithecus boisei* are equally common in fluvial and lake margin environments.

The stratigraphic catalogue (Fig. 2.5), combined with the microstratigraphic sections, provides evidence for the various levels of resolution of time within the hominid sample. Hominids found at the 'same stratigraphic level' (with respect to marker horizons, i.e. isochronous tuffs) may have been buried at different times, whereas specimens from widely spaced localities and separated by several vertical metres may have been buried at the same time. The sedimentary and taphonomic record cannot at this point determine whether any two hominids lived in the same place at the same time. It is, however, possible to say that certain hominid morphotypes occur throughout the same stratigraphic interval, and this is the meaning of 'contemporaneous' for the Koobi Fora faunal record. At present, in considerations of hominid evolution it is probably most valid to group all hominids between the apparently equivalent major tuffs as 'contemporaneous', although further chronological division of the fossil assemblages will certainly be possible when details of the stratigraphy are better known.

SOME COMMENTS ON THE TAXONOMY OF THE FOSSIL HOMINIDS

The annual increment to the fossil hominid collection from the Koobi Fora region has led us to become increasingly cautious in taxonomic interpretations. With only a few specimens, conclusions appeared relatively straightforward and unequivocal. As the collection grew, it became more and more apparent that this was not the case and it is most probable that hominid evolution is far more complex than even at present we imagine it to be.

The original specimens collected in 1968 and 1969 were referred to recognized genera from Olduvai Gorge and the Transvaal. KNM-ER 406 and the robust mandibles were thus assigned to *Australopithecus* cf. *boisei*; KNM-ER 407 was thought to be either *Homo* or a gracile australopithecine, but was too damaged to identify with any certainty (Leakey, 1970).

In the following year, 1970, a number of specimens were collected; they included postcranial elements for the first time. Most of the specimens were assigned to the robust *Australopithecus*, but two mandibles, KNM-ER 730 and 731, and a femur were attributed to *Homo*. The recovery of KNM-ER 732 suggested a marked degree of sexual dimorphism in the robust australopithecines, and after reconstruction KNM-ER 407 was reconsidered as a female robust *Australopithecus*. Specific attribution of the specimens was not attempted (Leakey, 1971).

In 1972 the discovery of KNM-ER 1470 demonstrated the advanced nature of the cranium of *Homo* in the earlier deposits, while the femora KNM-ER 1481 and 1742 showed a morphological pattern not unlike that of modern man (Leakey, 1973). These discoveries in particular confirmed the coexistince of *Homo* and *Australopithecus* which had already been suggested on the evidence of material from Olduvai Gorge.

The recovery in 1973 of a small gracile cranium, KNM-ER 1813, with a dentition remarkably similar to that of *Homo*, but with a small cranial capacity, posed new problems. This could either be considered as *Homo*, which would imply a high degree of variation in cranial capacity, or it could represent a third taxon. The striking resemblance of this specimen to some of the Olduvai material assigned to *Homo habilis*, OH 24 and OH 13, suggested that a revaluation of the Olduvai specimens was required since the type mandible of *H. habilis*, OH 7, closely resembled mandibles from Koobi Fora considered to belong with crania such as KNM-ER 1470 (Leakey, 1974).

By the end of 1973, we proposed that at least three hominid taxa were contemporary at Koobi Fora: *Homo* sp., best represented by KNM-ER 1470, 1590, and 1802; *Australopicus boisei*, best represented by KNM-ER 406, 732, and 729; and a third taxon whose affinities were probably closest to *A. africanus* from South Africa, best represented by KNM-ER 1813 and 992 (Leakey, 1974). Since the period covered in this volume, two crania have been recovered which establish the presence of *Homo erectus* in the upper member of the Koobi Fora Formation: KNM-ER 3733 and 3883 (Leakey and Walker, 1976; Leakey, in prepn.).

CONCLUSIONS

The hypotheses formulated by the end of 1974 have been confirmed rather than altered by subsequent finds. These ideas have been summarized recently (Leakey, 1976*a*) and will be put forward in more detail shortly. A brief summary is given below.

Three hominid taxa occupied the Koobi Fora region contemporaneously for a period of at least one million years.

(1) The robust australopithecine, *Australopithecus boisei*, can probably be considered to be specifically distinct from *A. robustus* of South Africa. This lineage became extinct some time after its last appearance below the Chari Tuff. This species is very distinctive, being characterized by hyper-robust mandibles, large molars and premolars relative to the anterior dentition, cranial capacity values less than 550 cm³, and sexual dimorphism manifested in superficial cranial characters such as sagittal and nuchal crests. Some postcranial features are also distinctive. This lineage is best represented at Koobi Fora by the crania KNM-ER 406 and 732, the mandibles KNM-ER 729 and 3230, and the femora KNM-ER 815, 1503, and 993.

(2) The small-brained gracile hominid appears to have its closest affinities with the South African species *Australopithecus africanus*. The characteristics of this hominid taxon are not clearly defined at present but they appear to include a cranial capacity of about 600 cm³ or less, sagittal crest rare or non-existent, small molars and premolars, and gracile mandibles. At Koobi Fora this hominid is best represented by KNM-ER 1813 and certain mandibles such as KNM-ER 1501, 1502, 1507, and 992.

(3) This lineage includes all the specimens attributed to *Homo*. In the earlier levels at Koobi Fora the species is characterized by relatively large anterior teeth, with equally large but not buccolingually expanded cheek teeth, moderately robust and externally buttressed mandibles that have everted basal margins, cranial capacity values exceeding 750 cm³, and a high vaulted skull with slight postorbital waisting and no sagittal crest. The postcranial morphology is similar to that of modern man. The crania KNM-ER 1470 and 1590, the mandible KNM-ER 1802, the femora KNM-ER 1481 and 1472, and the recently discovered innominate, KNM-ER 3228 (Leakey, 1976*b*), are good examples from Koobi Fora. This material is similar to OH 7 from Olduvai Gorge and as such might be considered as *Homo habilis*. The very complete skull of *H. erectus*, KNM-ER 3733, recovered recently from later sediments (Leakey and Walker, 1976) may have evolved from this earlier stage of the *Homo* lineage.

REFERENCES

BOWEN, B. E. and VONDRA, C. G. 1973. Stratigraphical relationships of the Plio–Pleistocene deposits, East Rudolf, Kenya. *Nature, Lond.* **242**, 391–3.

BEHRENSMEYER, A. K. (in press). The habitat of Plio–Pleistocene hominids in East Africa: taphonomic and microstratigraphic evidence. In *African Hominidae of the Plio–Pleistocene, evidence, problems and strategies* (ed. C. Jolly). Duckworth, New York.

LEAKEY, R. E. F. 1970. Fauna and artefacts from a new Plio–Pleistocene locality near Lake Rudolf in Kenya. *Nature, Lond.* **226**, 223–4.

——. 1971. Further evidence of Lower Pleistocene hominids from East Rudolf, North Kenya. *Nature, Lond.* **231**, 241–5.

——. 1973. Evidence for an advanced Plio–Pleistocene hominid from East Rudolf, Kenya. *Nature, Lond.* **242**, 447–50.

——. 1974. Further evidence of Lower Pleistocene hominids from East Rudolf, North Kenya, 1973. *Nature, Lond.* **248**, 653–6.

——. 1976a. Hominids in Africa. *American Scientist*, **64**, 174–8.

——. 1976b. New fossil hominids from the Koobi Fora Formation, Northern Kenya. *Nature, Lond.* **261**, 574–6.

—— and WALKER, A. C. 1976. *Australopithecus, Homo erectus*, and the single species hypothesis. *Nature, Lond.* **261**, 572–4.

THE CATALOGUE

For Key to Reference Sections, see p. 170

KNM-ER 164 (A–C)

A: Fragment of left parietal showing sagittal and lambdoid sutures on its medial and posterior borders respectively. The internal surface is encrusted with a hard matrix.

B: Two proximal phalanges firmly cemented by matrix in a crossed position. A fragment of bone (probably from the shaft of a third phalanx) lies between their distal ends, and the head of a metacarpal lies in articulation with the shorter phalanx.

C: A seventh cervical and a first thoracic vertebra firmly cemented together by matrix a little out of alignment.

Discovery: (A) H. Stradling, 1969. (B–C) M. G. Leakey, 1971.
Area: 104. Aerial photo 1449.
Stratigraphic position: Upper member, above major erosion surface (collection unit 4).
Environment of deposition: Probably delta margin, distributary, ADP.
Reference: K.F.R.P. Publ. Nos. 6, 12, 27.

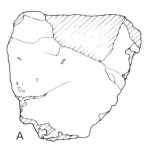

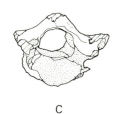

0 _____ 5 cm

FIG. 5.1. KNM-ER 164A, external.
KNM-ER 164B, dorsal.
KNM-ER 164C, superior.

KNM-ER 403

Right side of the body of a large robust mandible broken posteriorly through M_3. The broken and abraded crowns of P_3–M_3 remain and the roots of I_1–$\bar{C}$. The mandibular body is massive (Table 2) and the teeth large. Dental measurements have been estimated from interstitial wear facets on individual teeth (Tables 14, 15, 16, 17).

Discovery: M. Muoka, 1968.
Area: 103. Aerial photo 1341.
Stratigraphic position: Upper member, above major erosion surface, 12–15 m below the base of the Koobi Fora Tuff (collection unit 4).
Environment of deposition: Large distributary channel, ADP. Reference Section 1.
References: K.F.R.P. Publ. Nos. 1, 6, 10.

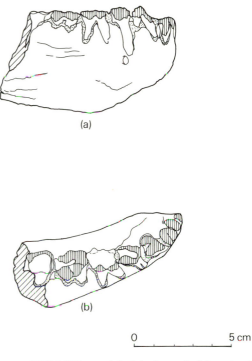

(a)

(b)

0   5 cm

FIG. 5.2. KNM-ER 403 (a) right lateral, (b) occlusal.

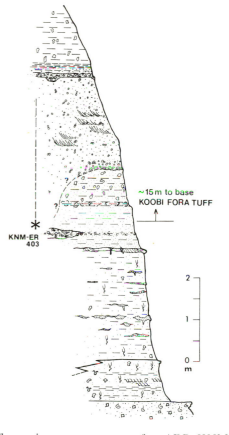

~15 m to base
KOOBI FORA TUFF

KNM-ER
403

1. The section represents part of an ADP. KNM-ER 403 was found on the outcrops of a channel, and its matrix matches the channel sand. The channel is presumed to be a major distributary.

KNM-ER 404

Right side of the body of a large robust mandible broken posteriorly behind M_3. The broken crowns of M_2–M_3 and the partial roots of P_3–M_1 are preserved. Measurements of the mandible, which shows surface weathering and expansion cracks: Table 2. Dimensions of the tooth crowns, which are damaged and expanded: Tables 17, 18.

Discovery: K. Kimeu, 1968.
Area: 7A. Aerial photo 1401.
Stratigraphic position: Ileret Member, 8–9 m below the base of the Chari Tuff (collection unit 5).
Environment of deposition: Interdistributary, ACP. Reference Section 2.
References: K.F.R.P. Publ. Nos. 1, 6, 10.

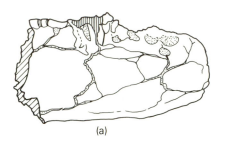

(a)

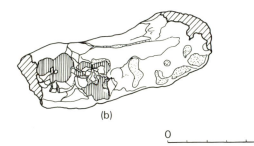

(b)

0 _____ 5 cm

FIG. 5.3. KNM-ER 404 (a) right lateral, (b) occlusal.

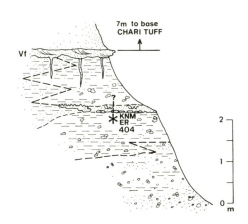

2. KNM-ER 404 was found on outcrops of ACP environments, below the sub Chari transgression. The matrix is sandy, and is referable to interdistributary sheet sands.

KNM-ER 405

Almost complete palate with parts of the maxilla showing details of the inferior nasal region, the maxillary air sinuses, the alveolar processes, and the roots of the maxillary teeth. The floors of both right and left maxillary sinuses and of the nasal cavity are exposed. The floor of the left maxillary sinus is divided into two portions by a septum, while the right has only a partial septum. The palate is deep (Table 1). On the right side, the roots of M^1–M^3 are intact, those of P^4 and I^2 are incomplete, and those of I^1, $\underline{C}$, and P^3 are missing. On the left side, only partial roots of I^1–M^3 remain. Measurements of the mesiodistal diameters of P^3–M^3, estimated by measuring from the mid-point between two adjacent roots, are given in Tables 7–10.

Discovery: N. Mutiwa, 1968.

Area: 105. Aerial photo 1590.

Stratigraphic position: Upper member, above post-KBS erosion surface (collection unit 4).

Environment of deposition: Channel, AVP. Reference Section 3.

References: K.F.R.P. Publ. Nos. 1, 6, 10.

PLATE 1. KNM-ER 405, occlusal.

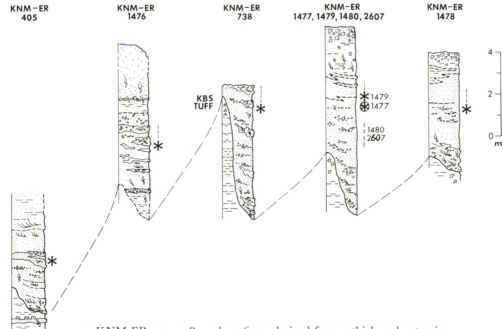

3–7. KNM-ER 405, 738, and 1476 are derived from a thick and extensive channel complex. The matrix indicates association with finer grain sizes of sand in the channels.

KNM-ER 1477, 1478 and 1479 occurred in the upper, relatively fine-grained channel deposits, indicating burial on levees or floodplain depressions (swales). The channels are part of a major alluvial valley plain deposit overlying the post-KBS erosion surface.

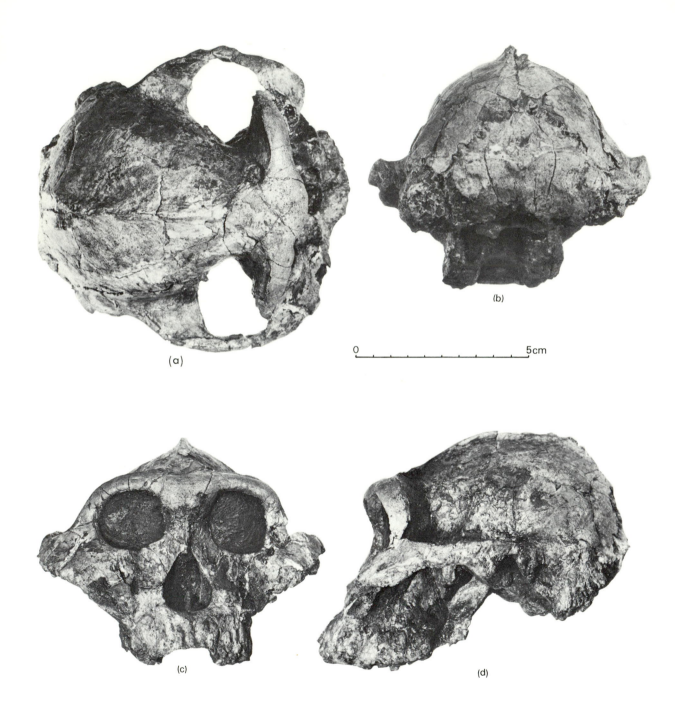

PLATE 2. KNM-ER 406 (a) superior, (b) posterior,
(c) frontal, (d) left lateral.

KNM-ER 406

Almost complete cranium. The mastoid processes and right occipital condyle have been abraded. Cortical bone is missing from the anterior and alveolar regions of the maxilla. The dentition is represented by complete or partial roots only. The cranium has sagittal and nuchal crests, well-developed mastoid processes and a strikingly broad robust face. The zygomatic arches are laterally flared but rather slender. The post-orbital constriction is very marked. The temporal ridges are strongly developed and fuse to form the sagittal crest some way anterior to lambda. The nuchal crests merge with the supra-mastoid crests which form the most laterally projecting points in the posterior region of the cranium. The mandibular fossae are wide and deep. The supraorbital tori are thick anteroposteriorly but not vertically, and the superior surfaces of the tori are flattened. The orbits are wider than they are high. The glabella is very prominent. The palate is deep and the teeth were large. Measurements of the cranium are given in Table 1. Accurate volumetric determinations have not been possible because the cranium is filled with a hard sandstone matrix, but Holloway (1973) has made an estimate of 510 cm³. There is a small round hole with an upturned lip in the left frontal just posterior to the supraorbital torus, which is considered to be pathological and may represent the site of a metastatic abscess.

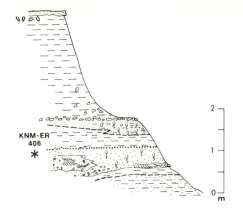

8. The section represents shoreline sediments of an LHE environment. KNM-ER 406 is derived from medium to coarse sands of a small distributary channel.

Discovery: R. E. Leakey, 1969.
Area: 10. Aerial photo 1521.
Stratigraphic position: Ileret Member, between the projected levels of 12/T II and the base of the Lower/Middle Tuff (collection unit 4).
Environment of deposition: Small distributary, LHE. Reference Section 8.
References: K.F.R.P. Publ. Nos. 1, 6, 10, 26, 91.

95

KNM-ER 407

Partial calvaria crushed and severely fragmented by pressures *in situ* and post-erosional weathering. The basicranium and parietals are preserved, but most of the frontals including the supraorbital tori are missing. The vault is small and lacks sagittal and nuchal crests. The weakly developed temporal lines can be identified anteriorly but they do not meet in the midline. The mastoids are pneumatized and large and there is a distinct supramastoid crest. Table 1.

Discovery: M. Muoka, 1969.
Area: 10. Aerial photo 1521.
Stratigraphic position: Ileret Member, approximately midway between the projected levels of 12/T II and the base of the Lower/Middle Tuff (collection unit 4).
Environment of deposition: Transgressive shoreline, LHE. Reference Section 9.
References: K.F.R.P. Publ. Nos. 6, 49.

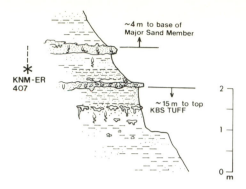

9. KNM-ER 407 occurred in sediments representing fluctuating lacustrine and subaerial conditions in an LHE environment. The specimen is probably derived from a thin transgressive beach sand.

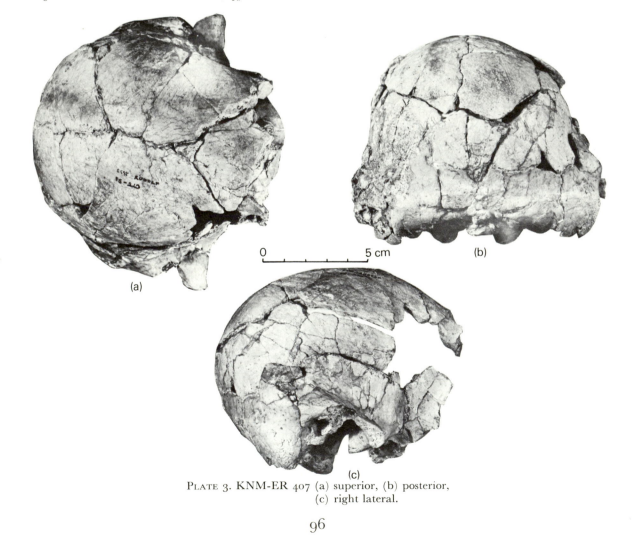

0   5 cm

PLATE 3. KNM-ER 407 (a) superior, (b) posterior, (c) right lateral.

KNM-ER 417

Fragment of left parietal. A small portion of the squamous suture is visible on the inferior margin and part of the lambdoid suture is preserved on the broken posteroinferior margin. The bone at the latter margin is thickened and pneumatized.
Discovery: N. Mutiwa, 1968.
Area: 129. Aerial photo 1752.
Stratigraphic position: Lower member, below 129/T IV (collection unit 3).
References: K.F.R.P. Publ. Nos. 6, 10.

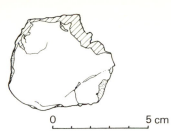

FIG. 5.4. KNM-ER 417, external.

KNM-ER 725

Left side and symphysis of the body of a robust mandible with the roots of P_4–M_3 and a partial root of P_3 preserved. Alveolar bone is missing except in the region of the molars. The specimen is cracked and expanded and lacks surface detail. Table 2.

Discovery: N. Mutiwa, 1970.
Area: 1. Aerial photo 1398.
Stratigraphic position: Ileret Member, *c.* 1–2 m above the local top of the Lower/Middle Tuff (collection unit 5).
Environment of deposition: Floodplain associated with $CaCO_3$ nodule horizon, AVP. Reference Section 10.
References: K.F.R.P. Publ. Nos 6, 11.

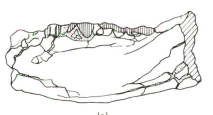

(a)

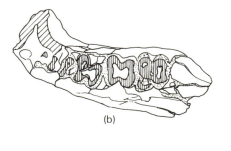

(b)

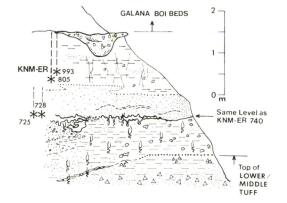

10. The section includes channel, levee, and floodplain deposits attributable to an AVP. KNM-ER 725, 728, and 740 were found on a surface formed by a soil-carbonate caliche horizon, in association with floodplain sands. KNM-ER 993 and 805 are derived from channel and levee sediments slightly higher in the section.

FIG. 5.5. KNM-ER 725 (a) left lateral, (b) occlusal.

KNM-ER 726

Left side of the body of a robust mandible with the roots of P₄–M₃ and the distal root of P₃ preserved. Alveolar bone is almost entirely missing and most surface details have been lost owing to weathering. Measurements, which have also been affected by expansion cracks, are in Table 2.

KNM-ER 727

Fragment of the right side of the body of a robust mandible with broken roots of M_1–M_2 and the distal root of P_4. The surface is damaged through solution weathering. Table 2.

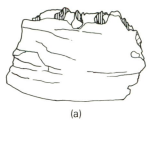

(a)

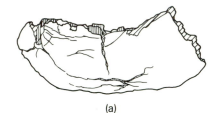

(a)

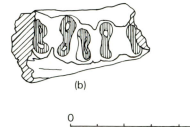

(b)

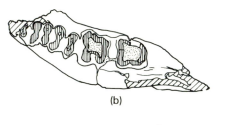

(b)

FIG. 5.7. KNM-ER 727 (a) right lateral, (b) occlusal.

FIG. 5.6. KNM-ER 726 (a) left lateral, (b) occlusal.

Discovery: H. Mutua, 1970.
Area: 6A. Aerial photo 1467.
Stratigraphic position: Ileret Member, 5 m below the base of the Lower/Middle Tuff (collection unit 4).
Environment of deposition: Distributary channel, ACP. Reference Section 11.
References: K.F.R.P. Publ. Nos. 6, 11.

Discovery: H. Mutua, 1970.
Area: 11. Aerial photo 1521.
Stratigraphic position: Ileret Member, *c.* 4 m above the top of the Lower/Middle Tuff (collection unit 5).
Environment of deposition: Channel, AVP.
References: K.F.R.P. Publ. Nos. 6, 11.

11. KNM-ER 727 occurred on an isolated outcrop of a gravel and sand channel deposit, 20–30 m distant from and stratigraphically above a 'cluster' of hominids which includes the other nine catalogue entries. All of the last-mentioned specimens are derived from a small channel deposit representing a distributary in the ACP environment.

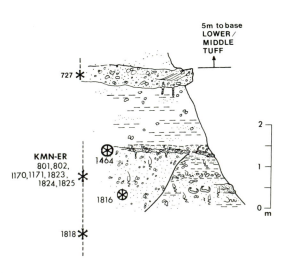

KNM-ER 728

Badly weathered fragment of the right side of the body of a mandible with the exposed roots of M_1–M_3 and a fragment of the M_3 crown which shows advanced wear. Table 2.

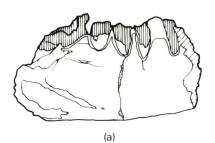

(a)

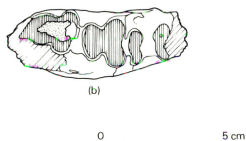

(b)

0 —————————— 5 cm

FIG. 5.8. KNM-ER 728 (a) right lateral, (b) occlusal.

Discovery: K. Kimeu, 1970.
Area: 1. Aerial photo 1398.
Stratigraphic position: Ileret Member, 1–2 m above the local top of the Lower/Middle Tuff (collection unit 5).
Environment of deposition: Floodplain associated with $CaCO_3$ nodule horizon, AVP. Reference Section 10.
References: K.F.R.P. Publ. Nos. 6, 11.

KNM-ER 729 (A–G)

A: Robust mandible with nearly complete dentition and an almost complete right ascending ramus. Much of the left side of the mandible is badly weathered. The right canine root and crown base, the crowns of the right P_4–M_3, and the crowns of the left P_3–P_4 and M_2–M_3 are all preserved. The crown of the left M_1 appears to have been lost in life prior to the eruption of P_4: the alveolar bone in this region shows resorption and the distal root plate (C) appears to show wear polishing. The two central incisors and the left canine were recovered separately and because the superior aspect of the symphysial region has been damaged they can be located only approximately in the mandible.

B: Mesial root of M_1.
C: Distal root of M_1.
D: Part of root and crown of right P_3.
E: Right I_1.
F: Left I_1.
G: Left $\overline{C}$.

Mandible: Table 2. Dentition: Tables 11 and 13–18.

Discovery: P. Abell, 1970.
Area: 8. Aerial photo 1466.
Stratigraphic position: *In situ*. Ileret Member, lower part of the Lower/Middle Tuff (collection unit 5).
Environment of deposition: Floodplain, channel edge, ACP. Reference Section 12.
References: K.F.R.P. Publ. Nos. 6, 11.

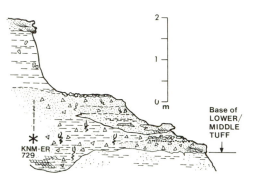

12. KNM-ER 729 is derived from floodplain tuffaceous sands associated with small-scale channels in the ACP.

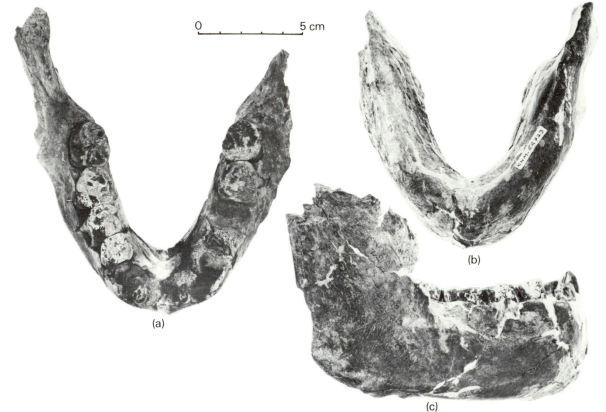

PLATE 4. KNM-ER 729 (a) occlusal, (b) inferior, (c) right lateral.

KNM-ER 730

Mandibular body with the right side broken off posterior to P₄ and the left side complete to the base of the ascending ramus. The roots of the right lateral incisor and right and left $\overline{\text{C}}$–P₄ are present. The crowns for the left M₁–M₃ are in place but heavily worn. There is evidence for extensive periodontal disease; alveolar resorption and intraosseous pocketing has exposed the roots of the molar teeth. There is a slight 'chin'. Mandible: Table 2. Teeth: Tables 16–18.

Discovery: M. G. Leakey, 1970.
Area: 103. Aerial photo 1341.
Stratigraphic position: Upper member, above major erosion surface, *c.* 4–6 m below the base of the Koobi Fora Tuff (collection unit 4).
Environment of deposition: Delta margin, ACP. Reference Section 13.
References: K.F.R.P. Publ. Nos. 6, 22, 70.

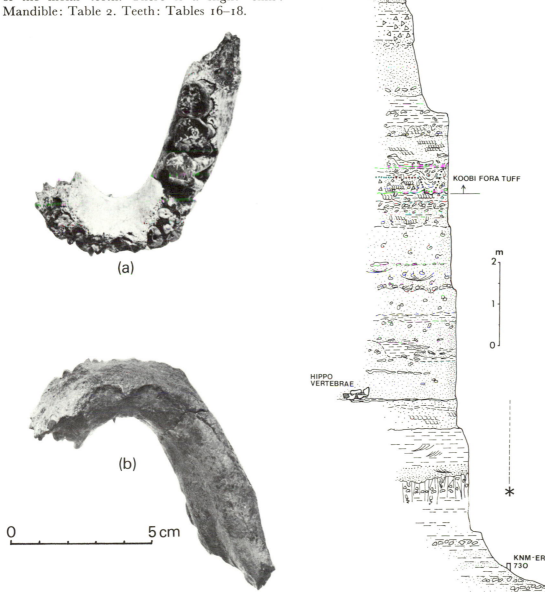

PLATE 5. KNM-ER 730 (a) occlusal, (b) inferior.

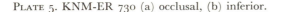

13. The section represents typical ACP deposits. KNM-ER 730 was derived from local transgressive sediments overlying a mud-cracked subaerial surface or from within the silty clay soil horizon.

KNM-ER 731

Edentulous fragment of the left side of the body of mandible broken anteriorly at the symphysis and posteriorly at the level of M_1. Alveolar resorption and a large cavity in the region of the canine alveolus suggest the presence of severe peridontal disease. Table 2.

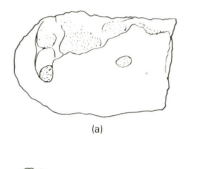

(a)

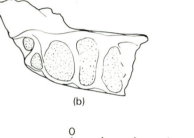

(b)

0   5 cm

FIG. 5.9. KNM-ER 731 (a) left lateral, (b) occlusal.

Discovery: K. Kimeu, 1970.
Area: 6A. Aerial photo 1398.
Stratigraphic position: Ileret Member, approximately midway between the Lower/Middle Tuff and the Chari Tuff (collection unit 5).
Environment of deposition: AVP.
References: K.F.R.P. Publ. Nos. 6, 22.

KNM-ER 732 (A–D)

A: Partial cranium consisting of most of the right facial skeleton, frontoparietal region and temporal bone and part of the left frontal and parietal. The right occipital condyle and parts of the occipital bone, together with some other fragments, have not yet been reconstructed. The right maxilla is damaged anterior to the level of P³. The dentition is represented by only half of the P⁴ crown and parts of the roots of P⁴–M³. The cranium is small with an estimated cranial capacity of 506 cm³ (K.F.R.P. Publ. No. 91). The temporal lines can be followed posteriorly and appear to reach their closest proximity when still about 15 mm apart. The postorbital constriction is marked, and the mastoid process is large and deep. The orbits are wider than they are high. Table 1.

B: Right occipital condyle.

C: Incisor crown, probably right I¹.

D: Skull fragments.

PLATE 6. KNM-ER 732 (a) superior, (b) frontal, (c) right lateral.

Discovery: H. Mutua, 1970.
Area: 10. Aerial photo 1521.
Stratigraphic position: *In situ*. Ileret Member, approximately midway between the projected levels of 12/T II and the base of the Lower/Middle Tuff, 5–6 m above KNM-ER 406 (collection unit 4).
Environment of deposition: Distributary channel or overbank, LHE. Reference Section 14.
References: K.F.R.P. Publ. Nos. 6, 11, 26, 91.

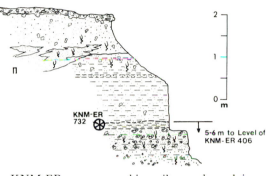

14. KNM-ER 732 occurred in a silty sand overlying a zone of CaCO₃ nodules probably formed in temporarily emergent deltaic deposits of the LHE environment.

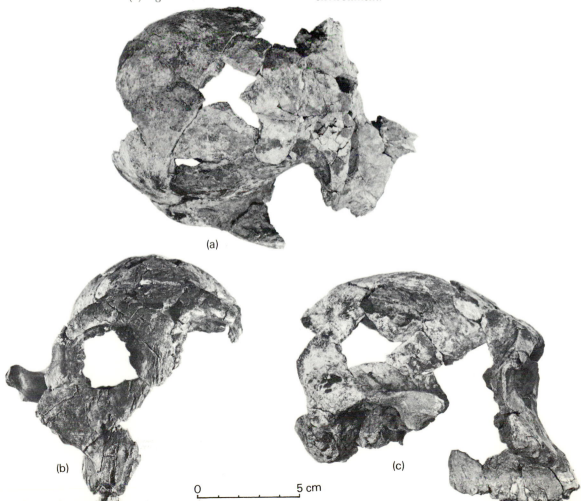

(a)

(b)   (c)

0   5 cm

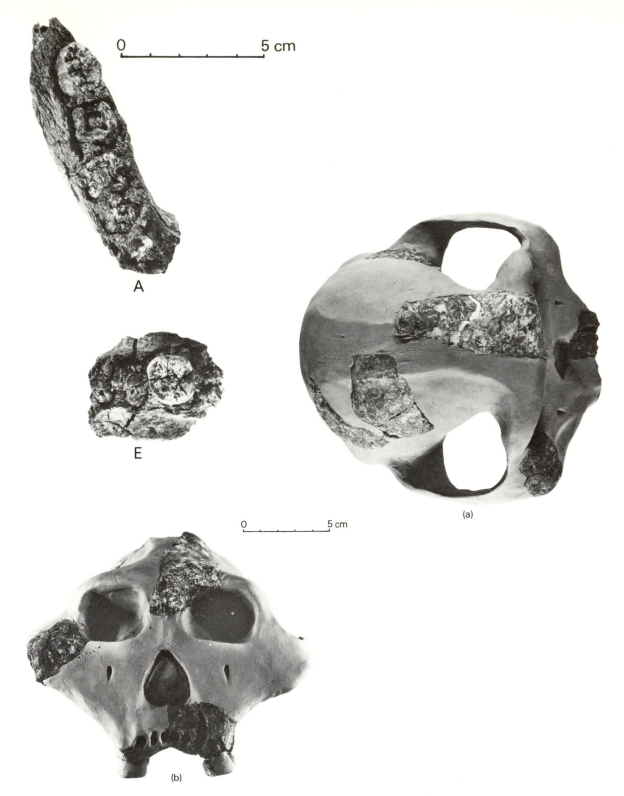

0　5 cm

A

E

(a)

0　5 cm

(b)

PLATE 7. KNM-ER 733A, occlusal. 733B–J (a) superior, (b) frontal. 733E, occlusal.

KNM-ER 733 (A–J)

Associated cranial fragments.

A: Right side of the body of a mandible with the broken crown of M_3 and the roots of P_3–M_2. The specimen shows surface weathering and expansion cracks.

B: Fragment of right parietal.

C: Fragment of cranial vault.

D: Half crown of left P^4.

E: Alveolar process and body of the left maxilla extending from the midline to the mesial roots of M^2 and including the crown of M^1.

F: Fragment of left supraorbital torus, glabella, and parts of left cranial vault.

G: Fragment of left side of occipital.

H: Fragment of right zygomatic.

I: Fragment of right parietal.

J: Fragment of left temporal.

These fragments represent the remains of a generally large and robust skull. The temporal lines, however, are not well developed and apparently had not developed a sagittal crest although the third molars are erupted. Tables 2, 8, 18.

Discovery: R. E. Leakey, 1970.

Area: 8. Aerial photo 1466.

Stratigraphic position: Ileret Member, within the Lower/Middle Tuff (collection unit 5).

Environment of deposition: Small channel or levee on flood plain, ACP. Reference Sections 15 and 22.

References: K.F.R.P. Publ. Nos. 6, 23.

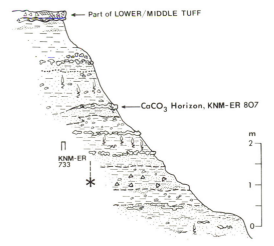

15. The section represents deposits of a small-scale channel and floodplain complex (ACP). KNM-ER 733 occurred in association with tuffaceous sands, below a marker horizon of CaCO₃ nodules which is also present at the site of KNM-ER 807 (see Reference Section 22).

KNM-ER 734

Small fragment of left parietal showing markings of the interparietal and coronal sutures along the medial and anterior margins respectively.

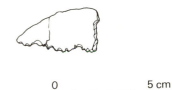

0 _____ 5 cm

FIG. 5.10. KNM-ER 734, external.

Discovery: R. E. Leakey, 1970.

Area: 103. Aerial photo 1341.

Stratigraphic position: Upper member, above major erosion surface, just below the Koobi Fora Tuff (collection unit 4).

Environment of deposition: Delta margin, ACP.

Reference: K.F.R.P. Publ. No. 6.

KNM-ER 736

Partial shaft of a massive left femur broken proximally just above the lesser trochanter and distally just proximal to the divergence of the supracondylar lines. The shaft is almost straight and is platymetric with a strongly developed linea aspera. Table 24.

Discovery: M. G. Leakey, 1970.
Area: 103. Aerial photo 1341.
Stratigraphic position: Upper member, above major erosion surface, 2–4 m below the projected level of the base of the Koobi Fora Tuff (collection unit 4).
Environment of deposition: Probably small distributary channel, ACP. Reference Section 16.
References: K.F.R.P. Publ. Nos. 6, 11, 41.

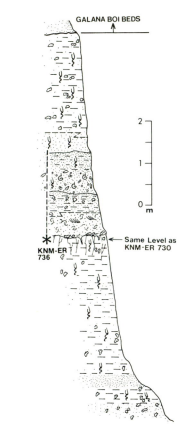

16. KNM-ER 736 occurred within the same transgressive sands and subaerial surface as KNM-ER 730, but the sites were separated by about 1 km.

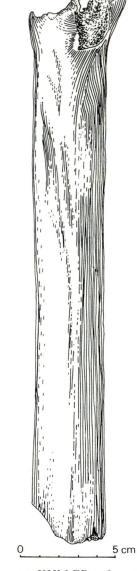

FIG. 5.11. KNM-ER 736, posterior.

KNM-ER 737

Shaft of a left femur, lacking the head, greater trochanter, lesser trochanter, and much of the neck. Distally part of the shaft and both femoral condyles are missing. The shaft is flattened antero-posteriorly throughout its length; this is exaggerated in the subtrochanteric region by the swelling for the gluteal tuberosity. Table 24.

Discovery: R. E. Leakey, 1970.
Area: 103. Aerial photo 1341.
Stratigraphic position: Upper member, within the base of the Koobi Fora Tuff (collection unit 5).
Environment of deposition: Transgressive shoreline deposits, ACP. Reference Section 17.
References: K.F.R.P. Publ. Nos. 6, 22, 71, 89.

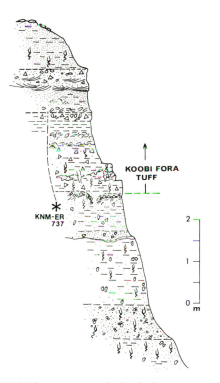

17. KNM-ER 737 was derived from transgressive tuffaceous sands that occur at the base of the Koobi Fora Tuff.

0   5 cm

FIG. 5.12. KNM-ER 737, posterior.

KNM-ER 738

Proximal portion of a left femur including the head, neck, lesser trochanter, and part of the shaft. The head is small and nearly hemispherical. The neck is long, and compressed anteroposteriorly. The linea aspera is strongly developed. There is evidence of a fracture callus on the shaft. Table 24.

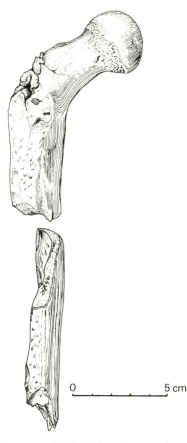

FIG. 5.13. KNM-ER 738, posterior.

Discovery: B. Ngeneo, 1970.
Area: 105. Aerial photo 1591.
Stratigraphic position: Upper member, above post-KBS erosion surface (collection unit 4).
Environment of deposition: Channel, AVP. Reference Section 5.
References: K.F.R.P. Publ. Nos. 6, 11, 41.

KNM-ER 739

Right humerus complete except for the head and a small portion of the proximal end of the shaft. The specimen is remarkable in its robustness and strongly marked muscle impressions. Table 21.

Discovery: H. Mutua, 1970.
Area: 1. Aerial photo 1467.
Stratigraphic position: Ilertet Member, *c.* 4 m above the local top of the Lower/Middle Tuff (collection unit 5).
Environment of deposition: Channel, AVP. Reference Section 18.
References: K.F.R.P. Publ. Nos. 6, 11.

McHenry, H. 1973. Early hominid humerus from East Rudolf, Kenya. *Science* **180**, 739–41.

McHenry, H. and Corruccini, R. S. 1975. Distal humerus in hominid evolution. *Folia Primatol.* **23**, 227–44.

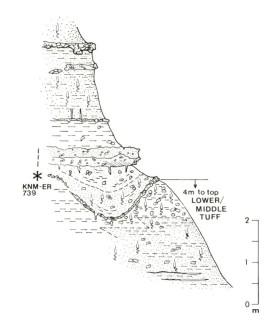

18. KNM-ER 739 occurred in association with a coarse channel lens and extensive carbonate-cemented sheet sands.

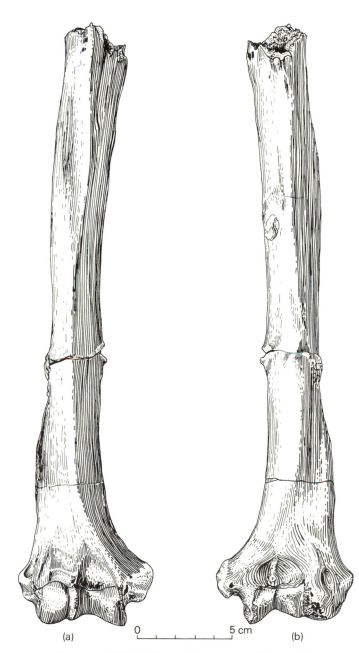

FIG. 5.14. KNM-ER 739 (a) anterior, (b) posterior.

KNM-ER 740

Fragment of a left humerus including the medial half of the distal portion of the shaft with the medial condyle abraded.

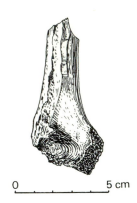

FIG. 5.15. KNM-ER 740, posterior.

Discovery: W. M. Garland, 1970.
Area: 3. Aerial photo 1398.
Stratigraphic position: Ileret Member, 1–2 m above the top of the Lower/Middle Tuff (collection unit 5).
Environment of deposition: Floodplain, associated with $CaCO_3$ nodule horizon, AVP. Reference Section 19.
References: K.F.R.P. Publ. Nos. 6, 11.

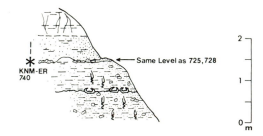

19. Both KNM-ER 740 and 1815 occurred above a soil-carbonate horizon which can be correlated stratigraphically with the carbonate ($CaCO_3$) horizon associated with KNM-ER 725 and 728 (Reference Section 10). The two localities are about 300 m apart.

KNM-ER 741

Proximal half of a left tibia in which the margins of the articular surfaces have been abraded. The anterior border of the shaft is strikingly developed. Table 25.

FIG. 5.16. KNM-ER 741, anterior.

Discovery: M. D. Leakey, 1970.
Area: 1. Aerial photo 1398.
Stratigraphic position: Ileret Member, *c.* 2–4 m above the top of the Lower/Middle Tuff (collection unit 5).
Environment of deposition: Fluvial, probably the edge of a channel, AVP. Reference Section 20.
References: K.F.R.P. Publ. Nos. 6, 11.

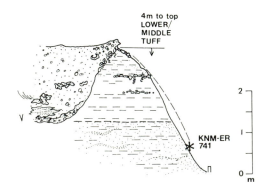

20. The sand matrix on KNM-ER 741, a surface find, indicates association with the channel lens rather than more proximal fine-grained sediments.

KNM-ER 801 (A–D)

A: Right side of the body of a robust manbible with the complete M_2, almost complete M_3, roots of M_1, and part of the distal root of P_4.

B: Broken crown of the left M_2.

C: Broken crown of the left M_3.

D: Complete right I_2.

The mandible shows some surface weathering and expansion cracks (Table 2). Dentition: Tables 12, 17, 18.

After the discovery of this specimen extensive sieving of the site yielded a number of hominid specimens including several isolated teeth and numerous dental fragments. The isolated teeth were found to represent at least three mature individuals: KNM-ER 801, KNM-ER 802, and KNM-ER 3737, as well as a juvenile individual,

KNM-ER 1171. The postcranial elements, KNM-ER 1464, 1823, 1824, and 1825, and some cranial fragments, KNM-ER 1170, have been considered as separate specimens, although some may well be associated with each other or with the dental specimens. Subsequently, in 1973, an additional mandible, KNM-ER 1816, was discovered on the lower slope of the site.

Discovery: R. E. Leakey, 1971.

Area: 6A. Aerial photo 1398.

Stratigraphic position: Ileret Member, *c.* 6–7 m below the base of the Lower/Middle Tuff (collection unit 4).

Environment of deposition: Distributary channel, ACP. Reference Section 11.

References: K.F.R.P. Publ. Nos. 12, 23.

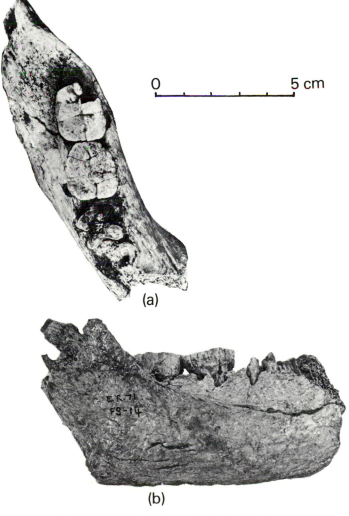

0 _____ 5 cm

(a)

(b)

PLATE 8. KNM-ER 801A (a) occlusal, (b) right lateral.

III

KNM-ER 802 (A–J)

Isolated upper and lower teeth, apparently from one individual (see KNM-ER 801).

A: Crown of right P$_4$.
B: Crown of left P$_4$.
C: Broken crown of right M$_1$.
D: Broken crown of left M$_2$.
E: Broken crown of left M$_3$.
F: Crown of right M$_3$.
G: (see KNM-ER 3737).
H: Partial crown of C, mesiodistal length 8.8 mm, labiolingual breadth 9.1 mm.
I: Crown of left P^3.
J: (see KNM-ER 3737).
Tables 6, 15, 16, 17, 18.

Recent study of the teeth originally included in this specimen has shown that some were misidentified and that two must belong to another individual; see KNM-ER 3737.

Discovery: Discovered while sieving for fragments of KNM-ER 801, 1971.

Area: 6A. Aerial photo 1398.

Stratigraphic Member: Ileret Member, *c.* 6–7 m below the base of the Lower/Middle Tuff (collection unit 4).

Environment of deposition: Distributary channel, ACP. Reference Section 11.

References: K.F.R.P. Publ. Nos. 12, 23.

KNM-ER 803 (A–T)

Associated parts of a skeleton of an adult individual.

A: Partial shaft of left femur.
B: Partial shaft of left tibia.
C: Partial shaft of left ulna.
D: Fragment of mid-shaft of left radius.
E: Fragment of left talus.
F: Proximal left metatarsal V.
G: Portion of left tibia medial condyle.
H: Crown of left C̲.
I: Crown of right I^1.
J: Left metatarsal III lacking head.
K: Intermediate toe phalanx ?III.
L: Intermediate toe phalanx ?II.
M: Terminal toe phalanx.
N: Fragment of left fibula shaft.
O: Fragment of right fibula shaft.
P: Fragment of radius shaft.
Q: Fragment of shaft of proximal phalanx of great toe.
R: Fragment of proximal phalanx (?II or III).
S: Fragment of phalanx shaft.
T: Fragment of proximal metacarpal.
Tables 3, 5, 22, 24, 28, 29.

Discovery: M. G. Leakey, 1971.

Area: 8. Aerial photo 1465.

Stratigraphic position: Ileret Member, within the Lower/Middle Tuff (collection unit 5).

Environment of deposition: Levee or floodplain, ACP. Reference Section 21.

References: K.F.R.P. Publ. Nos. 12, 27.

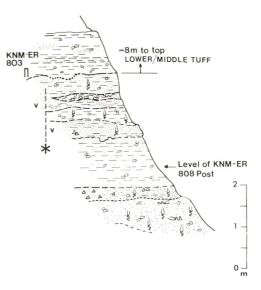

21. The numerous skeletal parts of KNM-ER 803 were closely associated on the surface, but excavation failed to reveal any specimens *in situ*. Sediments indicate burial in levee or floodplain deposits in the ACP environment. KNM-ER 808 occurred about 100 m from this section at the indicated level.

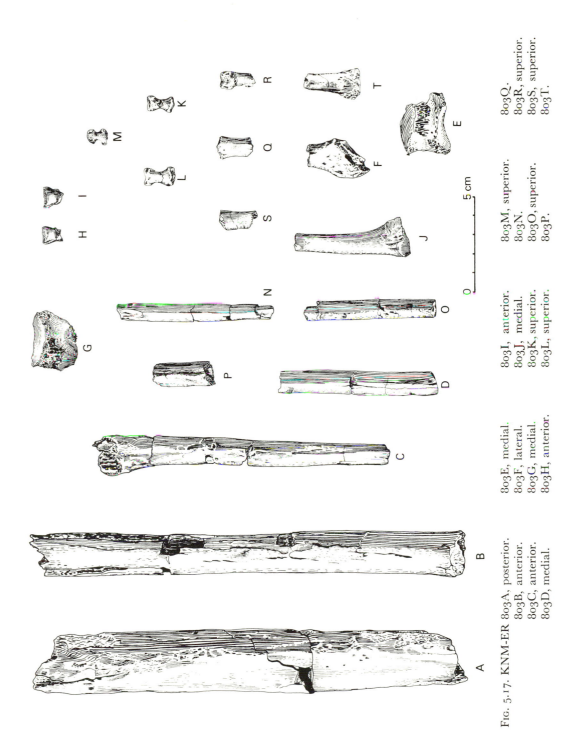

FIG. 5.17. KNM-ER 803A, posterior.
803B, anterior.
803C, anterior.
803D, medial.

803E, medial.
803F, lateral.
803G, medial.
803H, anterior.

803I, anterior.
803J, medial.
803K, superior.
803L, superior.

803M, superior.
803N.
803O, superior.
803P.

803Q.
803R, superior.
803S, superior.
803T.

KNM-ER 805 (A–B)

A: Weathered fragment of the left side of the body of a robust mandible broken through the mesial root of M_1 and posterior to M_3. The roots for M_1–M_3 are preserved.

B: Small fragment of the lateral region of the right side of the body of the mandible.

Table 2.

Discovery: K. Kimeu, 1971.

Area: 1. Aerial photo 1467.

Stratigraphic position: Ileret Member, 2–3 m above the top of the Lower/Middle Tuff (collection unit 5).

Environment of deposition: Floodplain or small channel, AVP. Reference Section 10.

References: K.F.R.P. Publ. Nos. 12, 23.

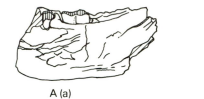

A (a)

B (a)

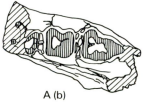

A (b)

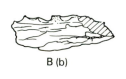

B (b)

0   5 cm

FIG. 5.18. KNM-ER 805A (a) left lateral, (b) occlusal.
805B (a) right lateral,
(b) occlusal.

KNM-ER 806 (A–F)

Associated teeth from an adult individual.

A: Crown of left M_3.
B: Crown of left M_2.
C: Crown of left M_1.
D: Crown of right M_3.
E: Broken crown of right P_3.
F: Crown of left P_3.

Tables 14, 16, 17, 18.

Discovery: H. Mutua, 1971.

Area: 8. Aerial photo 1465.

Stratigraphic position: Ileret Member, within the Lower/Middle Tuff (collection unit 5).

Environment of deposition: ACP.

References: K.F.R.P. Publ. Nos. 12, 20.

114

KNM-ER 807 (A–B)

A: Fragment of the body of a right maxilla with complete M^3, half M^2, and including the adjacent posterolateral part of the palatine process.

B: Fragment of right maxilla with almost complete M^1.

Tables 8, 9, 10.

Discovery: (A) N. Mutiwa, 1971; (B) K. Kimeu, 1973.
Area: 8A. Aerial photo 1465.
Stratigraphic position: Ileret Member, within the Lower/Middle Tuff (collection unit 5).
Environment of deposition: Floodplain or levee, ACP. Reference Sections 22 and 15.
References: K.F.R.P. Publ. Nos. 12, 20 (A only).

PLATE 9. KNM-ER 807A, occlusal.

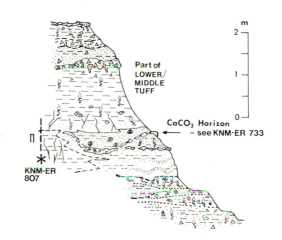

22. The CaCo₃ marker horizon at the site of KNM-ER 807 can be traced to the site of KNM-ER 733 (Reference Section 15), which is about 200 m distant. KNM-ER 807 is derived from floodplain or levee deposits in the ACP environment.

KNM-ER 808 (A–H)

Part of the associated upper dentition from an immature individual.

A: Worn right dI^1 lacking tip of root.
B: Worn left dI^1 lacking part of root.
C: Right P^3 germ.
D: Right I^2 germ.
E: Distal half of left I^2 germ.
F: Enamel flake from the buccal surface of I^1 germ.
G: Broken crown of right M^1.
H: Partial crown of right dM^1.

Tables 4, 6, 8, 19.

Discovery: N. Mutiwa, 1971.
Area: 8. Aerial photo 1465.
Stratigraphic position: Ileret Member, within the Lower/Middle Tuff (collection unit 5).
Environment of deposition: ACP. Reference Section 21.
References: K.F.R.P. Publ. Nos. 12, 20.

KNM-ER 809 (A–B)

A: Almost complete crown of a left lower molar (published as M_1); buccolingual breadth 12.7 mm.

B: Dental fragments.

Discovery: K. Kimeu, 1971.
Area: 8. Aerial photo 1465.
Stratigraphic position: Ileret Member, within the Lower/Middle Tuff (collection unit 5).
Environment of deposition: ACP.
References: K.F.R.P. Publ. Nos. 12, 20.

KNM-ER 810 (A–B)

A: Part of the left side of a robust mandible joined to a small part of the right side by the inferior portion of the symphysial region. The body is cracked and expanded particularly posteriorly. The almost complete roots of the left P_4–M_3 and the right canine, and the partial roots of both P_3s and right I_2 are preserved.

B: Complete but detached crown of M_3.

Tables 2, 18.

Discovery: K. Kitibi, 1971.
Area: 104. Aerial photo 1450.
Stratigraphic position: Upper member, above major erosion surface (collection unit 4).
Environment of deposition: Channel, ADP. Reference Section 23.
References: K.F.R.P. Publ. Nos. 12, 23.

5 cm

PLATE 10. KNM-ER 810, occlusal.

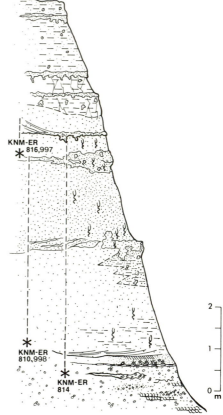

23. The hominids in this section are derived from major channel lenses of an ADP. The channels therefore reflect deposition in major distributaries. KNM-ER 810, 814, and 998 were found on erosion surfaces well below KNM-ER 816 and 997, but all could have been derived from the same horizon. All finds occurred within an area of about 100 × 100 m.

116

KNM-ER 811

Small undiagnostic fragment of parietal.
Discovery: B. Ngeneo, 1971.
Area: 104. Aerial photo 1450.
Stratigraphic position: Uncertain.
Reference: K.F.R.P. Publ. No. 12.

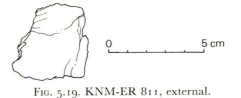

Fig. 5.19. KNM-ER 811, external.

KNM-ER 812

Fragment of the left side of the body of an immature mandible with roots of $d\overline{C}$–dM_2. Weathering of the surface of the bone has partially exposed the germs of I_1–P_4 in their crypts, and the mesial wall of the crypt of M_1, which has a large buccolingual breadth, is seen on the posterior fracture. A fragment of the right I_1 germ is seen in the anterior broken section.

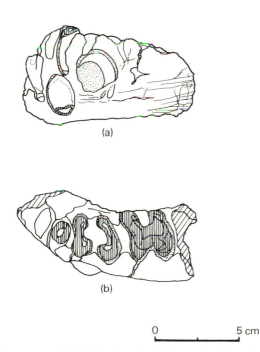

(a)

(b)

FIG. 5.20. KNM-ER 812 (a) left lateral, (b) occlusal.

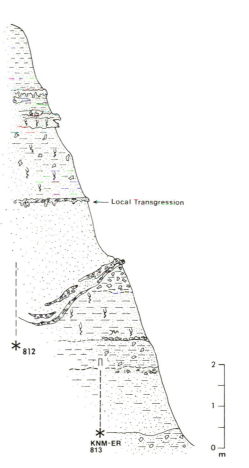

← Local Transgression

✱ 812

✱
KNM-ER
813

Discovery: B. Ngeneo, 1971.
Area: 104. Aerial photo 1450.
Stratigraphic position: Upper member, above major erosion surface (collection unit 4).
Environment of deposition: Channel, ADP. Reference Section 24.
References: K.F.R.P. Publ. Nos. 12, 23.

24. Both KNM-ER 812 and 813 occurred in association with channels in the ADP environment. The two localities are several hundred metres apart, and the section represents the composite stratigraphy of these localities. The 'local transgression' represents a major lacustrine incursion in the Koobi Fora Formation (see Fig. 2.6).

117

KNM-ER 813 (A–B)

A: Right talus damaged in the posterolateral portion of the body and on the inferomedial aspect of the head.

B: Fragment of distal portion of the shaft of a right tibia.

Table 27.

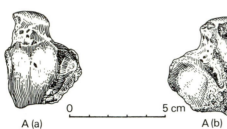

FIG. 5.21. KNM-ER 813A (a) superior, (b) inferior. 813B.

Discovery: B. Ngeneo, 1971.
Area: 104. Aerial photo 1450.
Stratigraphic position: Upper member, above major erosion surface (collection unit 4).
Environment of deposition: Near the top of a channel, ADP. Reference Section 24.
References: K.F.R.P. Publ. Nos. 12, 20, 31, 33, 70, 71 (A only).

KNM-ER 814 (A–D)

A: Small fragment of cranial vault including a suture margin.

B: Fragment of right frontal including most of the supraorbital torus which is thin in anterior view.

C–D: Badly cracked and distorted fragments of cranial vault.

These cranial fragments were found near the mandible KNM-ER 810 and may be parts of the same individual.

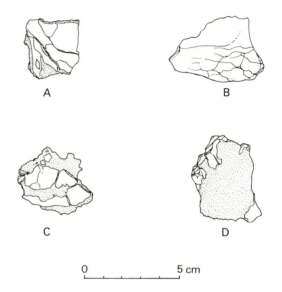

FIG. 5.22. KNM-ER 814A–D, external.

Discovery: B. Ngeneo, 1971.
Area: 104. Aerial photo 1450.
Stratigraphic position: Upper member, above major erosion surface (collection unit 4).
Environment of deposition: Channel, ADP. Reference Section 23.
References: K.F.R.P. Publ. Nos. 12, 23.

KNM-ER 815

Fragment of the proximal region of a left femur, including the neck, most of the lesser trochanter and part of the shaft. The neck is long and shows marked anteroposterior flattening. The shaft is very platymetric as far as the posterior break, and the medullary cavity at this break is small. Table 24.

FIG. 5.23. KNM-ER 815, posterior.

Discovery: A. Hill, 1971.
Area: 10. Aerial photo 1521.
Stratigraphic position: Ileret Member (collection unit 4).
Environment of deposition: Delta margin, probably distributary or offshore, LHE.
References: K.F.R.P. Publ. Nos. 12, 23, 41.

KNM-ER 817

Weathered fragment of the left side of the body of a mandible with the roots of M_1, the broken root of M_2, and the alveoli of $\bar{C}$, P_3, and P_4. Table 2.

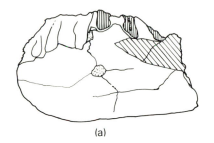

(a)

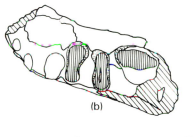

(b)

FIG. 5.24. KNM-ER 817 (a) left lateral, (b) occlusal.

Discovery: N. Mutiwa, 1971.
Area: 124. Aerial photo 1584.
Stratigraphic position: Above major erosion surface (collection unit 4).
Environment of deposition: AVP.
References: K.F.R.P. Publ. Nos. 12, 20.

KNM-ER 816 (A–E)

A: Complete left $\bar{C}$.
B–E: Dental fragments.
Table 5.
Discovery: N. Mutiwa, 1971.
Area: 104. Aerial photo 1450.
Stratigraphic position: Upper member, above major erosion surface (collection unit 4).
Environment of deposition: Upper part of a channel, ADP. Reference Section 23.
Reference: K.F.R.P. Publ. No. 12.

KNM-ER 818

Left side of the body of an extremely massive robust mandible which includes the broken crowns of the left P$_3$–M$_3$, and the broken roots of the right and left I$_1$, and the left I$_2$–C̄.

Large matrix-filled cracks affect the measurements of both the teeth and the body. Tables 2, 14, 15, 16, 17, 18.

Discovery: B. Ngeneo, 1971.
Area: 6A. Aerial photo 1398.
Stratigrahic position: Ileret Member, within the Lower/Middle Tuff (collection unit 5).
Environment of deposition: ACP.
References: K.F.R.P. Publ. Nos. 12, 23.

(a)

(b)

PLATE 11. KNM-ER 818 (a) occlusal, (b) left lateral.

KNM-ER 819

Fragment of the left side of the body of a mandible in which the roots of P₃–M₂ are preserved. The specimen is severely cracked and weathered.
Discovery: H. Mutua, 1971.
Area: 1. Aerial photo 1467.
Stratigraphic position: Ileret Member, below the base of the Lower/Middle Tuff.
Environment of deposition: Floodplain, ACP.
References: K.F.R.P. Publ. Nos. 12, 23.

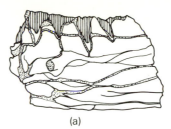

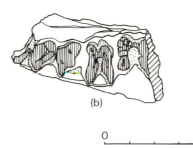

FIG. 5.25. KNM-ER 819 (a) left lateral, (b) occlusal.

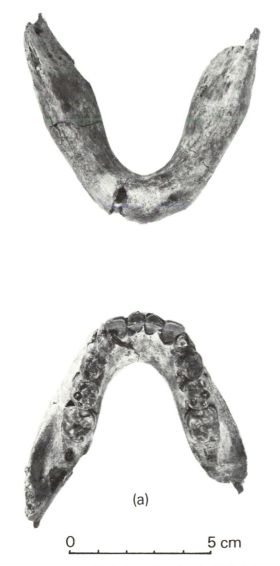

(a)

0   5 cm

PLATE 12. KNM-ER 820 (a) occlusal, (b) inferior.

KNM-ER 820

Well-preserved mandibular body with dentition and part of the left ascending ramus of an immature individual. The dentition includes the complete crowns of I₁, I₂, dM₁, dM₂, and M₁ on both sides. The crown of the left deciduous canine is broken, the crown of the right dC̄ is missing. Bone damage on part of the anterior region has exposed the germ of the left permanent canine. Radiographs show that the M₂s are partially developed in their crypts. The crypt for M₃ is already defined. Tables 2, 11, 12, 16, 20.
Discovery: H. Mutua, 1971.
Area: 1. Aerial photo 1467.
Stratigraphic position: *In situ*. Ileret Member, below the Lower/Middle Tuff (collection unit 4).
Environment of deposition: Floodplain, ACP. Reference Section 25.
References: K.F.R.P. Publ. Nos. 12, 20.

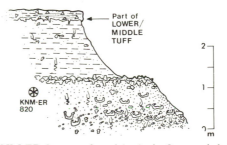

25. KNM-ER 820 was found *in situ* in fine sands below a zone of irregular CaCO₃ nodules which probably formed as soil carbonate. The environment of burial was a floodplain, probably part of the ACP.

KNM-ER 992 (A–D)

Both sides of a mandible broken in the symphysial region where several matrix-filled fractures have distorted the basal contour of the mandible.

A: Right side of the mandibular body and part of the ascending ramus, with complete C–M_3 and the empty alveoli for I_1 and I_2.

B: Left side of the mandible lacking the condyle and with part of the ascending ramus damaged. The dentition is represented by the empty alveolus of I_1, the root of I_2, the chipped $\overline{C}$, and the complete P_3–M_3.

C: Crown of the left incisor (published as I_2). Mesiodistal length 7.0 mm, labiolingual length 6.9 mm.

D: Fragments of the ascending rami.

Tables 2, 13, 14, 15, 16, 17, 18.

Discovery: B. Ngeneo, 1971.

Area: 3. Aerial photo 1398.

Stratigraphic position: Ileret Member, most probably below the Chari Tuff (collection unit 5), but possibly derived from Galana Boi beds.

Environment of deposition: Channel, AVP. Reference Section 26.

References: K.F.R.P. Publ. Nos. 12, 20, 32, 70.

Groves, P. C. and Mazak, V. 1975. An approach to the taxonomy of the Hominidae: gracile Villafranchian hominids of Africa. *Casopis pro mineralogii a geologii* **20**, 225–47.

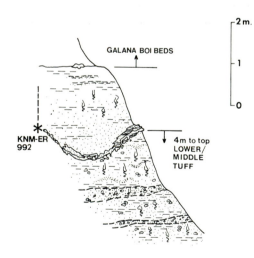

26. KNM-ER 992 occurred on the surface of the basal portion of a channel lens with fining-upward textural gradation. Owing to the proximity of Galana Boi deposits (Holocene), derivation of the specimen from younger sediments cannot be ruled out, but the excellent state of preservation and close association of the major fragments at the channel base argue against a younger age. The Koobi Fora Formation channel is associated with an AVP, and is probably part of the same channel system associated with KNM-ER 739 and 741 (Reference Sections 18 and 20).

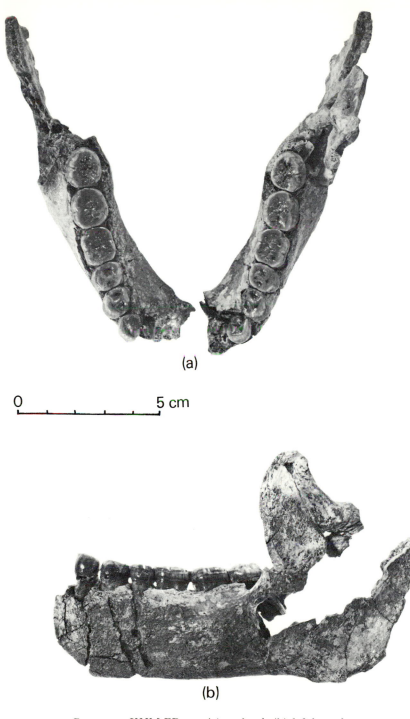

0 _____ 5 cm

PLATE 13. KNM-ER 992 (a) occlusal, (b) left lateral.

123

KNM-ER 993

Distal three-quarters of a right femur broken proximally just below the lesser trochanter. The specimen is abraded in patches and this is particularly heavy on the condyles and supra-patellar area. Table 24.

KNM-ER 997

Proximal portion of a left third metatarsal. The articular surface is damaged.

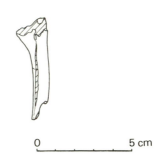

FIG. 5.27. KNM-ER 997, medial.

Discovery: N. Mutiwa, 1971.
Area: 104. Aerial photo 1450.
Stratigraphic position: Upper member, above major erosion surface (collection unit 4).
Environment of deposition: Fluvial, probably channel, ADP. Reference Section 23.
Reference: K.F.R.P. Publ. No. 12.

KNM-ER 998

Right I². Table 4.
Discovery: K. Kitibi, 1971.
Area: 104. Aerial photo 1450.
Stratigraphic position: Upper member, above major erosion surface (collection unit 4).
Environment of deposition: Fluvial, probably channel, ADP. Reference Section 23.
Reference: K.F.R.P. Publ. No. 12.

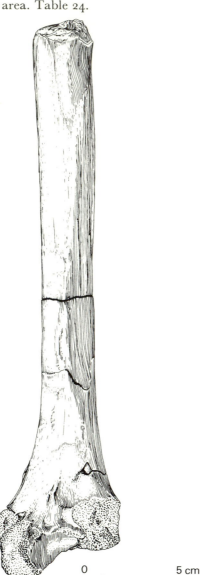

FIG. 5.26. KNM-ER 993, posterior.

Discovery: K. Kimeu, 1971.
Area: 1. Aerial photo 1398.
Stratigraphic position: Ileret Member, 1–2 m above the top of the Lower/Middle Tuff (collection unit 5).
Environment of deposition: Floodplain, AVP. Reference Section 10.
References: K.F.R.P. Publ. Nos. 12, 23, 41.

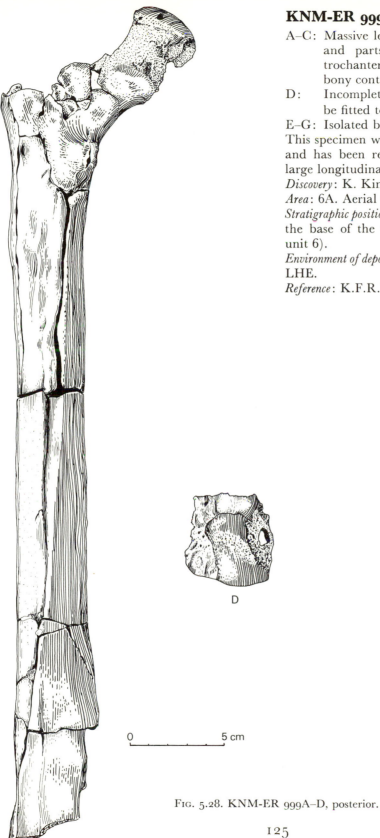

KNM-ER 999 (A–G)

A–C: Massive left femur, lacking the distal end and parts of the head, neck, greater trochanter, and lower shaft. There are bony contacts between the pieces A–C.

D: Incomplete medial condyle which cannot be fitted to the rest of the femur.

E–G: Isolated bone fragments.

This specimen was recovered in many fragments and has been reconstructed. There are several large longitudinal cracks in the shaft. Table 24.

Discovery: K. Kimeu, 1971.

Area: 6A. Aerial photo 1398.

Stratigraphic position: Approximately 9–11 m above the base of the Guomde Formation (collection unit 6).

Environment of depositon: Lake margin, beach sands, LHE.

Reference: K.F.R.P. Publ. No. 27.

FIG. 5.28. KNM-ER 999A–D, posterior.

KNM-ER 1170 (A–I)

Nine cranial fragments that do not piece together but which are probably from a single individual (see KNM-ER 801).
Discovery: While sieving for pieces of KNM-ER 801, 1971.
Area: 6A. Aerial photo 1398.

Stratigraphic position: Ileret Member, *c.* 6–7 m below the base of the Lower/Middle Tuff (collection unit 4).
Environment of deposition: Distributary channel, ACP. Reference Section 11.
Reference: K.F.R.P. Publ. No. 12.

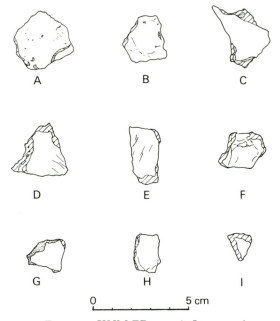

Fig. 5.29. KNM-ER 1170A–I, external.

KNM-ER 1171 (A–D)

Isolated upper and lower teeth and germs apparently from a single juvenile individual (see KNM-ER 801).
A: Right I^2 lacking tip of root.
B: Germ of left P_4.
C: Fragment of crown of left M_1.
D: Partial crown of right M_1.
E: Germ of left M_2.
F: Germ of right M_2.
G: Germ of left M^2.
H: Germ of right M^2.
I: Partial germ of right $\underline{C}$.
The surface of the enamel of the M_2 and P^4 germs is slightly expanded by numerous small cracks. Tables 4, 5, 9, 15, 16, 17.
Discovery: While sieving for fragments of KNM-ER 801.
Area: 6A. Aerial photo 1398.
Stratigraphic position: Ileret Member, *c.* 6–7 m below the base of the Lower/Middle Tuff (collection unit 4).
Environment of deposition: Distributary channel, ACP. Reference Section 11.
References: K.F.R.P. Publ. Nos. 12, 23.

KNM-ER 1462

Worn isolated left M_3. Table 18.
Discovery: N. Mutiwa, 1972.
Area: 130. Aerial photo 1752.
Stratigraphic position: Lower member, below 130/T I (collection unit 3).
References: K.F.R.P. Publ. Nos. 16, 28.

126

KNM-ER 1463

Almost complete shaft and neck of a right femur. The neck is long and anteroposteriorly compressed. The specimen is cracked and weathered, with much of the cortical bone lost, particularly distally. Table 24.

Fig. 5.30. KNM-ER 1463, posterior.

Discovery: K. Kimeu, 1972.
Area: 1. Aerial photo 1398.
Stratigraphic position: Ileret Member, within the Lower/Middle Tuff (collection unit 5).
Environment of deposition: Floodplain, ACP.
References: K.F.R.P. Publ. Nos. 16, 49.

KNM-ER 1464

Complete and undistorted right talus (Table 27). This specimen was found just eroding out of the sediment at the site of KNM-ER 801, which had been intensively swept and sieved the previous year. It is listed as a separate individual although it may be associated with any of the other eight specimens recovered from the same site.

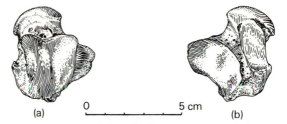

Fig. 5.31. KNM-ER 1464 (a) superior, (b) inferior.

Discovery: N. Mutiwa, 1972.
Area: 6A. Aerial photo 1398.
Stratigraphic position: *In situ*. Ileret Member, *c.* 6–7 m below the Lower/Middle Tuff (collection unit 4).
Environment of deposition: Edge of a distributary channel, ACP. Reference Section 11.
References: K.F.R.P. Publ. Nos. 16, 49.

KNM-ER 1465 (A–B)

A: Fragment of a left femur consisting of the proximal portion of the shaft and neck. The neck is anteroposteriorly compressed. Some surface bone is missing, particularly along the anterior aspect of the shaft.
B: Fragment of femoral head.

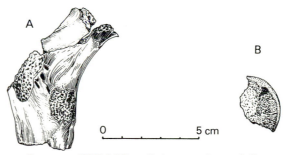

Fig. 5.32. KNM-ER 1465A, posterior. 1465B.

Discovery: K. Kimeu, 1972.
Area: 11. Aerial photo 1465.
Stratigraphic position: Ileret Member, *c.* 8–10 m below the base of the Chari Tuff (collection unit 5).
Environment of deposition: Delta margin, probably shoreline silts, ACP.
References: K.F.R.P. Publ. Nos. 16, 49.

KNM-ER 1466

Fragment of a left frontoparietal showing a prominent temporal line and part of the coronal suture. The bone is thick.

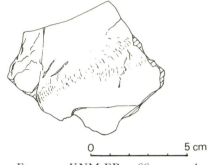

FIG. 5.33. KNM-ER 1466, external.

Discovery: B. Ngeneo, 1972.
Area: 6. Aerial photo 1398.
Stratigraphic position: Ileret Member, 6–7 m above the local top of the Lower/Middle Tuff (collection unit 5).
Environment of deposition: Channel, AVP. Reference Section 27.
References: K.F.R.P. Publ. Nos. 16, 49.

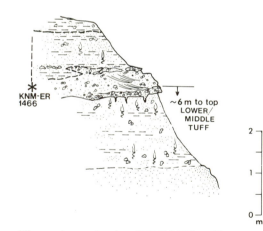

27. The section at the site of KNM-ER 1466 represents the AVP environment. The specimen was probably derived from silty sand near the top of a channel lens.

KNM-ER 1467

Weathered unworn crown of a left M_3. Table 18.
Discovery: N. Mutiwa, 1972.
Area: 3. Aerial photo 1398.
Stratigraphic position: Ileret Member, below the Chari Tuff (collection unit 5).
References: K.F.R.P. Publ. Nos. 16, 49.

KNM-ER 1468

Right side of the body of a robust mandible including the roots of P_4–M_3 and the distal root of P_3. The specimen shows surface weathering and expansion cracks. Table 2.

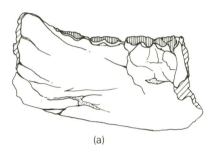

(a)

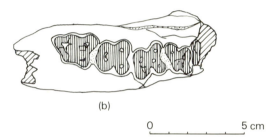

(b)

FIG. 5.34. KNM-ER 1468 (a) right lateral, (b) occlusal.

Discovery: B. Ngeneo, 1972.
Area: 11. Aerial photo 1465.
Stratigraphic position: Ileret Member, within the upper part of the Lower/Middle Tuff or possibly just above (collection unit 5).
Environment of deposition: Channel, AVP.
References: K.F.R.P. Publ. Nos. 16, 49.

KNM-ER 1469

Left side of the body of a mandible with the posterior fracture passing through the ascending ramus. The roots of P_3–M_3 are in place and the broken crowns of M_2 and M_3. The specimen shows some surface weathering and many expansion cracks. Table 2.

Discovery: K. Kimeu, 1972.
Area: 131. Aerial photo 1650.
Stratigraphic position: Lower member, *c.* 10–12 m below 131/T I (collection unit 3)
Environment of deposition: Distributary channel, ADP. Reference Section 28.
References: K.F.R.P. Publ. Nos. 16, 49.

28. KNM-ER 1496 was found in association with a distributary channel in the ADP environment. KNM-ER 1803 occurred on the surface of deposits underlying the channel at a distance of about 50 m from KNM-ER 1496. The two fragments may be from the same level.

PLATE 14. KNM-ER 1469 (a) occlusal, (b) left lateral.

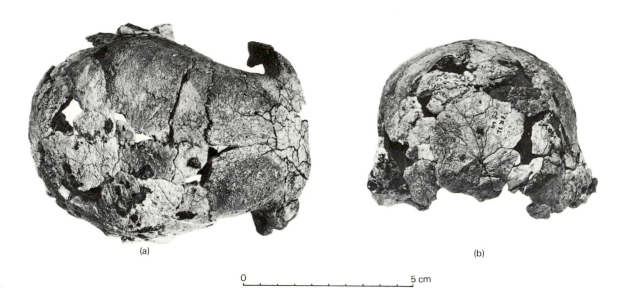

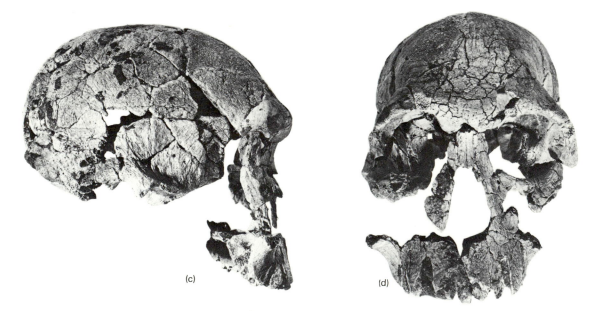

PLATE 15. KNM-ER 1470 (a) superior, (b) posterior, (c) right lateral, (d) frontal.

KNM-ER 1470 (A–D)

Relatively complete cranium.
A: Facial fragment including maxilla.
B: Calvaria.
C: Occipital fragment including the margin of the foramen magnum.
D: Cranial fragments not yet fitted to the cranium.

The cranium has been reconstructed from many fragments. The base of the calvaria and parts of the facial skeleton are missing. The calvaria is slightly distorted so that while there are bony contacts between the face and the rest of the skull, the orientation of the face relative to the calvaria cannot be accurately determined. There are no tooth crowns preserved but the premolar roots and the left M^1 roots and the mesial root of M^2 are in place. The maxilla is broken at M^2 on the left and at M^1 on the right. The incisors, canines, and right M^1 were apparently lost prior to fossilization and only parts of the alveoli for these teeth remain. The contact between the occipital fragment (C)—which includes the margin of the foramen magnum—and the main portion of the occipital is not entirely satisfactory and it is possible that a small amount of bone is missing.

The cranium belongs to an adult individual and has an estimated endocranial volume of 770–775 cm³ (R. Holloway, pers. comm.). The supraorbital tori are not strongly developed, and the temporal lines are weak. There is only moderate postorbital constriction, and the frontal bones rise in the midline in a gently convex curve to bregma. The frontal air sinus is well developed. The orbits are nearly circular and there is little subnasal prognathism. Table 1.

Discovery: B. Ngeneo, 1972.
Area: 131. Aerial photo 1650.
Stratigraphic positon: Lower member, *c.* 35–6 m below 131/T I (collection unit 3).
Environment of deposition: Upper part of distributary channel, ACP or LHE. Reference Section 29.
References: K.F.R.P. Publ. Nos. 16, 18, 26, 29, 70.

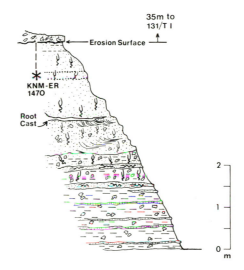

29. KNM-ER 1470 occurred as a closely associated assemblage of fragments on the outcrop surface of a channel sand. Matrix on the specimen matches fine sand near the top of the channel. The channel represents a distributary in the ADP or LHE environment. Mollusc-bearing sands above the site overlie the post-Tulu Bor erosion surface.

KNM-ER 1471

Proximal third of a right tibia. The margins of the condyles and the tibial tuberosity are extensively damaged and cortical bone has been lost in patches from much of the shaft, including the subcutaneous border. Table 25.

Discovery: B. Ngeneo, 1972.
Area: 131. Aerial photo 1650.
Stratigraphic position: Lower member, *c*. 27 m below 131/T I (collection unit 3).
Environment of deposition: Delta margin, ACP or LHE. Reference Section 30.
References: K.F.R.P. Publ. Nos. 16, 49.

0 ____ 5 cm

FIG. 5.35. KNM-ER 1471, anterior.

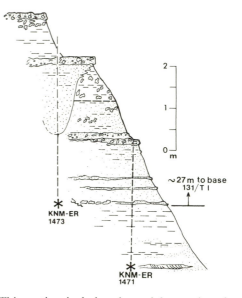

30. This section includes channel lenses, intraformational conglomerates with molluscs, and sandy clayey silts typical of the ADP or LHE environment. The range of possible source horizons for KNM-ER 1471 or 1473 covers several sub-environments.

KNM-ER 1472

Relatively complete right femur. Cancellous bone is exposed on parts of the head, neck, greater trochanter, and margins of the condyles. A variable thickness of cortical bone has been lost on the shaft and neck. The neck is subcircular. The shaft is platymetric and peculiarly straight. Table 24.

Discovery: J. M. Harris, 1972.
Area: 131. Aerial photo 1650.
Stratigraphic position: Lower member, *c*. 30 m below 131/T I (collection unit 3).
Environment of deposition: Delta margin, probably lagoon, shoreline, ACP or LHE. Reference Section 31.
References: K.F.R.P. Publ. Nos. 16, 18, 29.

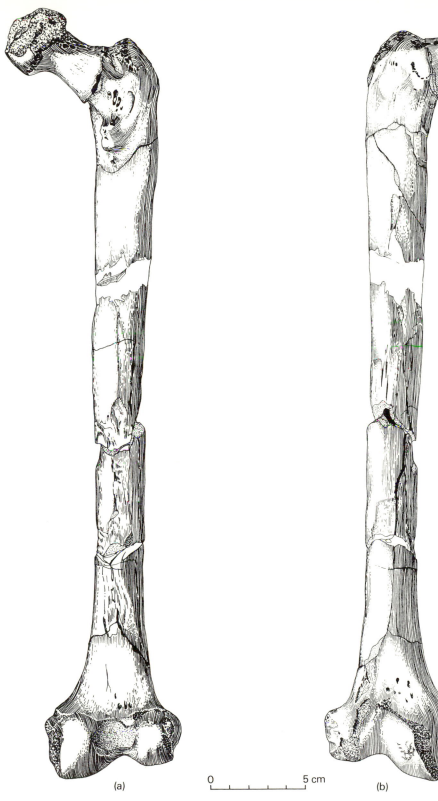

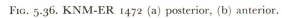

(a)   0   5 cm   (b)

FIG. 5.36. KNM-ER 1472 (a) posterior, (b) anterior.

KNM-ER 1473

Head, anatomical neck and tuberosities of a right humerus. The bone has been abraded extensively in the region of the anatomical neck and in patches on the head and greater tuberosity. Table 21.

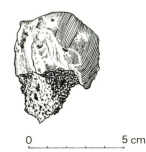

FIG. 5.37. KNM-ER 1473, anterior.

Discovery: B. Ngeneo, 1972.
Area: 131. Aerial photo 1650.
Stratigraphic position: Lower member, *c*. 25 m below 131/T I (collection unit 3).
Environment of deposition: Delta margin, ACP or LHE. Reference Section 30.
References: K.F.R.P. Publ. Nos. 16, 49.

KNM-ER 1474

Fragment of parietal.

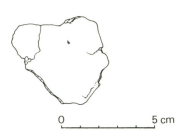

FIG. 5.38. KNM-ER 1474, external.

Discovery: B. Ngeneo, 1972.
Area: 131. Aerial photo 1650.
Stratigraphic position: Lower member, *c*. 30 m below 131/T I (collection unit 3).
Environment of deposition: Probably delta margin, ACP or LHE. Reference Section 31.
Reference: K.F.R.P. Publ. No. 16.

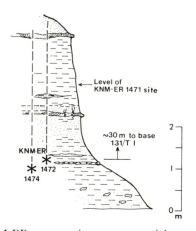

31. KNM-ER 1472 and 1474 occurred in association with deltaic sands and silts of ACP or LHE environments. These specimens were found in the same small drainage area as KNM-ER 1471 and 1475. Exact source horizons could not be determined.

134

KNM-ER 1475 (A–B)

A: Fragment of proximal right femur, broken just distal to the lesser trochanter and lacking the head and both trochanters. The neck is subcircular.

B: Badly weathered fragment of femoral shaft. Table 24.

KNM-ER 1476 (A–C)

A: Left talus damaged in the superomedial part of the head and the posteromedial corner of the trochlea. (Table 27.)

B: Proximal left tibia in which the edges of the condyles are extensively abraded. (Table 25.)

C: Fragment of the shaft of a right tibia.

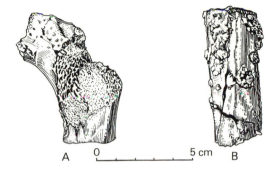

FIG. 5.39. KNM-ER 1475A–B, posterior.

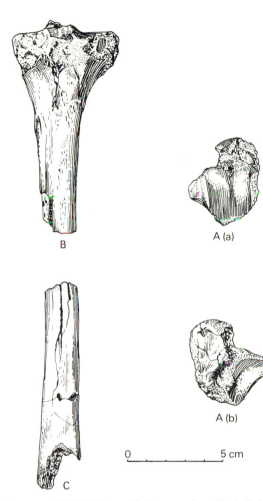

FIG. 5.40. KNM-ER 1476A (a) superior, (b) inferior. 1476B–C, anterior.

Discovery: K. Kimeu, 1972.
Area: 131. Aerial photo 1650.
Stratigraphic position: Lower member, *c.* 24 m below 131/T I (collection unit 3).
Environment of deposition: Delta margin, ACP or LHE.
References: K.F.R.P. Publ. Nos. 16, 18, 29.

Discovery: K. Kimeu, 1972.
Area: 105. Aerial photo 1590.
Stratigraphic position: Upper member, above post-KBS erosion surface (collection unit 4).
Environment of deposition: Channel, AVP. Reference Section 4.
References: K.F.R.P. Publ. Nos. 16, 49.

KNM-ER 1477 (A–D)

A: Body of an immature mandible broken posterior to M_1 on both sides. The deciduous canines and molars are preserved on both sides, the germs of the first molars are visible in their crypts, and the germs of the right P_3 and I_1 can be seen where the external mandibular surface is broken away. The external walls of the anterior alveoli are missing and on the left side the external surface of the mandible is damaged. Tooth germs from this region were recovered separately.

B: Germ of left I_1.

C: Germ of left $\overline{C}$.

D: Germ of left P_3.

Tables 2, 11, 13, 14, 16, 20.

Discovery: M. Mbithi, 1972.

Area: 105. Aerial photo 1590.

Stratigraphic position: *In situ*. Upper member, above post-KBS erosion surface (collection unit 4).

Environment of deposition: Channel, AVP. Reference Section 6.

References: K.F.R.P. Publ. Nos. 16, 49.

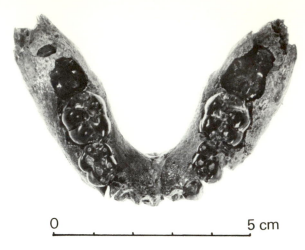

0   5 cm

PLATE 16. KNM-ER 1477, occlusal.

136

KNM-ER 1478 (A–J)

Associated weathered cranial fragments.

A: Fragment of the right maxilla with roots of M^1–M^3 and the distobuccal corner of the crown of M^2.

B: Fragment of the left maxilla with the roots of P^3–M^1 and the alveolus for $\underline{C}$.

C: Fragment of parietal.

D: Fragment of right temporal including both petrous and squamous portions and showing part of the mastoid process.

E: Bone fragment which is probably part of a petrous temporal.

F–J: Indeterminate cranial fragments.

Discovery: H. Mutua, 1972.
Area: 105. Aerial photo 1590.
Stratigraphic position: Upper member, above post-KBS erosion surface (collection unit 4).
Environment of deposition: Top of channel or flood-plain, AVP. Reference Section 7.
References: K.F.R.P. Publ. Nos. 16, 49.

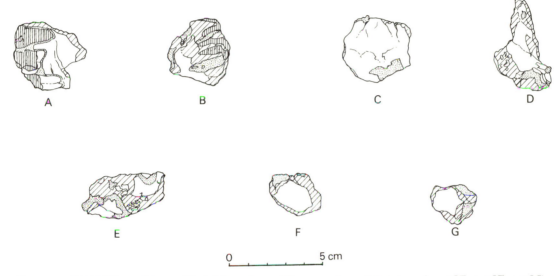

Fig. 5.41. KNM-ER 1478A. 1478B, left lateral. 1478C, external. 1478D, internal. 1478E. 1478F. 1478G.

KNM-ER 1479 (A–D)

Associated dental fragments.

A: Fragment of the crown of a left M_3.

B: Fragment of the crown of a right M_3.

C–D: Tooth fragments.

Discovery: N. Mutiwa, 1972.
Area: 105. Aerial photo 1590.
Stratigraphic position: Upper member, above post-KBS erosion surface (collection unit 4).
Environment of deposition: Upper part of channel or floodplain, AVP. Reference Section 6.
Reference: K.F.R.P. Publ. No. 16.

KNM-ER 1480

The crown and partially formed lingual roots of a right M_3. Table 18.

Discovery: J. M. Harris and A. K. Behrensmeyer, 1972.
Area: 105. Aerial photo 1590.
Stratigraphic position: Upper member, above post-KBS erosion surface (collection unit 4).
Environment of deposition: Channel, AVP. Reference Section 6.
References: K.F.R.P. Publ. Nos. 16, 28.

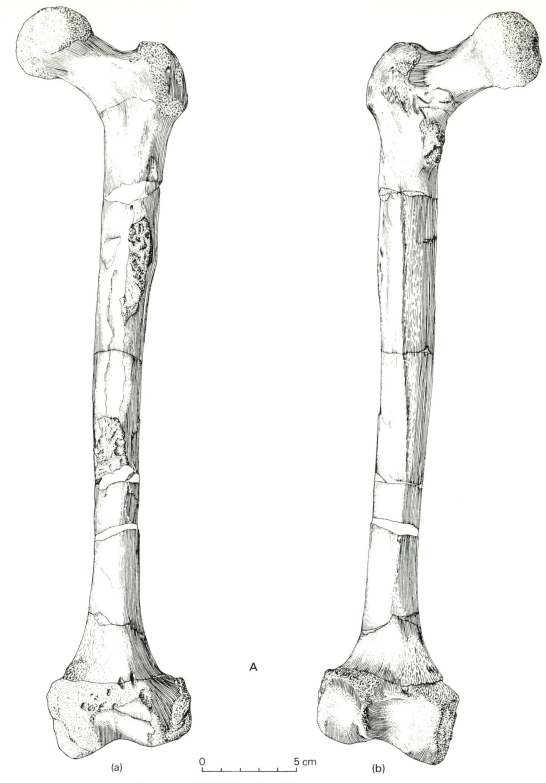

A

(a)   0   5 cm   (b)

FIG. 5.42. KNM-ER 1481A (a) anterior, (b) posterior.

KNM-ER 1481 (A–D)

Associated elements of a left lower limb of a single individual.

A: Virtually complete femur lacking some surface bone on the head, lesser trochanter, medial condyle and epicondyle, and the suprapatellar region. The head is large and the neck oval. The shaft is slender and platymeric.

B: Proximal tibia including the condyles and upper part of the shaft. The edges of the condyles and the tibial tuberosity are extensively damaged.

C: Distal tibia with the articular surface well preserved but much surface bone lost from parts of the non-articular surface.

D: Distal end of a fibula with slight loss of surface bone in the posterolateral region.

Tables 24, 25, 26.
Discovery: J. M. Harris, 1972.
Area: 131. Aerial photo 1650.
Stratigraphic position: Lower member, *c.* 10–13 m below 131/T I (collection unit 3).
Environment of deposition: Interdistributary or distributary, delta margin, ADP. Reference Section 32.
References: K.F.R.P. Publ. Nos. 16, 18, 29.

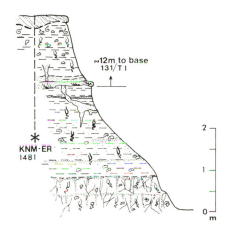

32. KNM-ER 1481 was associated with subaerial deltaic deposits of the ADP. The specimen may have been derived from a distributary channel that caps the local exposures or from underlying interdistributary deposits.

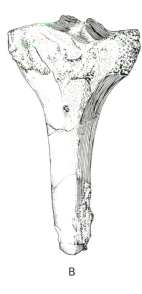

B

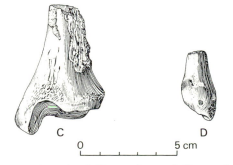

C   D

0   5 cm

Fig. 5.42 (cont.) 1481B, anterior. 1481C, anterior. 1481D, anterior.

KNM-ER 1482 (A–E)

A: Incomplete adult mandible including part of the left ascending ramus, the left side of the body, the symphysial region, and part of the right side of the body which is broken posterior to M_1. The roots of the lateral incisors, the right canine, P_3 and M_1, and the roots and partial crowns of the left $\overline{C}$–M_3 and the right P_4 are in place. The central incisors are missing.

B: Distal half of the crown of the right $\overline{C}$.

C: Distolingual quadrant of the left M_1.

D: Distolingual quadrant of the right M_1.

E: Enamel flake.

Tables 2, 14, 15, 17, 18.

Discovery: H. Muluila, 1972.

Area: 131. Aerial photo 1650.

Stratigraphic position: Lower member, *c.* 33 m below 131/T I, *c.* 3 m above KNM-ER 1470 (collection unit 3).

Environment of deposition: Delta margin, ACP or LHE. Reference Section 33.

References: K.F.R.P. Publ. Nos. 16, 26, 30.

(a)

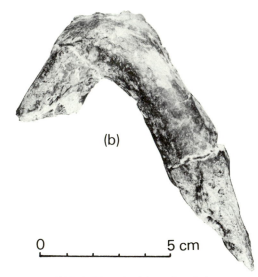

(b)

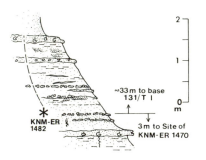

33. The deposits at the site of KNM-ER 1482 indicate shallow lacustrine conditions associated with the ACP or LHE environments. The mollusc-bearing sand at the base of the section can be correlated with the bed capping the section at the KNM-ER 1470 site, which is only some 80–100 m from KNM-ER 1482.

PLATE 17. KNM-ER 1482 (a) occlusal, (b) inferior.

0   5 cm

KNM-ER 1483 (A–E)

Associated parts of a mandible.

A: Fragment of the left side of the mandibular body including the roots of I_2–M_1.

B: Fragment of the left side of the mandibular body including the distal part of the M_3 alveolus.

C: Fragment of the right side of the mandibular body including the roots of I_1–P_4.

D: Fragment of the ascending ramus including part of the mandibular angle.

E: Partial crown of left M_2.

Tables 2, 17.

Discovery: W. Mangao, 1972.
Area: 131. Aerial photo 1650.
Stratigraphic position: Lower member, *c.* 0–3 m below the base of 131/T I (collection unit 3).
Environment of deposition: Channel or levee, ADP. Reference Section 34.
References: K.F.R.P. Publ. Nos. 16, 28.

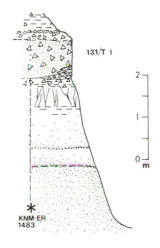

A (a)   B (a)

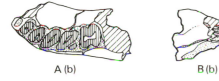

A (b)   B (b)

0 —————————— 5 cm

FIG. 5.43. KNM-ER 1483A–B (a) left lateral, (b) occlusal.

34. KNM-ER 1483 occurred in association with channel sands and floodplain deposits of the ADP. Matrix on the specimen was most similar to sands in the lower part of the section.

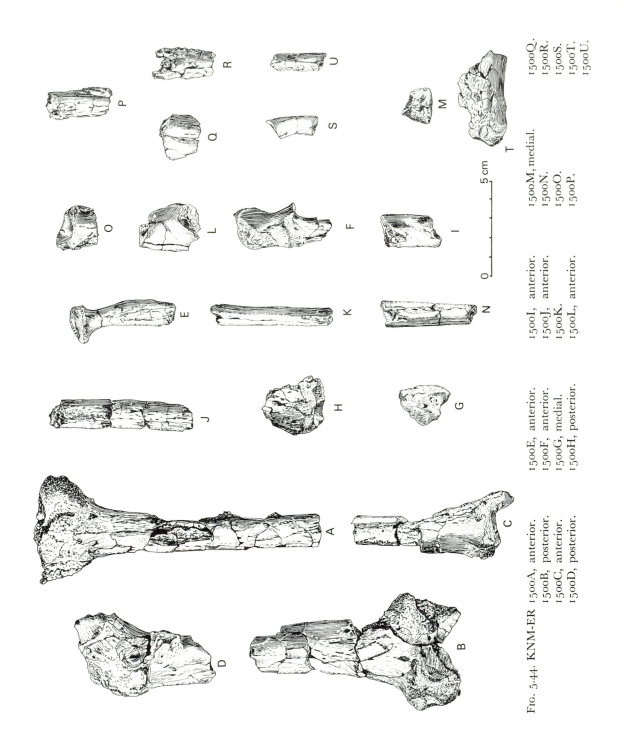

FIG. 5.44. KNM-ER 1500A, anterior. 1500B, posterior. 1500C, anterior. 1500D, posterior. 1500E, anterior. 1500F, anterior. 1500G, medial. 1500H, posterior. 1500I, anterior. 1500J, anterior. 1500K. 1500L, anterior. 1500M, medial. 1500N. 1500O. 1500P. 1500Q. 1500R. 1500S. 1500T. 1500U.

KNM-ER 1500 (A–T)

Associated skeletal elements of a small adult individual. All the fragments are heavily weathered showing numerous small cracks and abrasion of the surface bone.

A: Proximal third of a left tibia (Table 25).
B: Distal left femur.
C: Distal left tibia.
D: Proximal left femur including the neck which is anteroposteriorly compressed (Table 24).
E: Proximal right radius (Table 23).
F: Proximal right ulna (Table 22).
G: Distal right fibula.
H: Fragment of distal right tibia.
I: Fragment of right ulna shaft.
J: Fragment of right tibia shaft.
K: Fragment of right radius shaft.
L: Fragment of humerus shaft.
M: Fragment of proximal right metatarsal III (Table 28).
N: Bone fragment, probably radius shaft.
O: Fragment of glenoid cavity of left scapula.
P–S: Bone fragments.
T: Fragment of calcaneum.

Discovery: J. Kimengech, 1972.
Area: 130. Aerial photo 1752.
Stratigraphic position: Lower member, *c.* 2–5 m below the projected level of 130/T I (collection unit 3).
Environment of deposition: Channel, ACP. Reference Section 35.
References: K.F.R.P. Publ. Nos. 16, 49, 71.

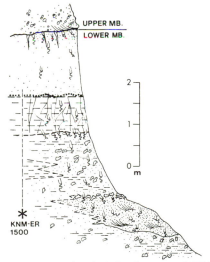

35. The many associated skeletal parts of KNM-ER 1500 were scattered over a relatively restricted area, indicating derivation from sands below the erosion unconformity which locally marks the contact between lower and upper members of the Koobi Fora Formation. The KBS Tuff is absent here owing to erosion but it crops out within 300 m of the site. Matrix on the specimen is a medium-grained sand.

KNM-ER 1501

Heavily weathered fragment of the right side of the body of a mandible including the roots of I_2–M_3. Table 2.

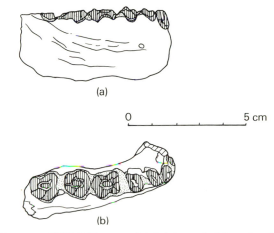

(a)

0   5 cm

(b)

FIG. 5.45. KNM-ER 1501 (a) left lateral, (b) occlusal.

Discovery: B. Ngeneo, 1972.
Area: 123. Aerial photo 1581.
Stratigraphic position: Upper member (provisional) (collection unit 4).
Environment of deposition: Probably delta margin. Reference Section 36.
References: K.F.R.P. Publ. Nos. 16, 28.

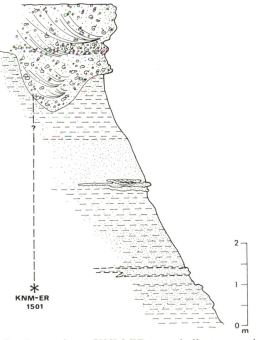

36. Sandy matrix on KNM-ER 1501 indicates association with the coarse mollusc-bearing channel lens rather than with finer underlying sediments. The channel represents a distributary cut into earlier lacustrine deposits.

(a)

(b)

0   5 cm

PLATE 18. KNM-ER 1502 (a) occlusal,
(b) right lateral.

KNM-ER 1502

Fragment of the right side of the body of a mandible with the crown of M_1 in place. The broken roots of M_2 and part of the crypt wall of M_3 are preserved. This specimen was found close to the site from which KNM-ER 1812 was subsequently found and may be the same individual. Tables 2, 16.

Discovery: W. Mangao, 1972.
Area: 123. Aerial photo 1581.
Stratigraphic position: Upper member (provisional) (collection unit 4).
Environment of deposition: Delta margin. Reference Section 37.
References: K.F.R.P. Publ. Nos. 16, 28.

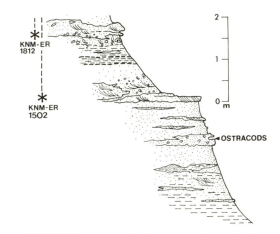

37. KNM-ER 1502 and 1812 were derived from a series of subaerial to shallow lacustrine deposits associated with a deltaic environment. It is possible that they come from the same horizon and represent the same individual.

KNM-ER 1503, 1504, 1505 (A–B)

KNM-ER 1503

Well-preserved fragment of the proximal end of a right femur including the head, neck, greater trochanter and lesser trochanter. The specimen is broken just below the lesser trochanter. The head is small and the neck is long and anteroposteriorly compressed. Table 24.

Discovery: KNM-ER 1503, M. Muluila, 1972. KNM-ER 1504, M. Mbithi, 1972. KNM-ER 1505, B. Ngeneo, 1972.
Area: 123. Aerial photo 1581.
Stratigraphic position: Upper member (provisional) (collection unit 4).
Environment of deposition: Delta margin. Reference Section 38.
References: K.F.R.P. Publ. Nos. 16, 49.
McHenry, H. 1975. Fossils and the mosaic nature of human evolution. *Science* **190**, 425–31.

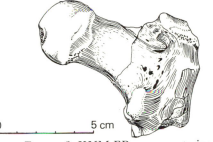

FIG. 5.46. KNM-ER 1503, posterior.

KNM-ER 1504

Well-preserved distal fragment of a right humerus. Table 21.

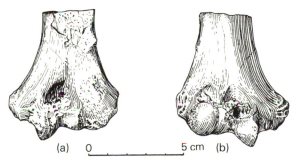

(a)   (b)

FIG. 5.47. KNM-ER 1504 (a) posterior, (b) anterior.

KNM-ER 1505 (A–B)

A: Head and part of the neck of a left femur. The neck is anteroposteriorly compressed. Table 24.
B: Fragment of the distal shaft of a left femur.

These specimens and KNM-ER 1822 were all found at the same locality although several metres apart. It is probable that they represent parts of a single individual.

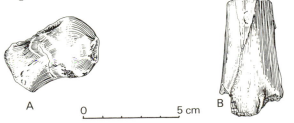

A   B

FIG. 5.48. KNM-ER 1505A–B, posterior.

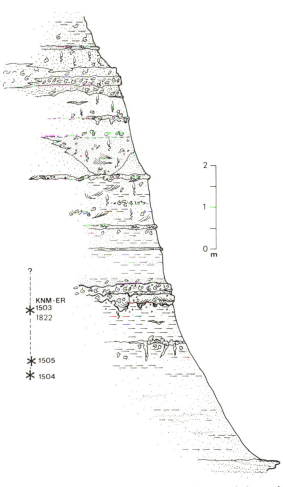

38. This section shows a typical association of channel lenses, mollusc-bearing sheet sands, caliche horizons, and fine-grained deposits. The environment was ADP to LHE, with fluctuating subaerial and aquatic conditions. KNM-ER 1503, 1504, and 1505 were derived from the lower part of this sequence, and may have come from the same horizon.

145

KNM-ER 1506 (A–D)

A: Fragment of the body of a right mandible with M_1 and M_2 in place. There is a well-developed contact facet on the distal margin of M_2 but no evidence of the roots of M_3, suggesting the loss ante mortem of M_3.

B: Crown of right P^4.

C: Crown of right P^3.

D: Tooth fragment.

Tables 6, 7, 16, 17.

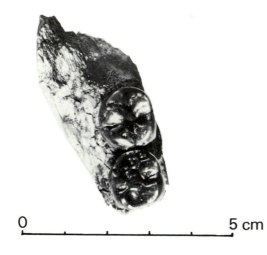

0 _____ 5 cm

PLATE 19. KNM-ER 1506A, occlusal.

Discovery: B. Ngeneo, 1972.
Area: 121. Aerial photo 1689.
Stratigraphic position: Upper member (provisional) (collection unit 4).
Environment of deposition: Distributary channel. Reference Section 39.
References: K.F.R.P. Publ. Nos. 16, 49.

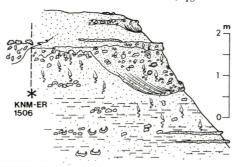

39. KNM-ER 1506 is derived from sediments that are primarily subaerial, associated with a deltaic plain environment. Algal stromatolites and molluscs indicate proximal lacustrine conditions. Distributary channel deposits are the most likely source of the specimen.

146

KNM-ER 1507

Weathered fragment of the left side of the body of a juvenile mandible with the crowns of dM_1, dM_2, and M_1 in place. The anterior break has exposed the germs of I_2 and $\bar{C}$ in their crypts, and the posterior break has exposed the M_2 germ. The germs of the premolars have been exposed in their crypts by surface weathering, which is particularly heavy on the inner surface and at the base. Tables 16, 20.

Discovery: N. Mutiwa, 1972.
Area: 127. Aerial photo 1739.
Stratigraphic position: Upper member, above major erosion surface (collection unit 4).
Environment of deposition: Channel, AVP. Reference Section 40.
References: K.F.R.P. Publ. Nos. 16, 28.

0   5 cm

(a)

(b)

40. KNM-ER 1507 and 1508 are derived from channel deposits associated with the AVP environment.

PLATE 20. KNM-ER 1507 (a) occlusal, (b) left lateral.

KNM-ER 1508

Isolated right molar (either M_1 or M_2) with roots. Matrix-filled cracks have caused slight distortion of the crown, which is 12.2 mm buccolingually and 13.6 mm mesiodistally.
Discovery: N. Mutiwa, 1972.
Area: 127. Aerial photo 1739.
Stratigraphic position: Upper member, above major erosion surface (collection unit 4).
Environment of deposition: Channel, AVP. Reference Section 40.
References: K.F.R.P. Publ. Nos. 16, 28.

KNM-ER 1509 (A–E)

Associated worn mandibular teeth.
A: Crown of left M_3.
B: Broken crown of left M_2 with partial distal roots.
C: Crown of left M_1.
D: Fragment of left P_4 crown.
E: Partial crown of left $\bar{C}$.
F: Tooth fragments.
Tables 16, 17, 18.
Discovery: H. Mutua, 1972.
Area: 119. Aerial photo 1540.
Stratigraphic position: Upper member, below Koobi Fora Tuff (collection unit 4).
Reference: K.F.R.P. Publ. No. 16.

147

KNM-ER 1515

Right I². Table 4.
Discovery: N. Mutiwa, 1972.
Area: 103. Aerial photo 1416.
Stratigraphic position: Upper member, above major erosion surface, *c*. 10 m below the Koobi Fora Tuff (collection unit 4).
Reference: K.F.R.P. Publ. No. 16.

KNM-ER 1590 (A–Q)

Fragments of a juvenile cranium with some teeth. Many of the fragments have been pieced together, but numerous small fragments still remain. The specimen was partially fragmented prior to fossilization.

A: Partial left and right parietals.
B: Left I¹.
C: Germ of left C̱.
D: Crown of right C̱.
E: Left dC̱ with tip of root broken.
F: Left dM² in fragment of maxilla showing part of the crypt for P⁴.
G: Left P³ with partial roots.
H: Crown of right P³.
I: Left P⁴ with partial roots.
J: Germ of right P⁴.
K: Left M¹ in maxilla fragment with partial crypt for P⁴.
L: Right M¹ in maxilla fragment.
M: Left M² germ.
N–O: Frontal fragments.
P: Tooth fragments.
Q: Cranial fragments.
Tables 3, 5, 6, 7, 8, 9, 19.
Discovery: B. Ngeneo, 1972.
Area: 12. Aerial photo 1523.
Stratigraphic position: Lower member, *c*. 10 m below 12/T II (collection unit 3).
Environment of deposition: Delta margin, LHE. Reference Section 41.
References: K.F.R.P. Publ. Nos. 16, 26, 49, 70.

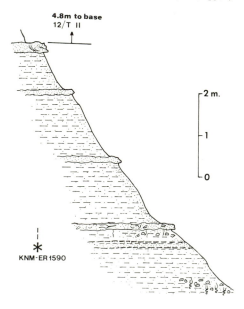

41. The cranial fragments of KNM-ER 1590 were scattered over an area of about 20 × 20 m on low outcrops of fine-grained sands and silts. A mud-cracked horizon overlain by mollusc-bearing sands is the most likely source of the specimen.

(a)

0   5 cm

(b)

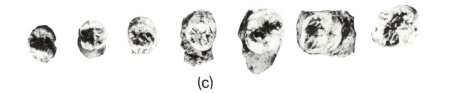

(c)

PLATE 21. KNM-ER 1590 (a) superior, (b) lingual,
(c) occlusal.

KNM-ER 1591 (A–D)

Shaft and distal end of a right humerus.

A–C: Proximal, middle and distal portions of the shaft with poor bony contacts between the three pieces.

D: Weathered distal articular region.

Discovery: H. Mutua, 1972.
Area: 12. Aerial photo 1523.
Stratigraphic position: Ileret Member, above the projected level of 12/T II (collection unit 4).
Environment of deposition: Delta margin, distributary sand, LHE.
Reference: K.F.R.P. Publ. No. 16.

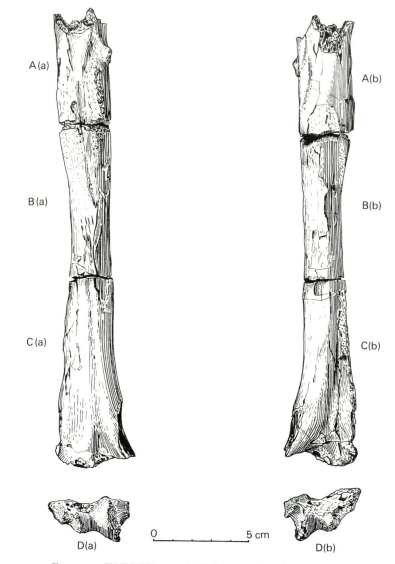

0 _____ 5 cm

FIG. 5.49. KNM-ER 1591A–D (a) anterior, (b) posterior.

KNM-ER 1592

Distal half of a right femur. The specimen is severely weathered with much of the surface bone broken into small fragments which are displaced and encrusted in matrix.

Discovery: N. Mutiwa, 1972.
Area: 12. Aerial photo 1523.
Stratigraphic position: Ileret Member, *c.* 12–18 m above the projected level of 12/T II (collection unit 4).
Environment of deposition: Distributary channel or deltaic plain, LHE. Reference Section 42.
References: K.F.R.P. Publ. No. 16.

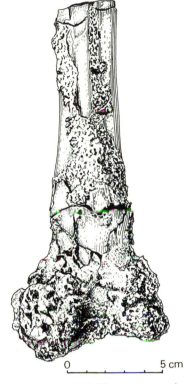

Fig. 5.50. KNM-ER 1592, anterior.

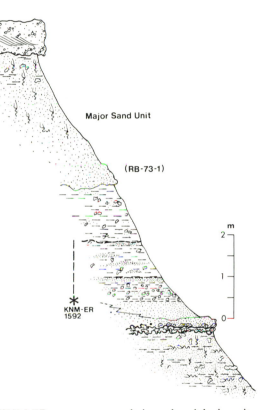

42. KNM-ER 1592 occurred in subaerial deposits associated with deltaic or coastal sedimentation in the LHE environment. The $CaCO_3$ matrix on the specimen matches nodules which occur in inter-distributary silty clays. The 'major sand unit' may represent a regressive shoreline associated with the post-KBS erosion surface. RB-73-1 indicates the position of a horizon that has yielded fossil pollen.

KNM-ER 1593 (A–C)

A: Fragment of left parietal showing markings of the coronal and sagittal sutures along its anterior and medial margins respectively.
B: Parietal fragment.
C: Fragment of the right side of a mandibular body with the partial remains of two molars, probably M_2 and M_3.

Discovery: W. Mangao, 1972.
Area: 12. Aerial photo 1523.
Stratigraphic position: Top of the lower member or base of the Ileret Member, in or just above the projected level of 12/T II (collection unit 4).
Environment of deposition: Delta margin, LHE.
References: K.F.R.P. Publ. Nos. 16, 49.

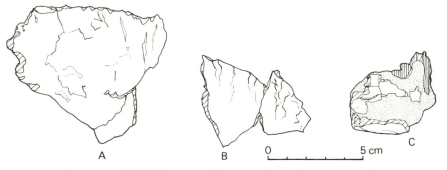

Fig. 5.51. KNM-ER 1593A–B, external. 1593C, right lateral.

KNM-ER 1648

Weathered cranial fragment with evidence of the temporal line.
Discovery: M. Muoka, 1971.
Area: 118. Aerial photo 1592.
Stratigraphic position: Upper member, above major erosion surface (collection unit 4).

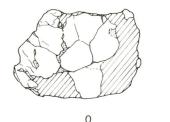

Fig. 5.52. KNM-ER 1648, external.

KNM-ER 1800 (A–W)

Associated small cranial fragments.
A: Parietal fragment with temporal line.
B: Right occipital fragment with lambdoid suture.
C–W: Undiagnostic cranial fragments.
Discovery: M. Muluila, 1973.
Area: 130. Aerial photo 1752.
Stratigraphic position: Lower member, below 130/T I (collection unit 3).
Environment of deposition: Delta margin, LHE or ACP. Reference Section 43.
Reference: K.F.R.P. Publ. No. 26.

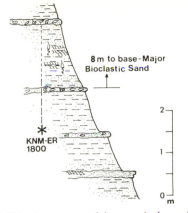

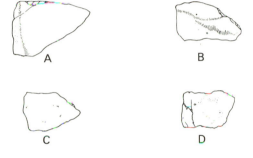

FIG. 5.53. KNM-ER 1800A–D, external.

43. KNM-ER 1800 occurred in association with fine-grained deposits interbedded with mollusc-bearing sheet sands. The environment was primarily lacustrine. The 'bioclastic sand' caps local outcrops and represents a major offshore bar or beach.

KNM-ER 1801

Weathered left side of the body of a mandible including the damaged crowns of P_4, M_1, and M_3, and the roots of $\bar{C}$, P_3, and M_2. Only the matrix-filled alveoli of I_1 and I_2 remain. The preserved tooth crowns are severely damaged by weathering. Tables 15, 16, 17, 18.
Discovery: W. Mangao, 1973.
Area: 131. Aerial photo 1651.
Stratigraphic position: Lower member, below 131/T I (collection unit 3).
Environment of deposition: LHE or ACP.
References: K.F.R.P. Publ. Nos. 26, 49.

PLATE 22. KNM-ER 1801, occlusal.

KNM-ER 1802 (A–B)

A: Mandibular body broken on both sides posterior to M_2 and damaged along the basal margin and on the superior surface of the symphysial region. The right and left P_4–M_2 and right P_3 are preserved in place, while only the roots of the left P_3 and the matrix-filled alveoli of the canines and left I_1 and I_2 remain.

B: Fragments of M_3.

Tables 2, 14, 15, 16, 17.

Discovery: J. M. Harris, 1973.
Area: 131. Aerial photo 1651.
Stratigraphic position: Lower member, *c.* 12 m below 131/T I (collection unit 3).
Environment of deposition: Delta margin, ACP or LHE. Reference Section 44.
References: K.F.R.P. Publ. Nos. 26, 49.

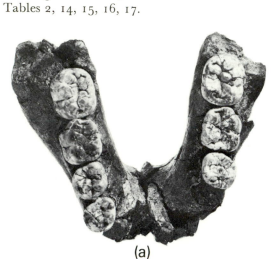

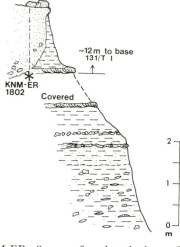

(a)

44. KNM-ER 1802 was found at the base of a channel lens but its surface association could also indicate derivation from a sheet sand truncated by the channel. The channel is a distributary associated with the ACP or LHE environment.

(b)

0   5 cm

PLATE 23. KNM-ER 1802 (a) occlusal, (b) inferior.

KNM-ER 1803

Weathered fragment of the right side of a mandibular body with the roots of P_3–M_1, broken posteriorly through the mesial root of M_2. Only the partial alveoli of I_2 and $\bar{C}$ remain. Table 2.

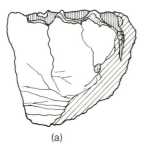

(a)

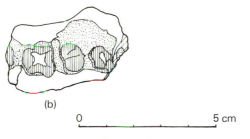

(b)

0   5 cm

FIG. 5.54. KNM-ER 1803 (a) right lateral, (b) occlusal.

Discovery: W. Mangao, 1973.
Area: 131. Aerial photo 1651.
Stratigraphic position: Lower member, *c.* 10–12 m below 131/T I (collection unit 3).
Environment of deposition: Delta margin, probably shallow offshore, ADP. Reference Section 28.
References: K.F.R.P. Publ. Nos. 26, 49, 89.

KNM-ER 1804

Fragment of left maxilla with the worn crowns of P^3–M^2 in place and the broken canine root. The bone has suffered extensive cracking and fragmentation with matrix filling the cracks. Tables 6, 7, 8, 9.

0   5

PLATE 24. KNM-ER 1804, occlusal.

Discovery: R. Holloway, 1973.
Area: 104. Aerial photo 1450.
Stratigraphic position: Upper member, above major erosion surface (collection unit 4).
Environment of deposition: Channel, ADP. Reference Section 45.
References: K.F.R.P. Publ. Nos. 26, 49.

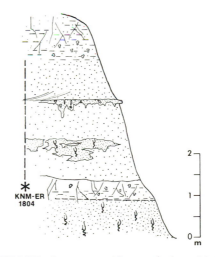

45. KNM-ER 1804 occurred in association with fining-upward channel deposits of the ADP. The locality is only 20–30 m from the KNM-ER 814 site, and all specimens indicated on Reference Section 23 may be from the same level as KNM-ER 1804. The local 'marker horizon' can be correlated between the two sections.

A (a)

A (b)

B (a)

A (c)

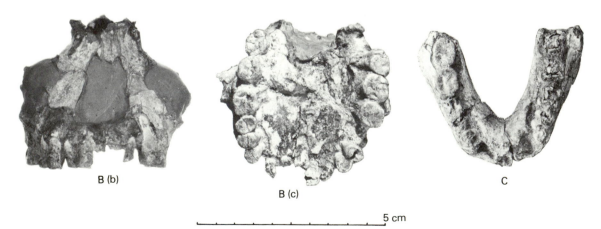

B (b)

B (c)

C

5 cm

PLATE 25. KNM-ER 1805A (a) superior, (b) posterior, (c) left lateral. 1805B (a) right lateral, (b) frontal, (c) occlusal. 1805C, occlusal.

KNM-ER 1805 (A–F)

Associated parts of a cranium.

A: Calvaria broken through the orbital cavities and lacking much of the basi-occipital. The frontal bone rises gently in a convex curve from the anterior break in the midline to bregma. The postorbital constriction appears to have been slight and the temporal lines can be traced from the anterior break posteriorly to a point 30 mm behind bregma, where they form para-sagittal crests. The nuchal crest is well developed and merges with very prominent mastoid crests. The preserved left mastoid process is moderately developed. The estimated endocranial volume is 582 cm³ (R. Holloway, pers. comm.).

B: Palate and part of the facial region. The palate is distorted but the dentition lacks only the right P⁴ and the left I¹ crown. The lateral incisors lie obliquely and show oblique wear facets. The interorbital width appears to have been large.

C: The body of a mandible damaged in the basal and alveolar regions. The crowns of the right M₂ and M₃ are in place and the roots of the right and left P₃–M₃. Very little surface bone remains.

D: Occipital fragment with part of the left side of the foramen magnum and condyle.

E: Tooth fragments.

F: Cranial fragments.

Tables 1, 3, 4, 5, 6, 7, 8, 9, 10, 17, 18.

Discovery: P. Abell, 1973.
Area: 130. Aerial photo 1752.
Stratigraphic position: *In situ.* Upper member, above major erosion surface, just below the base of the Okote Tuff (collection unit 4).
Environment of deposition: Channel, AVP. Reference Section 46.
References: K.F.R.P. Publ. Nos. 26, 49.

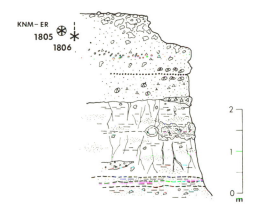

46. The section represents fluvial deposits in the AVP environment. KNM-ER 1805 and 1806 occurred in tuffaceous sands heavily cemented by soil carbonate nodules. The sands represent a channel deposit stabilized by soil processes.

KNM-ER 1806 (A–E)

Associated weathered fragments of a robust mandible with poor bony contacts between the pieces A–D.

A–B: Fragments of the left (A) and right (B) sides of the mandibular body, each with partial roots of C–M_2 preserved and broken posteriorly behind M_2.

C–D: Fragments of the posterior portion of the right (C) and left (D) sides of the mandibular body, each with the roots of M_3 preserved and part of the ascending ramus.

E: Fragment of the right ascending ramus.

Table 2.

Discovery: M. G. Leakey, 1973.

Area: 130. Aerial photo 1752.

Stratigraphic position: Upper member, above major erosion surface, just below the base of the Okote Tuff. The specimen was within 3 m laterally of KNM-ER 1805 and at the same stratigraphic level (collection unit 4).

Environment of deposition: Channel, AVP. Reference Section 46.

References: K.F.R.P. Publ. Nos. 26, 49.

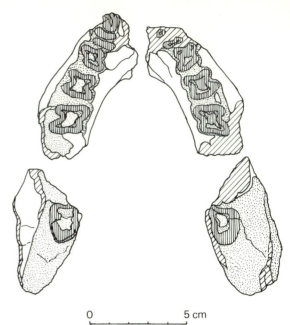

0   5 cm

FIG. 5.55. KNM-ER 1806, occlusal.

KNM-ER 1807

Distal two-thirds of the shaft of a right femur.

Discovery: K. Kimeu, 1973.

Area: 103. Aerial photo 1416.

Stratigraphic position: Upper member, *c.* 20–2 m above the top of the Koobi Fora Tuff (collection unit 5).

Environment of deposition: Large channel, ACP. Reference Section 47.

References: K.F.R.P. Publ. Nos. 26, 49.

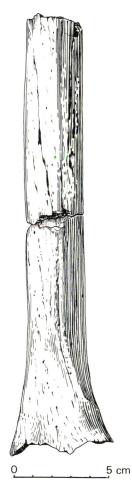

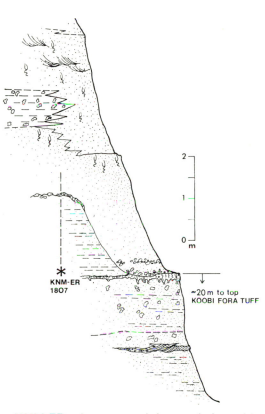

47. KNM-ER 1807 occurred in association with a large-scale channel deposit, from which it was probably derived.

FIG. 5.56. KNM-ER 1807, posterior.

KNM-ER 1808 (A–Z, AA, AB)

Associated parts of a skeleton of an adult individual which shows pathological disorders of the long bones.

A: Fragment of left side of the mandibular body with roots of M_2 and M_3.
B: Fragment of mandibular body with tooth roots.
C: Fragment of maxilla with roots of left premolar.
D: Right mandibular condyle.
E: Left lower canine.
F: Premolar crown.
G: Lower right molar crown, probably M_2. Mesiodistal length 13.6 mm, estimated buccolingual length 12.0 mm.
H: Upper right molar crown, probably M^2. Mesiodistal length 11.6 mm, estimated buccolingual length 13.4 mm.
I: Tooth fragments.
J: Right temporal fragment.
K: Left occipital fragment.
L: Frontal fragment.
M: Distal half of femur shaft.
N: Proximal fragment of right femur shaft and part of neck.
O: Proximal fragment of right femur shaft and part of the lesser trochanter.
P: Fragment of left femur shaft.
Q: Shaft of a long bone, possibly humerus.
R: Fragment of left ilium.
S: Fragment of right ilium.
T: Distal fragment of humerus.
U: Fragment of fibula.
V: Fragment of long bone, probably tibia.
W: Fragment of long bone, probably radius.
X: Fragment of long bone, probably radius.
Y: Fragment of long bone, probably ulna.
Z: Fragment of atlas vertebra.
AA: Small cranial fragments.
AB: Small postcranial fragments.

Sieving of the site has not been completed and further fragments may be recovered.

Discovery: K. Kimeu, 1973.
Area: 103. Aerial photo 1416.
Stratigraphic position: Upper member, above major erosion surface, 10–11 m below the base of the Koobi Fora Tuff (collection unit 4).
Environment of deposition: Delta margin, probably distributary or transgressive sand, ADP.
Reference: K.F.R.P. Publ. No. 26.

KNM-ER 1809

Shaft of a small right femur with a small part of the neck but lacking the greater and lesser trochanters and the distal end. Table 24.

0 _____ 5 cm

FIG. 5.57. KNM-ER 1809, posterior.

Discovery: K. Kimeu, 1973.
Area: 121. Aerial photo 1689.
Stratigraphic position: Upper member (provisional) (collection unit 4).
Environment of deposition: Delta margin, probably distributary channel.
References: K.F.R.P. Publ. Nos. 26, 49.

KNM-ER 1810

Proximal portion of a left tibia heavily abraded on the margins of the condyles. Table 25.

FIG. 5.58. KNM-ER 1810, anterior.

Discovery: M. Muluila, 1973.
Area: 123. Aerial photo 1580.
Stratigraphic position: Upper member (provisional) (collection unit 4).
Environment of deposition: Delta margin, probably transgressive sand.
References: K.F.R.P. Publ. Nos. 26, 49.

KNM-ER 1811 (A–B)

Weathered mandibular fragments.
A: Fragment of the left side of the body of a mandible with the roots of I_2–P_4 preserved. Table 2.
B: Fragment of the basal region of the mandibular body.

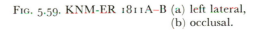

FIG. 5.59. KNM-ER 1811A–B (a) left lateral, (b) occlusal.

Discovery: R. E. Leakey, 1973.
Area: 123. Aerial photo 1580.
Stratigraphic position: Upper member (provisional) (collection unit 4).
Environment of deposition: Delta margin, probably distributary channel. Reference Section 48.
References: K.F.R.P. Publ. Nos. 26, 49.

48. The section at the site of KNM-ER 1811 includes mollusc-bearing coarse to medium sands with mudclasts and sandy silt deposits. The sands represent a distributary on a deltaic plain. KNM-ER 1811 is probably derived from the channel deposits.

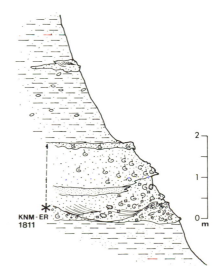

KNM-ER 1812 (A–D)

A: Anterior portion of the right side of a mandibular body with the partial roots of I_1–P_3.

B: Crown of a left I_2.

C: Crown of a left molar, probably M_3. Mesiodistal length 14.4 mm, buccolingual breadth 12.5 mm.

D: Head of a radius broken distally across the neck.

Tables 12, 23.

This specimen was found close to the site from which KNM-ER 1502 was recovered and it may represent parts of the same individual.

Discovery: W. Mangao, 1973.

Area: 123. Aerial photo 1581.

Stratigraphic position: Upper member (provisional) (collection unit 4).

Environment of deposition: Delta margin. Reference Section 37.

References: K.F.R.P. Publ. Nos. 26, 49.

KNM-ER 1813 (A–B)

A: Relatively complete cranium lacking part of the left side of the face, much of the sphenoid and part of the left occipital. The dentition is incomplete: on the left side $\underline{C}$–M^3 are preserved in good condition, while only the root tip of I^1 and the empty alveolus of I^2 remain. On the right side I^2, $\underline{C}$ and M^3 are in good condition, while only the broken crowns of I^1,M^1, and M^2 and the roots of P^3 and P^4 remain.

The skull is relatively small and lightly built, with an estimated endocranial volume of 505–510 cm^3 (R. Holloway, pers. comm.). The supraorbital tori are not particularly salient, and the glabella is not prominent. There is a slight postglabella sulcus and the frontal bone then rises gently in the midline in a convex curve to bregma. The postorbital constriction is moderate and the temporal lines remain far apart and can be traced posteriorly. The nuchal crests are weak, and the mastoid process small. Tables 1, 3, 4, 5, 6, 7, 8, 9, 10.

B: Cranial fragments.

Discovery: K. Kimeu, 1973.

Area: 123. Aerial photo 1580.

Stratigraphic position: *In situ*. Upper member (provisional) (collection unit 4).

Environment of deposition: Delta margin, offshore or interdistributary. Reference Section 49.

References: K.F.R.P. Publ. Nos. 26, 49.

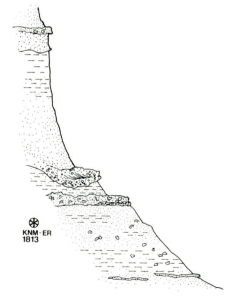

49. KNM-ER 1813 occurred *in situ* in silty fine-grained sands associated with typical delta margin deposits. $CaCO_3$ nodules within the unit indicate periodic subaerial exposure. The overall environment was alluvial, coastal, or deltaic plain, and KNM-ER 1813 was buried either by floodplain or shallow, offshore sedimentation.

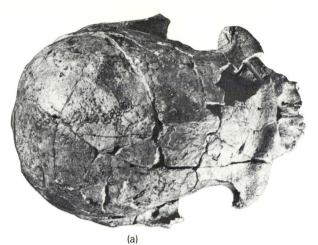

(a)

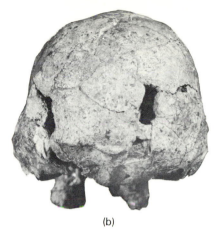

(b)

(c)

(d)

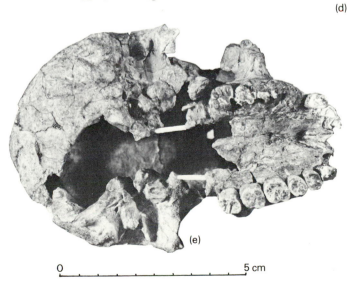

(e)

0   5 cm

PLATE 26. KNM-ER 1813 (a) superior, (b) posterior, (c) right lateral, (d) frontal, (e) inferior.

163

KNM-ER 1814 (A–C)

Associated elements of the lower dentition (originally published as upper dentition) encrusted in matrix.

A: Crowns of the right P_3 and P_4 and the mesial half of M_1.

B: Distal fragment of the crown of M_1, the cracked and expanded crown of M_2, and the mesial portion of the crown of M_3.

C: Worn incisor crown.

Tables 14, 15, 16.

Discovery: N. Mutiwa, 1973.

Area: 127. Aerial photo 1739.

Stratigraphic position: Upper member, above major erosion surface (collection unit 4).

Environment of deposition: Flood plain, AVP.

Reference: K.F.R.P. Publ. No. 26.

KNM-ER 1816 (A–F)

Weathered fragments of the mandibular body of an immature individual. The specimen was found *in situ* but in very poor condition with the bone almost reduced to powder. No morphological features of the bone were discernable and so it was decided to extract the preserved tooth crowns and germs. Although also badly cracked and weathered, these provide some information.

A: Fragment of the left side of the mandibular body with P_3, dM_2, and M_1.

B: Roots of left M_1.

C: Germ of left M_2.

D: Germ of left P_4.

E: Fragment of the right side of the mandibular body with a tooth which is probably M_1.

F: Germ of right P_4.

The teeth are all distorted by cracks: Tables 14, 15, 16, 17.

Discovery: B. A. Wood, 1973.

Area: 6A. Aerial photo 1398.

Stratigraphic position: *In situ*. Ileret Member, *c.* 8 m below the base of the Lower/Middle Tuff. From the lower slope of the site from which KNM-ER 801, 802, etc. were recovered (collection unit 4).

Environment of deposition: Distributary channel, ACP. Reference Section 11.

Reference: K.F.R.P. Publ. Nos. 26, 49.

KNM-ER 1817

Very severely weathered fragment of the left side of a mandibular body with some tooth roots. No details can be discerned.

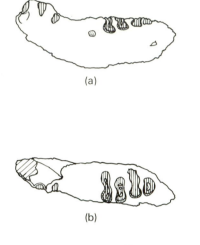

(a)

(b)

0   5 cm

FIG. 5.60. KNM-ER 1817 (a) left lateral, (b) occlusal.

Discovery: A. Kilonzo, 1973.

Area: 1. Aerial photo 1467.

Stratigraphic position: Ileret Member, just below the base of the Lower/Middle Tuff (collection unit 4).

Environment of deposition: Floodplain, ACP.

Reference: K.F.R.P. Publ. No. 26.

KNM-ER 1818

Weathered left I^1. Table 3.

Discovery: M. Muluila, 1973.

Area: 6A. Aerial photo 1398.

Stratigraphic position: Ileret Member, *c.* 10 m below the Lower/Middle Tuff. Found within 30 m laterally of the site from which KNM-ER 801, 802, etc. were recovered (see Reference Section 11) (collection unit 4).

Reference: K.F.R.P. Publ. No. 26.

KNM-ER 1819

Broken left M_3 crown. Table 18.

Discovery: B. Ngeneo, 1973.

Area: 3. Aerial photo 1467.

Stratigraphic position: Ileret Member, probably below the Lower/Middle Tuff (collection unit 4).

Reference: K.F.R.P. Publ. No. 26.

KNM-ER 1820

Fragment of the left side of the body of a mandible of an immature individual with the crowns of dM_2 and M_1 and the roots of dM_1, $d\bar{C}$, and dI_2 preserved. The bone is cracked and on the outer surface the cracks are large and matrix-filled. Surface bone is missing in places, exposing the germ of P_3. The I_1 germ is exposed in its crypt at the anterior break. Tables 16, 20.

The M_1 crown was not discovered until 1975, subsequent to the publication of a description of this specimen (K.F.R.P. Publ. No. 49).

Discovery: K. Kimeu, 1973.
Area: 103. Aerial photo 1416.
Stratigraphic position: Upper member, below the Koobi Fora Tuff (collection unit 4).
Environment of deposition: ADP.
References: K.F.R.P Publ. Nos. 26, 49.

(b)

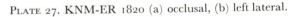

(a)

0   5 cm

PLATE 27. KNM-ER 1820 (a) occlusal, (b) left lateral.

KNM-ER 1821

Parietal fragment with sutural markings on two of its borders.
Discovery: N. Mutiwa, 1973.
Area: 123. Aerial photo 1581.
Stratigraphic position: Upper member (provisional) (collection unit 4).
Reference: Unpublished.

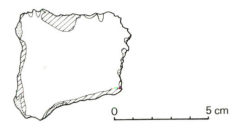

0   5 cm

FIG. 5.61. KNM-ER 1821, external.

KNM-ER 1822

Fragment of the midshaft region of a femur (probably right). It was found at the same locality as KNM-ER 1503, 1504, and 1505. Probably these specimens represent parts of a single individual.
Discovery: K. Kimeu, 1973.
Area: 123. Aerial photo 1581.
Stratigraphic position: Upper member (provisional) (collection unit 4). Reference Section 38.
Reference: K.F.R.P. Publ. No. 49.

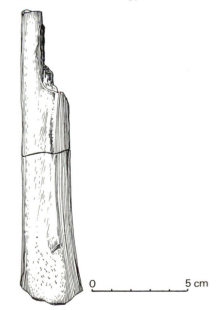

0   5 cm

FIG. 5.62. KNM-ER 1822, posterior.

KNM-ER 1823, 1824, 1825

KNM-ER 1823
Proximal portion of a metatarsal.

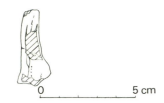

FIG. 5.63. KNM-ER 1823.

KNM-ER 1824
Distal articular surface of a right humerus.

FIG. 5.64. KNM-ER 1824, distal.

KNM-ER 1825
Fragment of an atlas vertebra.

(a)　　　　　　　　(b)

FIG. 5.65. KNM-ER 1825 (a) inferior, (b) superior.

These specimens were all recovered from the site of KNM-ER 801. They are considered as separate individuals but they may be part of a single individual or be associated with any of the other specimens from this site: KNM-ER 801, 802, 1170, 1171, 1464, 1816.
Discovery: While sieving for fragments of KNM-ER 801, 1971.
Area: 6A. Aerial photo 1398.
Stratigraphic position: Ileret Member, *c.* 6–7 m below the Lower/Middle Tuff (collection unit 4).
Environment of deposition: Distributary channel, Reference Section 11.
Reference: K.F.R.P. Publ. No. 49 (KNM-ER 1823).

KNM-ER 2592 (A–B)

A: Fragment of parietal with sutural markings on two of its borders.
B: Cranial fragment.

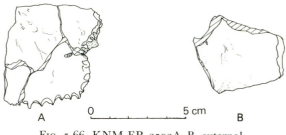

FIG. 5.66. KNM-ER 2592A–B, external.

Discovery: M. Muluila, 1974.
Area: 6. Aerial photo 1398.
Stratigraphic position: Ileret Member, probably below the Lower/Middle Tuff (collection unit 4).
Reference: K.F.R.P. Publ. No. 78.

KNM-ER 2593

Tooth fragment.
Discovery: N. Mutiwa, 1974.
Area: 6. Aerial photo 1398.
Stratigraphic position: Ileret Member, just in or above the Lower/Middle Tuff (collection unit 5).
Reference: K.F.R.P. Publ. No. 78.

KNM-ER 2595

Parietal fragment with sutural markings on two of its borders.

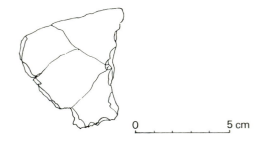

FIG. 5.67. KNM-ER 2595, external.

Discovery: B. Ngeneo, 1974.
Area: 1A. Aerial photo 1397.
Stratigraphic position: Ileret Member, probably below the Lower/Middle Tuff (collection unit 4).
Reference: K.F.R.P. Publ. No. 78.

KNM-ER 2596

Distal end of a left tibia expanded by several cracks.

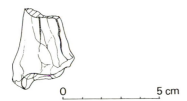

0   5 cm

FIG. 5.68. KNM-ER 2596, anterior.

Discovery: B. Ngeneo, 1974.
Area: 15. Aerial photo 1523.
Stratigraphic position: Approximately at the level of 15/T IV (collection unit 4).
Reference: K.F.R.P. Publ. No. 78.

KNM-ER 2597

Lower molar (either M_2 or M_3), weathered and cracked.
Discovery: K. Kimeu, 1974.
Area: 15. Aerial photo 1523.
Stratigraphic position: Approximately at the level of 15/T IV (collection unit 4).
Reference: K.F.R.P. Publ. No. 78.

KNM-ER 2598

Fragment of occipital with markings of the lambdoid suture on the superior margin. The bone is remarkably thickened and sharply angled.

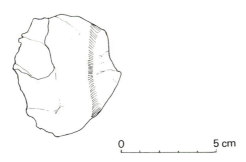

0   5 cm

FIG. 5.69. KNM-ER 2598, external.

Discovery: N. Mutiwa, 1974.
Area: 15. Aerial photo 1523.
Stratigraphic position: Approximately at the level of 15/T IV (collection unit 4).
Reference: K.F.R.P. Publ. No. 78.

KNM-ER 2599

Lingual portion of a left P_4.
Discovery: M. Muluila, 1974.
Area: 15. Aerial photo 1523.
Stratigraphic position: Approximately at the level of 15/T IV (collection unit 4).
Reference: K.F.R.P. Publ. No. 78.

KNM-ER 2600

Partial lower molar.
Discovery: M. Mbithi, 1974.
Area: 130. Aerial photo 1752.
Stratigraphic position: Lower member, below 130/T I (collection unit 3).
Reference: K.F.R.P. Publ. No. 78.

KNM-ER 2601

Crown of a right lower molar.
Discovery: B. Ngeneo, 1974.
Area: 130. Aerial photo 1752.
Stratigraphic position: Lower member, below 130/T I (collection unit 3).
Reference: K.F.R.P. Publ. No. 78.

KNM-ER 2602 (A–G)

Isolated cranial fragments.

A: Fragment of occipital which spans the midline; the left superior portion includes part of the lambdoid suture and a portion of the left parietal. Parts of the right and left nuchal crests are also shown.

B: Cranial fragment including some of the left and right parietal and sagittal crest.

C: Parietal fragment with part of the sagittal crest on the medial border.

D–G: Cranial fragments.

Discovery: W. Mangao, 1974.
Area: 117. Aerial photo 1455.
Stratigraphic position: Lower member, just above 117/T III (collection unit 2).
Reference: K.F.R.P. Publ. No. 78.

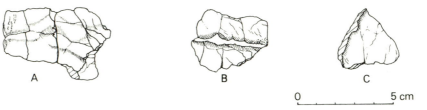

Fig. 5.70. KNM-ER 2602A–C, external.

KNM-ER 2603, 2604, 2605, 2606

Isolated tooth fragments.
Discovery: KNM-ER 2603, K. Kimeu, 1974. KNM-ER 2604, M. Muluila, 1974. KNM-ER 2605, M. G. Leakey, 1974. KNM-ER 2606, Judy Harris, 1974.
Area: 117. Aerial photo 1530.
Stratigraphic position: Lower member, all below 117/T III except KNM-ER 2604 which is from just above (collection unit 2).
Reference: K.F.R.P. Publ. No. 78.

KNM-ER 2607

Fragment of enamel from the lingual aspect of a molar tooth (originally published as KNM-ER 1480B).
Discovery: J. M. Harris and A. K. Behrensmeyer, 1972.
Area: 105. Aerial photo 1590.
Stratigraphic position: Upper member, post-KBS erosion surface (collection unit 4).
Environment of deposition: Channel, AVP. Reference Section 6.
Reference: K.F.R.P. Publ. No. 28.

KNM-ER 3230

Robust mandibular body with complete dentition, discovered *in situ* during the excavation of an archaeological site. The bone is in poor condition and is missing posteriorly and from the anterior alveoli. Most of the tooth crowns are complete. The mandible was originally very distorted with the anterior teeth displaced. However, since the incisor roots are preserved, it has been possible to replace these teeth fairly accurately in their original position. The cheek teeth are large and the anterior teeth small. Tables 11, 12, 13, 14, 15, 16, 17, 18.
Discovery: K. Kitibi, 1974, in archaeological site excavated by J. W. K. Harris.
Area: 131. Archaeological site FxJj 20E. Aerial photo 1750.
Stratigraphic position: *In situ*. Upper member, within the Okote Tuff. The specimen was located 10-15 cm stratigraphically above the main archaeological horizon containing artefacts of the Karari Industry (collection unit 5).
Environment of deposition: Floodplain, AVP.
Reference: K.F.R.P. Publ. No. 78.

PLATE 28. KNM-ER 3230 (a) occlusal, (b) right lateral.

KNM-ER 3737 (A–B)

Isolated lower teeth.
A: Partial crown of right M₃.
B: Broken crown of right M₁.
These teeth were originally assigned to KNM-ER 802 as a left M₃ and a right M¹. Subsequent reassessment has, however, shown that more than one individual was represented.
Discovery: While sieving for fragments of KNM-ER 801, 1971.
Area: 6A. Aerial photo 1398.
Stratigraphic position: Ileret Member, *c.* 6–7 m below the base of the Lower/Middle Tuff (collection unit 4).
Environment of deposition: Distributary channel. Reference Section 11.
References: K.F.R.P. Publ. Nos. 12, 23 (as KNM-ER 802).

169

LITHOLOGY

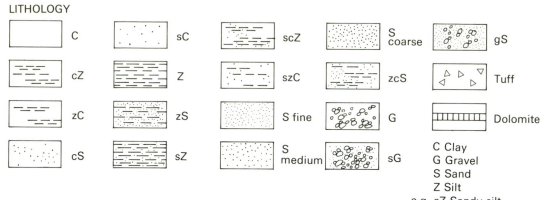

C Clay
G Gravel
S Sand
Z Silt
e.g. sZ Sandy silt

SEDIMENTARY STRUCTURES

CONTACTS

FOSSILS

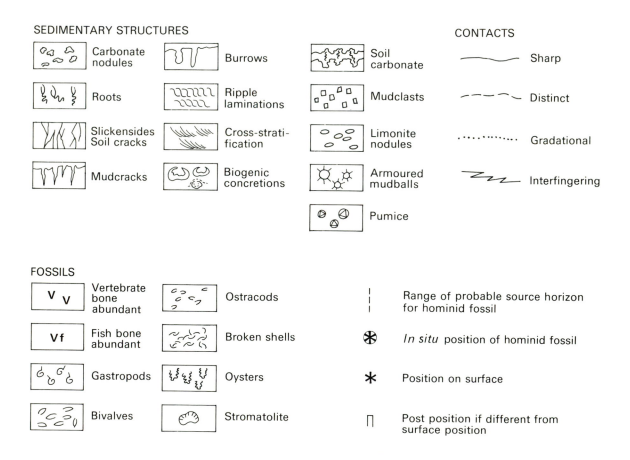

Key to the Reference Sections

TABLES

Abbreviations used in Tables 5.1–30

M/D, Mesiodistal
B/L, Buccolingual
L/L, Labiolingual
Rt, Lt, Right, Left
* Possible distortion of measurement caused by weathering, expansion cracks, or part missing.
( ) Estimated measurement.

KFRP Publ. No., Koobi Fora Research Project publication no.

TABLE 5.1. *Measurements (mm) of the cranium*

KNM-ER No.	405	406	407	732	1470	1805	1813
Length (glabella-opisthocranion)	—	163†	—	—	(170)	—	161†
Bregma-opisthocranion	—	(117)†	—	—	(124)†	108†	111†
Minimum frontal breadth	—	62·0	—	(60)	(80)	(88)	71
Maximum breadth across supra-mastoid crests	—	(140)	(118)	—	—	(130)	113·0
Length of palate (staphylion-orale)	67·0	(69)	—	—	—	—	(56)†
Maximum length of orbit	—	36·0	—	30·0	(39)	—	30·0
Maximum breadth of orbit	—	36·5	—	37·0	(40)	—	30·0
Interorbital breadth	—	27·0†	—	(21)	—	(38)	22·0
Maximum width of pyriform aperture	34·0	28·6†	—	—	(27)	(28)	21·5
Height at midline of pyriform aperture	—	(33)†	—	—	(36)	(34)	(27)
KFRP Publ. No.	10	10	49	23	29	49	49

† Not previously published.

TABLE 5.2A. *Mandibular measurements (mm): body breadth*

Measurements represent a parallel breadth taken perpendicular to the long axis of the corpus (Fig. 5.71(a)) at the points indicated (Fig. 5.71(b)). Measurements which would include the ascending ramus are not given. These measurements were taken by T. White and are previously unpublished.

KNM-ER No.	P₃	P₃/P₄	P₄	P₄/M₁	M₁	M₁/M₂	M₂	M₂/M₃	M₃
403	—	—	—	28·8(+1)	29·5(+1)	30·8(+1)	30·8(+1)	32·1(+1)	—
404	—	—	—	—	—	30(±2)	31(±2)	—	—
725	—	—	26·2(±1)	26·9(±1)	27·0(±1)	29·0(±1)	30·9(±1)	32·4(±1)	—
726	—	—	—	30·0(±1)	29·8(±1)	28·7(±1)	29·6(±1)	32·3(±1)	—
727	—	—	—	21(+3)	22(+3)	23(+3)	—	—	—
728	—	—	—	—	24(+3)	24(+3)	26(+3)	—	—
729A Rt	—	—	—	—	—	—	28·8	29·8	—
Lt	27·6	28·0	28·3	28·2	26·9	28·3(−1)	—	—	—
730 Rt	19·8	—	—	—	—	—	—	—	—
Lt	20·1	19·2	19·1	—	18·9	18·5	18·6	18·2	18·3
731	17·5(+1)	—	—	—	—	—	—	—	—
733A	—	—	24(+2)	26(+2)	26(+2)	27(+2)	—	—	—
801A	—	—	27·6(±1)	26·6(±1)	26·7(±1)	26·4(±1)	29·0(±1)	—	—
805A	—	—	—	—	27·2(±1)	29(±2)	31·0(±1)	—	—
810A	—	—	—	23·1	23·2	23·8	27·4	—	—
817	16·8(+1)	16·6(+1)	16·6(+1)	16·2(+1)	—	—	—	—	—
818	31(−2)	—	32(−2)	35(−2)	35(−2)	35(−2)	35(±2)	—	—
820 Rt	14·6	14·5	14·9	14·9	16·2	—	—	—	—
Lt	15·4	14·5	14·2	15·1	16·0	—	—	—	—
992A Rt	20·4	20·4	—	20·1	20·0	20·7	21·5	—	—
992B Lt	—	20·9	20·3	19·6	19·8	18·5	19·9	—	—
1468	—	—	—	—	—	31(+2)	—	—	—
1469	29(−2)	28(−2)	28(−2)	29(−3)	30(−3)	32(−3)	—	—	—
1477 Rt	15·6(+1)	16·7	17·9	18·7	—	—	—	—	—
Lt	—	—	18·3	19·6	—	—	—	—	—
1482	20·9	20·4	20·2	19·1(+1)	19·3(+1)	20(+2)	21(+2)	—	—
1483	—	—	—	22·8	22·2	23·6	—	—	—
1501	—	—	—	—	—	—	17(±3)	—	—
1502	—	—	—	15·4(+1)	16·3	—	—	—	—
1507	—	—	15·3(+1)	16·2(+1)	18·3(+1)	—	—	—	—
1802	20·1	19·6	18·9	18·8	20·8	23·8	—	—	—
1803	—	—	24·4(±1)	25·2(±1)	—	—	—	—	—
1805	22·3	22·7	21·9	21·8	20·8(+1)	20·5(+1)	—	—	—
1806 Rt	—	—	—	—	27·4	28·4	—	—	—
Lt	27·6(±1)	27·5(±1)	27·4(±1)	27·5(±1)	28·0(±1)	—	—	—	—

(±) the estimated correction of the given measurement which is affected by breakage or distortion. The estimated correction is with 1 S.D.

(+) the estimated correction of the given minimum measurement.

(−) the estimated correction of the given measurement which includes matrix or expansion cracks.

KNM-ER 820, 1477, 1507: P₃ = dM₁, and P₄ = dM₂.

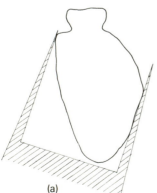

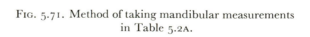

FIG. 5.71. Method of taking mandibular measurements in Table 5.2A.

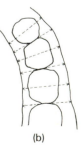

(a)

(b)

172

TABLE 5.2B. *Mandibular measurements (mm): minimum body height*

Measurements represent the minimum distance from the basal contour to the lateral alveolar margin at each crown or at each interproximal contact as indicated (Fig. 5.72(a), (b)). Measurements were taken perpendicular to the alveolar line defined by P_3 to M_3 or by analogous dental elements of younger individuals.

KNM-ER No.	P_3	P_3/P_4	P_4	P_4/M_1	M_1	M_1/M_2	M_2	M_2/M_3	M_3
403	—	—	—	—	47(+2)	47·5(+1)	45(+2)	45·0(+2)	—
404	—	—	—	—	—	—	50(±2)	47(±2)	47(±2)
725	—	—	—	40(±3)	40(±3)	42(±4)	36(±2)	36(±2)	33(±2)
726	—	—	—	46(±2)	45·8(+1)	45(±2)	43(+2)	43(+2)	41(+2)
727	—	—	—	34(+3)	34(+3)	35(+3)	35(+3)	–	—
728	—	—	—	—	—	37(+4)	37(+4)	—	—
729A Rt	50·3	49·6(+1)	49·3	49·1	44·8(±1)	44·5(+1)	45·6	44·4	47·4
Lt	49·1(±1)	48·7(+1)	—	—	—	—	32·8(R)	31·0(R)	31·9
730	31·4(R)								
733A	—	41(+2)	—	—	39(+3)	—			
801A	—	—	—	—	40(+3)	41(+2)	39·8(+1)	40·3(+1)	38·8(+1)
805A	—	—	—	—	38·6(+1)	39·6(+1)	38(±3)		
810A	—	44·4(±1)	40·3(+1)	41·6(+1)	40·6(+1)	38·7(+1)	37·0(+1)	37·5(±1)	38·8(±1)
812	22(+2)	—	—						
817	—	—	—	30·3(+1)	—	—	—	—	—
818	57(±2)	58(±2)	55(±2)	54(±2)	53(±2)	51(±2)	51(±2)	—	—
820 Rt	22·2	21·3	21·0	19·8	18·4	—	—	—	—
Lt	22·6	23·0	21·8	20·0	18·5	—	—	—	—
992A Rt	31·6(±1)	31·2(±1)	—	—	—	32·1	33·1	34·0	33·1(+1)
992B Lt			31·8(±1)	31·1	31·6	31·0	31·6	32·5	
1468	—	53(±2)	50(±2)	49(±3)	47(±3)	45(±3)	44(±2)	44(±2)	43·2(±1)
1469	46(±2)	47(±2)	—	45(±2)	43(±2)	42(±2)	—	—	41(±2)
1477A Rt	24·2	23·0	21·2	19·5	—	—	—	—	—
Lt	—	21·7	19·7	18·3	—	—	—	—	—
1482	—	36·1(±1)	32·7	34·1	32·6	30·8(+1)	28·1(+1)	—	28·5
1483	—	38·8	37·0	37·8	37·1	37·2	—	—	—
1502	—	—	—	28·2	27·4	26·0	—	—	—
1506	—	—	—	—	33·7(±1)	32·0	30·5	28·8	—
1507	27·2(+1)	26·7(+1)	22·9(+1)	21·1(+1)	18·9(+1)	—	—	—	—
1802	38(+3)	38·7(+1)	37·2	37·1(+1)	35(±2)	—	—	—	—
1803	—	—	—	—	41(±2)	—	—	—	—
1805	—	—	—	—	28·6(+1)	28·3(±1)	28·3(+1)	—	—
1806 Rt	—	—	—	46(±2)	—	—	—	—	—
Lt	—	—	—	47·0(±1)	—	—	—	—	—
1811	32·8(±1)	—	—	—	—	—	—	—	—

(±), (+), (−) as for Table 5.2A.
KNM-ER 820, 1477, 1507: $P^3 = dM^1$ and $P^4 = dM^2$.
(R) major alveolar resorption evident.

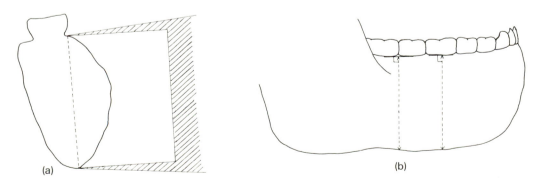

FIG. 5.72. Method of taking mandibular measurements in Table 5.2B.

TABLE 5.3.
Measurements (mm) of upper central incisor

KNM-ER No.	M/D	L/L	KFRP Publ. No.
803I	10·2	7·9	27
1590B	11·8*	8·1*	49
1805B	(12·0)	(6·5)	49
1813	9·0 max.	—	49
1818	9·0*	6·0*	—

TABLE 5.5.
Measurements (mm) of upper canine

KNM-ER No.	M/D	L/L	KFRP Publ. No.
803H	9·3	8·5	27
816A	8·4	9·6	—
1171I	(12·0)	—	23
1590C Lt	11·3	12·5	49
1590D Rt	11·4	12·2	
1805B Lt	8·3*	10·0*	49
Rt	8·2	10·0	
1813A Lt	8·0	8·4	49
Rt	8·2	8·4	

TABLE 5.4.
Measurements (mm) of upper lateral incisor

KNM-ER No.	M/D	L/L	KFRP Publ. No.
808D	7·9	7·7	20
998	7·3	6·2	—
1171A	6·9*	6·5*	—
1515	8·7	9·0	—
1805B Rt	5·6*	5·5*	49
Lt	5·6*	5·5*	
1813A	6·5	5·8	49

TABLE 5.6.
Measurements (mm) of upper third premolar

KNM-ER No.	M/D	B/L	KFRP Publ. No.
802I	11·7	14·0	23
808C	8·7*	12·5	20
1506C	8·2	11·7	49
1590G Lt	10·2	13·6	49
1590H Rt	10·1*	13·3	
1804	10·8	16·0	49
1805B Lt	7·7	(12·4)	49
Rt	(7·3)	(12·4)	
1813A	8·0	11·1	49

TABLE 5.7.
Measurements (mm) of upper fourth premolar

KNM-ER No.	M/D	B/L	KFRP Publ. No.
405	(10·8)	—	10
1506B	8·3	12·2	49
1590I Lt	10·5	13·6	49
1590J Rt	10·1*	14·0*	
1804	11·3	17·4	49
1805B	8·0	11·8*	49
1813A	9·0	11·3	49

TABLE 5.9.
Measurements (mm) of upper second molar

KNM-ER No.	M/D	B/L	KFRP Publ. No.
405	(15·9)	—	10
807A	—	(14)	20
1171G Lt	17·0*	17·3*	23
1171H Rt	18·1	17·5	
1590M	13·9	16·8	49
1804	15·5	18·2	49
1805B Lt	12·6	(13·5)	49
Rt	(13·2)	(14·5)	
1813A	12·2	13·6	49

TABLE 5.8.
Measurements (mm) of upper first molar

KNM-ER No.	M/D	B/L	KFRP Publ. No.
405	(14·3)	—	10
733E	15·3*	16·5*	23
807B	(13·0)	14·0*	—
808G	(13·2)	13·0	20
1590K Lt	13·5*	14·0*	49
1590L Rt	13·3*	13·8*	
1804	13·8	15·8	49
1805B Lt	12·6*	13·2	49
Rt	12·5*	13·2*	
1813A	12·2	12·5	49

TABLE 5.10.
Measurements (mm) of upper third molar

KNM-ER No.	M/D	B/L	KFRP Publ. No.
405	(14·2)	—	10
807A	11·0	13·0	20
1805B Lt	12·9	13·8	49
Rt	13·1	13·9	
1813A Lt	11·5	13·0	49
Rt	11·7	13·5	

TABLE 5.11.
Measurements (mm) of lower central incisor

KNM-ER No.	M/D	L/L	KFRP Publ. No.
729E Rt	—	(7·5)	—
729F Lt	—	(7·5)	—
820 Rt	6·1	6·4	20
Lt	6·0	6·2	
1477B	5·9	7·1	49
3230 Lt	5·1	6·5	78
Rt	5·1	6·2	

TABLE 5.13.
Measurements (mm) of lower canine

KNM-ER No.	M/D	L/L	KFRP Publ. No.
729G Lt	(8·5)	(10·0)	—
992B Lt	9·0	8·1	20
992A Rt	9·3	9·3	
1477C	7·9	7·1	49
3230 Lt	7·8	9·2	78
Rt	7·5	9·1	

TABLE 5.12.
Measurements (mm) of lower lateral incisor

KNM-ER No.	M/D	L/L	KFRP Publ. No.
801D	6·1	6·6	23
820 Lt	7·3	6·9	20
Rt	7·5	6·7	
1812B	7·0	6·4	49
3230 Lt	6·9	—	78
Rt	6·3	8·0	

TABLE 5.14.
Measurements (mm) of lower third premolar

KNM-ER No.	M/D	B/L	KFRP Publ. No.
403	(10·2)	—	10
729A	12·0	13·0	11
806F	9·2*	10·8	20
806E	8·6*	11·2	
818	(13·0)	—	23
992B Lt	9·5	11·1	20
992A Rt	9·2	11·2	
1477D	11·5*	11·3*	49
1482A	(8·4)	—	30
1802A	10·4*	12·1*	49
1814A	9·7*	11·3*	—
1816A	11·8	12·6*	49
3230 Lt	11·5	14·6*	78
Rt	11·0	14·1*	

TABLE 5.15.
Measurements (mm) of lower fourth premolar

KNM-ER No.	M/D	B/L	KFRP Publ. No.
403	(12·4)	—	10
729A Lt	14·0	15·0*	11
Rt	14·0	16·0*	
802B Lt	13·5*	14·0*	23
802A Rt	13·7	14·5	
818	14·5*	(16·0)	23
992B Lt	8·4	11·1	20
992A Rt	8·6	11·1	
1171B	(15·5)	(15·8)	23
1482A Lt	9·3*	12·2*	30
Rt	—	12·3*	
1801	9·3*	(11)	49
1802A Lt	11·4*	12·0*	49
Rt	11·3	12·1	
1814A	9·7*	11·4*	—
1816D Lt	14·0*	15·6*	49
1816F Rt	13·0*	14·4*	
3230 Lt	13·8	—	78
Rt	14·0	16·9	

TABLE 5.16.
Measurements (mm) of lower first molar

KNM-ER No.	M/D	B/L	KFRP Publ. No.
403	(15·0)	—	10
729A	15·5*	15·5*	11
730	>11·7*	11·7*	6
802C	(17·0)	(16·0)	23
806C	13·7	12·6	20
818	17·2*	—	23
820 Lt	12·3	10·7	20
Rt	12·2	10·8	
992B Lt	12·0	10·9	20
992A Rt	11·9	10·7	
1171D	(18·5)	—	23
1477A Lt	(15·0)	(12·0)	49
Rt	(15·0)	(12·0)	
1502	13·4*	11·4*	28
1506A	13·7	12·5	49
1507	13·3*	11·1*	28
1509C	14·5	14·3	—
1801	12·4*	13·3*	49
1802A Lt	14·7*	13·3*	49
Rt	14·6	13·2	
1814A	—	12·8*	—
1816A	16·6	13·8	49
1820	16·1	—	—
3230 Lt	(17·0)	—	78
Rt	16·6	15·4	

TABLE 5.17.

Measurements (mm) of lower second molar

KNM-ER No.	M/D	B/L	KFRP Publ. No.
403	(16·0)	—	10
404	< 19·0*	—	10
729A Lt	19·5*	18·0*	11
Rt	18·5	18·0	
730	> 12·0*	> 11·6*	6
801A	18·9*	16·5*	23
802D	(17·0)	(16·0)	23
806B	14·3	13·1	20
818	19·7*	(18·0)	23
992B Lt	13·0	12·3	20
992A Rt	13·2	12·5	
1171E Lt	19·0*	16·8*	23
1171F Rt	(19·5)	(16·5)	—
1482A	(14·9)	(14)	30
1483E	—	< 13	28
1506A	14·0	13·2	49
1509B	16·0*	13·0	—
1801	(13)	—	49
1802A Lt	16·6*	14·1*	49
Rt	16·5	14·3	
1805C	13·8	12·8	49
1816C	17·3*	16·2	49
3230 Lt	(20·0)	—	78
Rt	20·1	18·5	

TABLE 5.18.

Measurements (mm) of lower third molar

KNM-ER No.	M/D	B/L	KFRP Publ. No.
404	22·0*	—	10
729A Lt	20·0	19·0	11
Rt	22·0	19·0	
730	13·0	11·5	6
733A	(19·0)	—	23
801A	19·7*	15·9*	—
802F	18·7	16·3	23
806A Lt	14·7	12·1	20
806D Rt	14·0	12·2	
810B	17·5	15·6	23
818	(22·0)	(18·0)	23
992B Lt	12·8	12·3	20
992A Rt	13·0	12·1	
1462	14·5*	13·6*	28
1467	18·8*	15·5*	49
1480	15·3*	12·5*	28
1482A	—	14·6*	30
1509A	19·2*	15·7*	—
1801	16·5*	14·5*	—
1805C	14·4	12·2*	49
1819	21·5*	—	—
3230 Lt	20·5	16·2	78
Rt	21·2	16·9	

TABLE 5.19.
Measurements (mm) of upper deciduous central incisor, canine and molars

Tooth	KNM-ER No.	M/D	B/L	KFRP Publ. No.
dI^1	808A Rt	5·0	4·8	20
	808B Lt	5·7	4·9	
dC̱	1590E	7·1*	6·6*	49
dM^1	808H	9·2*	—	—
dM^2	1590F	11·4*	11·5*	49

TABLE 5.20.
Measurements (mm) of lower deciduous canine and molars

Tooth	KNM-ER No.	M/D	B/L	KFRP Publ. No.
dC̱	1477A	6·0	5·8	49
dM$_1$	820 Lt	9·0	7·9	20
	Rt	9·1	7·7	
dM$_1$	1477A Lt	11·0	8·9*	49
	Rt	11·0	9·2	
dM$_1$	1507	7·8	6·8*	28
dM$_2$	820 Lt	10·7	9·4	20
	Rt	11·0	9·4	
dM$_2$	1477A Lt	13·7*	12·3	49
	Rt	13·8	11·7	
dM$_2$	1507	11·3	9·1*	28
dM$_2$	1820	13·6	12·0	49

TABLE 5.21.
Measurements (mm) of the humerus

KNM-ER No.	739	1473	1504
Diameter of shaft			
(1) at m. lattissimus dorsi			
insertion transverse	29·5	—	—
antre/postre	31·0	—	—
(2) at spiral groove			
transverse	27·0	—	—
antre/postre	25·0	—	—
(3) at 50 mm above most distal point on trochlear margin			
transverse	38·5	—	30·5†
antre/postre	18·0	—	17·5†
Total biepicondylar width	71·5	—	60·0
Total condylar width	48·5	—	39·5†
Trochlear width	25·0	—	20·0†
Max. capitulum diameter	25·7	—	20·0†
Max. head diameter	—	43·3	—
KFRP Publ. No.	11	49	49

† Not previously published.

TABLE 5.22.
Measurements (mm) of the ulna.

KNM-ER No.	803C	1500F
Olecranon breadth	—	20·5*
Minimum diameter of trochlear surface	—	17·8*
Transverse diameter distal to coronoid tubercle	18·1	—
Antre/postre diameter distal to coronoid tubercle	20·8*	—
KFRP Publ. No.	27	49

TABLE 5.23.
Measurements (mm) of the radius

KNM-ER No.	1500E	1812D
Diameter of head	20·0*	18·5
KFRP Publ. No.	49	49

TABLE 5.24. *Measurements (mm) of the femur*

KNM-ER No.	736	737	738	803A	815	993	999	1463	1465	1472	1475	1481	1500D	1503	1505A	1809
Diameter of shaft																
(1) 0–20 mm below the lesser trochanter																
antre/postre	30·0*	27·1	22·5*	25·5*	19·6*†	25·5*	34·8*	23·5*	26·8*	22·0*	—	23·0	—	22·5*	17·2*	21·8*
med./lat.	40·0*	39·3	26·5*	23·6*	27·2*†	32·4*†	40·7*	28·0*	29·8*	32·0*	—	30·8	—	31·2*	—	27·4*
(2) Approx. at mid-shaft																
antre/postre	—	27·4	—	28·2*	—	27·1*	37·5*	23·0*	—	—	—	22·5*	—	—	—	24·5
med./lat.	—	32·6	—	32·1*	—	28·2*	24·4*	23·4*	—	—	—	25·3*	—	—	—	23·2
Diameter of neck (midway)																
antre/postre	—	—	16·5*	—	15·9*	—	—	15·0	18·0*	21·0*	22·0*	24·0	15·5*	18·0	—	—
rt. angles to above	—	—	26·5*	—	(25·0)	—	—	—	—	26·6*†	28·0*†	30·0*†	28·0	28·0	—	—
Angle of neck to long axis of shaft	—	—	130°	—	—	—	135°	—	—	(125°)	(125°)	123°	—	—	—	—
Neck length	—	—	—	—	—	—	105·0	—	—	—	—	32·0	—	88·0	—	—
Diameter of head	—	—	—	—	—	—	—	—	—	40·0*	—	>44	—	35·4	35·0	—
Width distal intercondylar fossa	—	—	—	—	—	25·0*	—	—	—	19·0*	—	24·0*	—	—	—	—
Width distal epiphysis																
med./lat.	—	—	—	—	—	(47·0)	—	—	—	53·0*†	—	61·3*†	—	—	—	—
antre/postre	—	—	—	—	—	(67·0)	—	—	—	69·2*†	—	73·5*†	—	—	—	—
Bicondylar length	—	—	—	—	—	—	—	—	—	(400)	—	395·0	—	—	—	—
KRFP Publ. No.	41	22	11	27	23	23	27	49	49	29	29	29	49	49	49	49

† Not previously published.

TABLE 5.25. *Measurements (mm) of the tibia*

KNM-ER No.	741	1471	1476B	1481C	1500A	1810
Bicondylar breadth at tibial tuberosity	69·0	58·8*	57·6*	—	52·2*	64·6*
Antre/postre diameter at tibial tuberosity	38·0†	35·0*	30·3*	—	—	35·3
Posterior lat./med. width of distal articular surface	—	—	—	19·0	—	—
Anterior lat./med. width of inferior articular surface	—	—	—	27·0	—	—
Antre/postre length of inferior articular surface	—	—	—	(25)	—	—
Inferior projection of tibial maleolus	—	—	—	18·0	—	—
KFRP Publ. No.	11	49	49	29	49	49

† Not previously published.

TABLE 5.26.
Measurements (mm) of the fibula

KNM-ER No.	1481D
Max. height of distal articular surface	19·5
Max. width of distal articular surface	17·0
KFRP Publ. No.	29

TABLE 5.27.
Measurements (mm) of the talus

KNM-ER No.	813A	1464	1476A
Mid-trochlear breadth	23·0	22·0	19·0
Length of trochlear surface at mid-point of ant. border	31·0	31·0†	27·0*†
Max. projection of lateral process	(8·0)	—	—
Length of posterior calcaneal articular surface	24·0	29·5†	25·5†
Max. width of posterior calcaneal articular surface	18·0	19·0†	15·5†
Angle of dip (average medial and lateral)	25·5°	19°	18°†
Angle of head torsion	48°	30°	30°
Horizontal angle	14°	25°	30°
Neck length	—	17·0	—
Length of fibular facet	—	22·0	—
Fibular facet projection	—	10·0	12·0
Medial head projection	—	9·5	—
KFRP Publ. No.	20	49	49

† Not previously published.

TABLE 5.28.
Measurements (mm) of the metatarsal

KNM-ER No.	803J	1500M	803F
M/t	III	III	V
Proximal end			
lat./med. breadth	13·3	12·9	20·0*
dorso-plantar depth	21·1*	18·0	13·5*
Mid-shaft			
lat./med. breadth	6·1	—	—
dorso-plantar depth	10·4	—	—
KFRP Publ. No.	27	49	27

TABLE 5.29. *Measurements (mm) of phalanges of the foot*

KNM-ER 803	K	L	M	Q	R
	intermediate		terminal	proximal	
Digit	?III	II	?IV or V	I	?II or III
Interarticular length	12·6	13·7	—	—	—
Mid-shaft diameter					
lat./med.	5·3*	5·7	4·2	9·9	6·9
dorso-plantar	4·5*	4·5	4·3	8·5	6·1
Proximal end diameter					
lat./med.	9·0	10·2	8·6*	—	—
dorso-plantar	7·9	8·2	7·0*	—	—
Distal end					
med./lat.	8·5	8·8	—	—	9·0
dorso-plantar	6·2	5·1	—	—	6·3
KFRP Publ. No.	27	27	27	27	27

TABLE 5.30. *Hominid specimens according to parts of the skeleton*

Craniae	406, 407, 732, 1470, 1805A, 1813
Cranial fragments	164A, 417, 733B, C, F–J, 734, 811, 814, 1170, 1466, 1474, 1478, 1590A, N, O, Q, 1593A, B, 1648, 1800, 1808J–L, 1821, 2592, 2595, 2598, 2602
Mandibles	403, 404, 725, 726, 727, 728, 729, 730, 731, 733A, 801, 805, 810, 812, 817, 818, 819, 820, 992, 1468, 1469, 1477, 1482, 1483, 1501, 1502, 1506, 1507, 1593C, 1801, 1802, 1803, 1805C, 1806, 1808A, B, D, 1811, 1812A, 1816, 1817, 1820, 3230
Maxillae	405, 733E, 807, 1478A, B, 1804, 1805B, 1808C
Isolated teeth	802, 803H, I, 806, 808, 809, 816, 998, 1171, 1462, 1467, 1479, 1480, 1508, 1509, 1515, 1590B–M, 1814, 1818, 1819, 2593, 2597, 2599, 2600, 2601, 2603, 2604, 2605, 2606, 2607, 3737
Associated skeletons	803, 1500, 1808
Vertebrae	164C, 1808Z, 1825
Scapula	1500O
Humeri	739, 740, 1473, 1500L, 1504, 1591, 1808T, 1824
Ulnae	803C, 1500F, I
Radii	803D, P, 1500E, K, 1812D
Metacarpal	803T
Innominates	1808R, S
Femora	736, 737, 738, 803A, 815, 993, 999, 1463, 1465, 1472, 1475, 1481A, 1500B, D, 1503, 1505, 1592, 1807, 1808M–P, 1809, 1822
Tibiae	741, 803B, G, 813B, 1471, 1476B, C, 1481B, C, 1500A, C, H, J, 1808Q, 1810, 2596
Fibulae	803N, O, 1481D, 1500G, 1808U
Calcaneum	1500T
Tali	803E, 813A, 1464, 1476A
Metatarsals	803F, J, 997, 1500M, 1823
Phalanges	164B, 803K, L, M, Q, R, S

BIBLIOGRAPHY

KOOBI FORA RESEARCH PROJECT

Catalogue of publications 1970 to 1976

1. LEAKEY, R. E. F. 1970. Fauna and artefacts from a new Plio–Pleistocene locality near Lake Rudolf in Kenya. *Nature, Lond.* **226**, 223–4.
2. BEHRENSMEYER, A. K. 1970. Preliminary geological interpretation of a new hominid site in the Lake Rudolf basin. *Nature, Lond.* **226**, 225–8.
3. FITCH, F. J. and MILLER, J. A. 1970. Radioisotopic age determinations of Lake Rudolf artefact site. *Nature, Lond.* **226**, 226–8.
4. LEAKEY, M. D. 1970. Early artefacts from the Koobi Fora area. *Nature, Lond.* **226**, 228–30.
5. LEAKEY, R. E. F. 1970. In search of man's past at Lake Rudolf. *National Geographic* **137**, 712–32.
6. LEAKEY, R. E. F. 1971. Further evidence of Lower Pleistocene hominids from East Rudolf, North Kenya. *Nature, Lond.* **231**, 241–5.
7. VONDRA, C. F., JOHNSON, G. D., BOWEN, B. E., and BEHRENSMEYER, A. K. 1971. Preliminary stratigraphical studies of the East Rudolf Basin. *Nature, Lond.* **231**, 245–8.
8. MAGLIO, V. J. 1971. Vertebrate faunas from the Kubi Algi, Koobi Fora and Ileret areas, East Rudolf, Kenya. *Nature, Lond.* **231**, 248–9.
9. ISAAC, G. LL., LEAKEY, R. E. F., and BEHRENSMEYER, A. K. 1971. Archaeological traces of early hominid activities, East of Lake Rudolf, Kenya. *Science* **173**, 1129–34.
10. LEAKEY, R. E. F., MUNGAI, J. M., and WALKER, A. C. 1971. New australopithecines from East Rudolf, Kenya. *Am. J. Phys. Anthrop.* **35**, 175–86.
11. LEAKEY, R. E. F., MUNGAI, J. M., and WALKER, A. C. 1972. New australopithecines from East Rudolf, Kenya (II). *Am. J. Phys. Anthrop.* **36**, 235–51.
12. LEAKEY, R. E. F. 1972. Further evidence of Lower Pleistocene hominids from East Rudolf, North Kenya, 1971. *Nature, Lond.* **237**, 264–9.
13. LEAKEY, R. E. F. and ISAAC, G. LL. 1972. Hominid fossils from the area East of Lake Rudolf, Kenya: photographs and a commentary on context. In *Perspectives on human evolution 2* (eds. S. L. Washburn and P. Dolhinow), pp. 129–40. Holt, Rinehart, and Winston, San Francisco.
14. MAGLIO, V. J. 1972. Vertebrate faunas and chronology of hominid bearing sediments East of Lake Rudolf, Kenya. *Nature, Lond.* **239**, 379–85.
15. LEAKEY, R. E. F. 1972. New evidence for the evolution of man. *Social Biology* **19**, 99–114.
16. LEAKEY, R. E. F. 1973. Further evidence of Lower Pleistocene hominids from East Rudolf, North Kenya, 1972. *Nature, Lond.* **242**, 170–3.
17. BOWEN, B. E. and VONDRA, C. F. 1973. Stratigrahpical relationships of the Plio–Pleistocene deposits, East Rudolf, Kenya. *Nature, Lond.* **242**, 391–3.
18. LEAKEY, R. E. F. 1973. Evidence for an advanced Plio–Pleistocene hominid from East Rudolf, Kenya. *Nature, Lond.* **242**, 447–50.
19. LEAKEY, R. E. F. 1973. Skull 1470. *National Geographic* **143**, 818–29.
20. LEAKEY, R. E. F. and WOOD, B. A. 1973. New evidence for the genus *Homo* from East Rudolf, Kenya (II). *Am. J. Phys. Anthrop.* **39**, 355–68.

21. JOHNSON, G. D. 1974. Cainozoic lacustrine stromatolites from hominid-bearing sediments east of Lake Rudolf, Kenya. *Nature, Lond.* **247**, 520–3.
22. DAY, M. H. and LEAKEY, R. E. F. 1973. New evidence for the genus *Homo* from East Rudolf, Kenya (I). *Am. J. Phys. Anthrop.* **39**, 341–54.
23. LEAKEY, R. E. F. and WALKER, A. C. 1973. New australopithecines from East Rudolf, Kenya (III). *Am. J. Phys. Anthrop.* **39**, 205–22.
24. LEAKEY, R. E. F. 1972. Man and sub-men on Lake Rudolf. *New Scientist* **56**, 385–7.
25. LEAKEY, M. G. and LEAKEY, R. E. F. 1973. New large Pleistocene Colobinae (Mammalia, Primates) from East Africa. In *Fossil Vertebrates of Africa*, Vol. III (eds. L. S. B. Leakey and R. J. G. Savage), pp. 211–38. Academic Press, London and New York.
26. LEAKEY, R. E. F. 1974. Further evidence of Lower Pleistocene hominids from East Rudolf, North Kenya, 1973. *Nature, Lond.* **248**, 653–6.
27. DAY, M. H. and LEAKEY, R. E. F. 1974. New evidence for the genus *Homo* from East Rudolf, Kenya (III). *Am. J. Phys. Anthrop.* **41**, 367–80.
28. LEAKEY, R. E. F. and WOOD, B. A. 1974. New evidence for the genus *Homo* from East Rudolf, Kenya (IV). *Am. J. Phys. Anthrop.* **41**, 237–44.
29. DAY, M. H., LEAKEY, R. E. F., WALKER, A. C., and WOOD, B. A. 1974. New hominids from East Rudolf, Kenya (I). *Am. J. Phys. Anthrop.* **42**, 461–76.
30. LEAKEY, R. E. F. and WOOD, B. A. 1974. A hominid mandible from East Rudolf, Kenya. *Am. J. Phys. Anthrop.* **41**, 245–50.
31. WOOD, B. A. 1974. A *Homo* talus from East Rudolf, Kenya. *J. Anat.* **117**, 203–4.
32. WOOD, B. A. 1974. Morphology of a fossil hominid mandible from East Rudolf, Kenya. *J. Anat.* **117**, 652–3.
33. WOOD, B. A. 1974. Evidence on the locomotor pattern of *Homo* from early Pleistocene of Kenya. *Nature, Lond.* **251**, 135–6.
34. BROCK, A. and ISAAC, G. LL. 1974. Palaeomagnetic stratigraphy and chronology of hominid-bearing sediments east of Lake Rudolf, Kenya. *Nature, Lond.* **247**, 344–8.
35. BEHRENSMEYER, A. K. 1975. The taphonomy and palaeoecology of Plio–Pleistocene vertebrate assemblages east of Lake Rudolf, Kenya. *Bull. Mus. Comp. Zool.* **146**, 473–578.
36. BEHRENSMEYER, A. K. (in press). The habitat of Plio–Pleistocene hominids in East Africa: taphonomic and microstratigraphic evidence. In *African Hominidae of the Plio–Pleistocene: evidence, problems and strategies* (ed. C. J. Jolly). Duckworth, New York.
37. LEAKEY, R. E. F. (in press). East Rudolf—a summary 1968–1973. *Ibid.*
38. ISAAC, G. LL. (in press). The archaeological evidence for the activities of early African hominids. *Ibid.*
39. (Paper withdrawn.)
40. LEAKEY, R. E. F. 1973. Australopithecines and hominines: A summary on the evidence from the early Pleistocene of Eastern Africa. *Symp. Zool. Soc. Lond.* **33**, 53–69.
41. WALKER, A. 1973. New *Australopithecus* femora from East Rudolf, Kenya. *Journal of Human Evolution* **2**, 545–55.
42. HARRIS, J. M. 1976. Pleistocene Giraffidae (Mammalia: Artiodactyla) from East Rudolf, Kenya. *Fossil Vertebrates of Africa*, Vol. IV (eds. R. J. G. Savage and S. C. Coryndon), pp. 283–332. Academic Press, London and New York.
43. HARRIS, J. M. 1976. Fossil Rhinocerotidae (Mammalia: Perissodactyla) from East Rudolf, Kenya. *Fossil Vertebrates of Africa*, Vol. IV (eds. R. J. G. Savage and S. C. Coryndon), pp. 147–72. Academic Press, London and New York.
44. HARRIS, J. M. 1976. Cranial and dental remains of *Deinotherium bozasi* (Mammalia: Probiscidae) from East Rudolf, Kenya. *J. Zool.* **178**, 57–75.

45. HARRIS, J. M. and WATKINS, R. T. 1974. A new early Miocene fossil mammal locality near Lake Rudolf, Kenya. *Nature, Lond.* **252**, 576–7.

46. HARRIS, J. M. 1974. Orientation and variability of the ossicones of African Sivatheriinae (Mammalia: Giraffidae). *Ann. S. Afr. Mus.* **65**, 189–98.

47. HURFORD, A. J. 1974. Fission track dating of a vitric tuff from East Rudolf, Kenya. *Nature, Lond.* **249**, 236–7.

48. FITCH, F. J., FINDLATER, I. C., WATKINS, R. T., and MILLER, J. A. 1974. Dating of the rock succession contributing fossil hominids at East Rudolf, Kenya. *Nature, Lond.* **251**, 213–5.

49. DAY, M. H., LEAKEY, R. E. F., WALKER, A. C., and WOOD, B. A. 1976. New hominids from East Turkana, Kenya. *Am. J. Phys. Anthrop.* **45**, 369–436.

50. LEAKEY, R. E. 1976. Hominids in Africa. *American Scientist* **64**, 174–8.

51. LEAKEY, R. E. F. (in press). Reconnaissance and Palaeontological exploration east of Lake Turkana 1968–1969. National Geographic Society Research Reports.

52. VONDRA, C. F. and BOWEN, B. E. 1976. Plio–Pleistocene deposits and environments, East Rudolf, Kenya. In *Earliest man and environments in the Lake Rudolf Basin: Stratigraphy, paleoecology and evolution* (eds. Y. Coppens, F. C. Howell, G. Ll. Isaac, and R. E. F. Leakey), pp. 79–93. Chicago University Press.

53. FINDLATER, I. C. 1976. Tuffs and the recognition of isochronous mapping units in the East Rudolf succession. *Ibid.* pp. 94–104.

54. CERLING, T. E. 1976. Oxygen-isotope studies of the East Rudolf volcanoclastics. *Ibid.* pp. 105–15.

55. Johnson, G. D. and RAYNOLDS, R. G. K. 1976. Late Cenozoic environments of the Koobi Fora Formation. *Ibid.* pp. 115–22.

56. FITCH, F. J. and MILLER, J. A. 1976. Conventional potassium–argon and argon-40/argon-39 dating of the volcanic rocks from East Rudolf. *Ibid.* pp. 123–47.

57. BROCK, A. and ISAAC, G. LL. 1976. Reversal stratigraphy and its application at East Rudolf. *Ibid.* pp. 148–62.

58. HARRIS, J. M. 1976. Rhinocerotidae from the East Rudolf succession. *Ibid.* pp. 222–4.

59. EISENMANN, V. 1976. A preliminary note on Equidae from the Koobi Fora Formation, Kenya. *Ibid.* pp. 234–50.

60. CORYNDON, S. C. 1976. Fossil Hippopotamidae from Pliocene–Pleistocene successions of the Rudolf Basin. *Ibid.* pp. 238–50.

61. COOKE, H. B. S. 1976. Suidae from Pliocene–Pleistocene strata of the Rudolf Basin. *Ibid.* pp. 251–63.

62. HARRIS, J. M. 1976. Giraffidae from the East Rudolf succession. *Ibid.* pp. 264–7.

63. HARRIS, J. M. 1976. Bovidae from the East Rudolf succession. *Ibid.* pp. 293–301.

64. LEAKEY, M. G. 1976. Carnivora of the East Rudolf succession. *Ibid.* pp. 302–13.

65. LEAKEY, M. G. 1976. Cercopithecoidea of the East Rudolf succession. *Ibid.* 345–50.

66. TCHERNOV, E. 1976. Crocodilians from the late Cenozoic of the East Rudolf Basin. *Ibid.* pp. 370–82.

67. BEHRENSMEYER, A. K. 1976. Fossil assemblages in relation to sedimentary environments in the East Rudolf succession. *Ibid.* pp. 383–401.

68. LEAKEY, R. E. 1976. An overview of the Hominidae from East Rudolf, Kenya. *Ibid.* pp. 476–83.

69. WALKER, A. 1976. Remains attributable to *Australopithecus* in the East Rudolf succession. *Ibid.* pp. 484–9.

70. WOOD, B. A. 1976. Remains attributable to *Homo* in the East Rudolf succession. *Ibid.* pp. 490–506.

71. DAY, M. H. 1976. Hominid postcranial remains from the East Rudolf succession. *Ibid.* pp. 507–521.

72. ISAAC, G. LL. 1976. Plio–Pleistocene artefact assemblages from East Rudolf, Kenya. *Ibid.* pp. 552–64.

73. ISAAC, G. LL., HARRIS, J. W. K., and CRADER, D. 1976. Archaeological evidence from the Koobi Fora formation. *Ibid.* pp. 533–51.

74. LUEDTKE, N. A., FASCHING, J. L., and ABELL, P. J. (in press). The elemental composition of palaeosol sediments from Lake Rudolf, Kenya. *Earth and Planetary Science Letters.*

75. LUEDTKE, N. A., FASCHING, J. L., HAMMOCK, J. P., ABELL, P. I., FINDLATER, I. C., and FITCH, F. J. (in press). A preliminary investigation of the elemental composition of tuffs from Lake Rudolf, Kenya. *Geochimica et Cosmochimica Acta.*

76. CERLING, T. E., BIGGS, D. L., VONDRA, C. V., and SVEC, H. J. 1975. Use of oxygen isotope ratios in correlation of tuffs, East Rudolf Basin, Northern Kenya. *Earth and Planetary Science Letters* **25**, 291–6.

77. FITCH, F. J., WATKINS, R. T., and MILLER, J. A. 1975. Age of a new carbonatite locality in Northern Kenya. *Nature, Lond.* **245**, 581–3.

78. LEAKEY, R. E. F. 1976. New fossil hominids from the Koobi Fora Formation, Northern Kenya. *Nature, Lond.* **261**, 574–6.

79. LEAKEY, M. G. and LEAKEY, R. E. F. 1976. Further Cercopithecinae (Mammalia, Primates) from the Plio–Pleistocene of East Africa. In *Fossil Vertebrates of Africa*, Vol. 4 (eds. R. J. Savage and S. C. Coryndon), pp. 121–46. Academic Press, London and New York.

80. HARRIS, J. W. K. and ISAAC, G. LL. 1975. The Karari Industry: early Pleistocene archaeological evidence from the terrain east of Lake Turkana, Kenya. *Nature, Lond.* **262**, 102–7.

81. ISAAC, G. LL. (in press). Researches in the area formerly known as 'East Rudolf': a commentary and classified bibliography. *Paleoecology of Africa.* Vol. 9 (ed. C. Van Zinderen Bakker).

82. FINDLATER, I. C. 1978. Isochronous surfaces within the Plio–Pleistocene sediments east of Lake Turkana, Kenya. In *Geological background to fossil man* (ed. W. W. Bishop). Geol. Soc. Lond. Special Publ. No. 6. Scottish Academic Press, Edinburgh.

83. WILLIAMSON, P. G. 1978. Evidence for the major features and development of rift palaeolakes in Neogene of East Africa from certain aspects of lacustrine mollusc assemblages. *Ibid.*

84. BEHRENSMEYER, A. K. 1978. Correlation in Plio–Pleistocene sequences of the northern Lake Turkana basin: a summary of evidence and issues. *Ibid.*

85. HARRIS, J. W. K. and HERBICH, I. 1978. Aspects of early Pleistocene hominid behaviour at East Rudolf, Kenya. *Ibid.*

86. FITCH, F. J., HOOKER, P. J., and MILLER, J. A. 1978. Geochronological problems and radioisotopic dating in the Gregory Rift Valley of East Africa. *Ibid.*

87. DAY, M. H. 1974. The early hominids from East Rudolf, North Kenya. *J. Anat.* **117**, 651.

88. DAY, M. H. 1975. The evolution of man. In *Racial Variation in Man.* Institute of Biology Symposium (ed. F. J. Ebling), pp. 3–7. London: Institute of Biology. Blackwells.

89. DAY, M. H. 1973. Locomotor features of the lower limb in hominids. *Symp. Zool. Soc. London* **33**, 29–51.

90. CURTIS, G. H., DRAKE, R., CERLING, T. E., and HAMPEL, J. H. 1975. Age of KBS tuff in Koobi Fora Formation, East Rudolf, Kenya. *Nature, Lond.* **358**, 395–8.

91. HOLLOWAY, R. L. 1973. New endocranial values for the East African early hominids. *Nature, Lond.* **243**, 97–9.

92. LEAKEY, R. E. and WALKER, A. C. 1976. *Australopithecus, Homo erectus* and the single species hypothesis. *Nature, Lond.* **261**, 572–4.

93. BONNEFILLE, R. 1976. Implications of pollen assemblages from the Koobi Fora Formation, East Rudolf, Kenya. *Nature, Lond.* **264**, 403–7.

94. LEAKEY, R. and ISAAC, GL. 1976. East Rudolf: An introduction to the abundance of new evidence. In *Human Origins: Louis Leakey and the East African Evidence* (eds. G. Ll. Isaac and E. R. McCown), pp. 307—32. W. A. Benjamin, Inc., Menlo Park, California.

95. ISAAC, G. LL. 1976. The activities of early African hominids: a review of archaeological evidence from the time span two and half to one million years ago. *Ibid.* pp. 483–514.

96. HARRIS, J. W. K. (unpublished). Karari Industry: its place in African prehistory. Ph.D. thesis, University of California, Berkeley.

97. FITCH, F. J., HOOKER, P. J., and MILLER, J. A. 1976. $^{40}Ar/^{39}Ar$ dating of the KBS Tuff in the Koobi Fora Formation, East Rudolf, Kenya. *Nature, Lond.* **263**, 740–4.

98. HURFORD, A. J., GLEADOW, A. J. W., and NAESER, C. W. 1976. Fission-track dating of pumice from the KBS Tuff, East Rudolf, Kenya. *Nature, Lond.* **263**, 738–40.

99. EISENMANN, V. 1976. Nouveaux cranes d'Hipparions (Mammalia, Perrissodactyla) Plio–Pléistocènes d'Afrique orientale (Ethiopie et Kenya): *Hipparion* sp., *Hipparion* cf. *ethiopicum*, et *Hipparion afarense* nov. sp. *Géobios* **9**, 577–605.

187

INDEX

Abell, P., 3, 100, 157
Acheulian Industry, 66, 67, 77
Aepyceros, 50, 55
aerial photographs, 3, 5, 8, 36, 38
Alcelaphini, 49–50
Alcelaphus, 49
Allia Bay, 1–3, 6, 7, 15, 19, 25, 36
    Tuff, 15, 19, 33–5
alluvial coastal plain (ACP), 19,
    22–4, 25, 29, 30
    delta plain (ADP), 19, 23, 24,
    25, 28–30, 70
    valley plain (AVP), 19, 22–5,
    28–30
Amphibia, 51
Antidorcas, 50, 55, 79
Antilopini, 50
Aonyx, 42
archaeological occurrences, 77, 78,
    79
    sites, 65–71 (*see also* BBS, GS,
    HAS, IHS, KBS, NMS,
    NS)
archaeology, 4, 9, 10, 64–85
artefacts, composition of in exca-
    vations, 73
    discovery of, 4, 9, 10
Artiodactyla, 45–50
Australopithecus, 54, 83, 87, 88, 89
Aves, 52

Bakate Gap, 2, 19, 27, 83
Barthelme, J., 10, 64, 78, 80, 84
BBS (Bruce Bowen Site), 66, 73,
    81
BBS Tuff, 15
Beatragus, 50, 55
Beden, M., 5
Behrensmeyer, A. K., 3, 4, 5, 9, 10,
    29, 51, 78, 86, 136, 168
bifaces, 73, 83
Black, C. C., 5
Bonnefille, R., 53
Bovidae, 5, 37, 39, 48–50, 59
Bowen, B. E., 4, 14, 15, 19, 32, 81,
    83

Brock, A., 5
Bura Hasuma, 2, 6, 36, 37

Camelidae, 47, 59
Camelus, 47, 55
Campbell, R. I. M., 3
Canidae, 41–2
Canis, 41, 54
Carnivora, 5, 39, 41–3, 57
casts, 12
Ceratotherium, 44–5, 54
Cercocebus, 40, 41, 54, 57
Cercopithecidae, 40–1, 57
Cercopithecoides, 41, 54
Cercopithecus, 41, 57
Cerling, T. E., 32
Chari Tuff, 15–21, 28, 33–5, 37,
    65, 89
Chelonia, 51
Chrysochloridae, 40
Clarius, 51, 82
collection units, *see* palaeonto-
    logical collection units
Colobinae, 41
Colobus, 41, 54, 57
Connochaetes, 50, 55
Cooke, H. B. S., 5
Cox, A., 6
Crader, D., 80, 84
cranial capacity, 89
Crocodylidae, 51
Crocodylus, 51, 60
Crocuta, 42, 54
Curtis, G. H., 11

Damaliscus, 39, 50
Dassenetch, 6, 10
dating methods, 11 (*see also*
    fission track, palaeomagne-
    tism, potassium–argon)
    of tuffs, 4, 5, 10, 11, 60, 77
Day, M. H., 5, 12, 13
Deinotheriidae, 43, 57
Deinotherium, 43, 54
Diceros, 39, 45, 54
Dinofelis, 43, 54, 57

East Rudolf, 1
East Rudolf Expedition, 5
ecological zones, 39
Eisenmann, V., 5
Elephantidae, 5, 43, 52, 57, 82
Elephas, 43–4, 54, 57
Enhydriodon, 42, 54
environments of deposition, 19, 20,
    22–4, 28, 30, 39, 86, 87
Equidae, 5, 39, 44, 58
Equus, 38, 39, 44, 54, 58
Erinacidae, 40
erosion surface, 30
    post-KBS, 20–1, 28, 30, 52
    post-Tulu Bor, 15, 28
Euthecodon, 51
excavations, 9, 38, 78
expeditions, 3–6

faulting, 28
Felidae, 42, 43, 57
Felis, 43, 54
Findlater, I. C., 5, 9, 32, 86
fire in archaeological sites, 83
fission-track dating, 11
Fitch, F. J., 4, 11
F.M. Consultants Ltd., 4
fossil collections, *see* palaeonto-
    logical collections

Gabra, 6
Galana Boi, 6
    beds, 10, 15, 29, 38, 61, 66
Garland, W. M., 110
Gazella, 39, 50, 55
Genetta, 42, 54
geographical names, 2, 6
geological studies, 4
Gifford, D., 10
Giraffa, 39, 47–8, 55
Giraffidae, 47–8, 59, 82
Gowlett, J., 81, 82
GS (Gravel Site), 66, 73, 78, 82
Guomde Formation, 15, 28, 29, 37,
    61, 64, 66, 86

Hadar, 42, 45, 48
Harris, J. M., 3, 5, 6, 132, 136, 139, 154, 168
Harris, Judy, 168
Harris, J. W. K., 72, 79, 80, 81, 82, 83, 169
HAS (Hippo and Artefact Site), 66, 68–70, 73, 79, 80
Hasuma Tuff, 15, 19, 25, 33–5, 52, 56 (see also Bura Hasuma)
Herbich, I., 82, 83
Hexaprotodon, 46, 47, 55, 58, 59
Hill, A., 10, 119
Hillhouse, J. D., 6
Hipparion, 44, 54, 58
Hippopotamidae, 5, 46, 47, 58–9, 79, 80, 82
Hippopotamus, 46, 47, 55, 59
Hippotragini, 49
Hippotragus, 49, 55
Höhnel, L. von, 1
Holloway, R., 95, 131, 155, 162
Holocene deposits, 10, 29
  sites, 64
hominid catalogue, 12, 86, 90–169
hominids, context, 14, 24, 38, 71, 72, 83, 86, 87
  depositional environments, 22, 23, 24, 31, 38
  description, 5, 12
  discovery, 3, 4, 5, 9
  distribution, related to archaeological sites, 68–72
  excavation of, 9, 71
  habits, 71, 84
  locations, 16, 17, 18, 20
  morphology, 89
  palaeoecology, 87
  stratigraphic position, 20, 21, 30, 86, 87
  taxonomy, 77, 88, 89
Homo, 54, 87, 88, 89
Homo erectus, 10, 89
  habilis, 88, 89
Homotherium, 43, 54
Huntings Survey Ltd., 5
Hyaena, 42, 54
Hyaenidae, 42
Hystrix, 79

IHS (Ingrid Herbich Site), 66, 73, 78, 82
Ileret, 2, 4, 6–8, 16–19, 25, 28, 30, 37, 65, 70, 73
  Member, 15, 37, 70, 84, 86

Il Erriet River, 8, 61
Insectivora, 40
invertebrates, 5, 52 (see also Mollusca)
Isaac, G. Ll., 4, 5, 10, 78, 80, 81
Johnson, G., 4

Kaiso, 53
KBS (Kay Behrensmeyer Site), 4, 5, 66, 68–70, 73, 78–80
  Industry, 66, 67, 72, 73, 75, 76, 77, 78
  Tuff, 4, 5, 9, 15–21, 28, 33–5, 37, 56, 65, 66, 70, 77, 79, 80
  dating of, 11, 60, 77
Kanapoi, 3
K–Ar dating, see potassium–argon
Karari escarpment, 2, 4, 8, 9, 19, 27, 28, 30, 65, 68, 70, 73, 77, 81, 82, 83
  Industry, 4, 9, 66–8, 71, 72–4, 75, 77, 78, 81, 83
  Tuff, 15–21, 33–5, 65, 68, 83
Kenya National Museum, Parks, etc., see National Museum, National Parks of Kenya
KFRP, see Koobi Fora Research Project
Kilonzo, A., 164
Kimengech, J., 143
Kimeu, K., 3, 78, 92, 99, 102, 114, 115, 124, 125, 127, 129, 135, 159, 160, 162, 165, 167, 168
Kitibi, K., 116, 124, 169
Kobus, 48, 49, 55, 79
Kokoi, 2, 8, 27, 37
Koobi Fora, 1–4, 6–8, 12, 14, 16–20, 25, 28, 64, 88
  Formation, 6, 10, 11, 15, 27, 28, 37, 38, 39, 40–53, 55–60, 64, 65, 66, 67, 75, 77, 86, 87
  Research Project, 1, 5, 60, 85
    monographs, 12, 60
  Ridge, 2, 4, 27, 70
  Tuff, 15, 19, 33, 35, 56
Kubi Algi, 8
  Formation, 6, 15, 25, 37, 40, 41, 43–5, 47–52, 56, 58, 61

lacustrine high-energy (LHE), 19, 22–4, 28, 29
  low-energy (LLE), 19, 24, 29

Lagomorpha, 41
lake levels, 25, 27, 28, 39, 52
Leakey, D. M., 3
Leakey, L. S. B., 1
Leakey, M. D., 110
Leakey, M. G., 5, 90, 101, 106, 112, 158, 168
Leakey, R. E., 78, 79, 81, 95, 105, 107, 111, 161
LHE, see lacustrine high-energy
Litocranius, 39
LLE, see lacustrine low-energy
locality reference, 8
Lothagam, 3
lower member, 15, 37, 70, 77
Lower/Middle Tuff, 15, 33–5, 65, 66, 70, 71
Loxodonta, 37, 44, 54, 57
Lutra, 42, 54, 57
Lycaon, 42, 54

Machairodontinae, 43
Madoqua, 50, 55
Maglio, V. J., 4, 5, 36, 37, 57
mammalian fossils, 38, 39, 40, 54
Mangao, W., 141, 144, 152, 153, 155, 162, 168
Mbithi, M., 136, 145, 167
Megalotragus, 49, 55
Megantereon, 43, 54
Mellorivinae, 42, 54
Menelikia, 49, 55
Mesochoerus, 37, 45, 46, 54
Metridiochoerus, 37, 46, 54–5, 79
microfauna, 5, 40
microstratigraphy, 4, 5, 36, 86, 87
Miller, J. A., 4, 11
millipedes, 52
Miocene deposits, 1, 3, 32
Mollusca, 28, 29, 52–3, 56, 60
  species of, 52, 56
monographs, KFRP, 12, 60
Mudoga, N., 80
Muluila, M., 140, 145, 153, 161, 164, 166, 167, 168
Muoka, M., 91, 96, 152
Mustelidae, 42
Mutiwa, N., 93, 97, 115, 119, 124, 126, 127, 128, 147, 148, 151, 164, 165, 166, 167
Mutua, H., 98, 103, 108, 114, 121, 137, 147, 150

National Museum of Kenya, 9, 12
National Parks of Kenya, 6

Nderati, 3
Ndombi, J., 5
Neolithic, 64
Neotragini, 50
Ngeneo, B., 108, 117, 118, 120, 122, 128, 131, 132, 134, 143, 145, 146, 148, 164, 166, 167
NMS (Nathaniel Mudoga Site), 80
NS (North Site), 66, 73, 78, 82
Notochoerus, 37, 45–6, 54
Nyanzochoerus, 45–6, 54
Nzube, P., 71, 84

Okote, 8
 Tuff, 4, 15–21, 33–5, 65, 66, 67, 68, 70, 71, 72, 75, 81, 83
Oldowan Industry, 72, 75, 77
Olduvai, 42–4, 46–51, 60, 72, 75, 77, 88, 89
Omo, 1, 40–53, 57–60
Onyango-Abuje, J., 79
Orycteropodidae, 44, 58
Orycteropus, 44, 54
Oryx, 39, 49, 55

palaeoenvironment, 5, 39, 60
palaeoflora, 53, 61, 79
palaeomagnetism, 5, 11
palaeontological collection areas, 7, 8, 20, 22–4, 33, 65, 66, 67
 collection units, 6, 35, 36, 37, 40–51, 53–5, 57, 59, 60, 69, 86
 collections, 3, 4, 5, 6, 8, 32, 36, 38
 marker horizons, 32, 33
palynology, 53
Panthera, 42, 43, 54, 57
Papio, 40, 54, 57
Parmularius, 49, 50, 55

Pelorovis, 48, 55
Perissodactyla, 44–5
Phacochoerus, 38, 39, 46
Pisces, 51
Potamochoerus, 45, 54
potassium–argon dating, 4, 11
Primates, 5, 37, 39, 40–1, 57
Proboscidea, 43–4
Pseudocivetta, 42, 54
publications, 12, 60, 86

Rabaticeras, 50, 55
Reduncini, 48, 82
Redunca, 49, 55
reference sections, 9, 20, 29, 30, 86, 87
Rendille, 6
Reptilia, 51
Rhinocerotidae, 44–5, 58
Rhynchotragus, 39, 49
Rodentia, 41
Rudolf, Lake, *see* Turkana, Lake

Savage, S. C., 5
sedimentary environments, *see* environments of deposition
sedimentation, 19, 24, 25–9
Shangilla, 6
Shungura Formation, 40–53, 57, 60
Sibilot, 8
Sivatherium, 47, 56, 59
Soricidae, 40
Squamata, 52
Standard African Site Enumeration System, 65
Stradling, H., 90
stratigraphical correlation, 14, 20, 86, 87 (*see also* tuffs, correlation of)
 framework, 5
 nomenclature, 14, 15, 32
 sections, *see* reference sections

Suidae, 5, 36, 37, 39, 45–6, 52, 58, 82
Suregei, 8
 Cuesta, 68, 83
 Tuff, 15, 19, 27, 33–5, 37, 56

taphonomy, 10, 38, 39, 89
Tapinochoerus, 46
taxonomy, 12, 54, 77, 88, 89
Tchernov, E., 51
Teleki, Count S., 1, 6
Theropithecus, 40, 54, 57
Tragelaphini, 48, 82
Tragelaphus, 39, 48, 55
Transvaal, 88
Trionyx, 51
Tubulidentata, 44
tuff labelling system, 32, 33, 36
tuffs, correlation of, 5, 15, 19, 20, 32, 34, 36, 86, 87 (*see also* Chari, KBS, etc.)
Tulu Bor, 8
 Tuff, 15–21, 27, 30, 33–5, 37, 56, 60, 68
Turkana, Lake, 1, 2, 6, 7, 16–18, 25, 32, 52

upper member, 15, 28, 37, 52, 70, 73, 77, 83

vegetation patterns, 39
Viverridae, 42
Vondra, C., 4, 15, 19, 32

Walker, A. C., 5, 12, 13
Wandibba, S., 83
Watkins, R., 5
White, T. D., 6, 172
Williamson, P. G., 5, 52
Wood, B. A., 3, 5, 12, 13, 164

zones, faunal, of Maglio, 36, 37 of Williamson, 52, 56